Partisan Realignment

A Westview Encore Edition

Partisan Realignment

Voters, Parties, and Government in American History

Jerome M. Clubb
William H. Flanigan
Nancy H. Zingale

Westview Press
BOULDER, SAN FRANCISCO, & OXFORD

35.00

16-2-90

Published in 1990 in the United States of America by Westview Press, Inc., 5500 Central Avenue, Boulder, Colorado 80301, and in the United Kingdom by Westview Press, Inc., 36 Lonsdale Road, Summertown, Oxford OX2 7EW

Library of Congress Cataloging-in-Publication Data
Clubb, Jerome M., 1928–   .
    Partisan realignment : voters, parties, and government in American
history / Jerome M. Clubb, William H. Flanigan, Nancy H. Zingale.
    p. cm.
    Includes index.
    ISBN 0-8133-1031-8
    1. Party affiliation—United States—History. 2. Political
parties—United States—History. 3. Elections—United States—
History. I. Flanigan, William H. II. Zingale, Nancy H.
III. Title.
JK2261.C59   1990
324'.0973—dc20   90-38667
                                                                                          CIP

Printed and bound in the United States of America

        The paper used in this publication meets the requirements
(∞)   of the American National Standard for Permanence of Paper
        for Printed Library Materials Z39.48-1984.

10   9   8   7   6   5   4   3   2   1

CONTENTS

To
Charlie's
and
Doro's

PREFACE TO
THE ENCORE EDITION

Ten years ago we undertook to explore those circumstances that cause some time periods to become known, in retrospect, as important watersheds of American politics. Almost unanimously, scholars view the Civil War, the 1890s, and the New Deal as occasions when something momentous happened in the governance of the American political system, leading to a fundamental re-structuring of the alignment of partisan forces in the nation. What else did these three periods have in common? What is the underlying dynamic in American politics that produces significant and lasting change at some points and returns to normality at others?

This was territory that had been traveled before by scholars to whom we gratefully acknowledged our debt (for example, W. Dean Burnham,[1] James Sundquist,[2] Paul A. Beck,[3] and, of course, V. O. Key,[4] who first brought the concept of realignment to the attention of the scholarly community). Our journey ended, however, at a somewhat different point than that of our predecessors, placing relatively less emphasis upon the behavior of the electorate and more upon the actions of political leaders. The three great partisan realignments had this in common: In each case, a crisis of considerable magnitude gave to one of the parties unified control over the elected agencies of the national government, and unified control over an increased proportion of the state governments. Unified control gave to that party an opportunity to take policy action that was popularly perceived as effectively addressing national problems. As both cause and consequence of these policy innovations, the partisan balance in the electorate was altered to the advantage of the party in power. A sustained period of unified control of government then ensued that was of sufficient length to allow institutionalization of policy change.

Each partisan realignment worked to produce a new issue agenda for the nation, displaced older problems and preoccupations, and brought new concerns and values to the fore. Each also worked to create a pattern of symbols—negative symbols surrounding the defeated party and attributing blame for crisis to that party, and positive symbols for the victors, attributing to them credit for improvement of national conditions. These symbols worked to sustain the electoral cleavages and alignments that grew out of the realignment.

The periods following realignments were marked, as we saw it, by progressive decay and deterioration of these electoral alignments and of the capacity of the symbols of the old realignment to sustain them. During each of these periods, new issues emerged that cut across the divisions produced by the realignment. As party loyalties weakened, split ticket voting increased, as did the number of independents and third party candidacies. As a consequence, divided control and governmental deadlock became more common, and capacity to take effective policy action diminished. This ineffectiveness, together with the expanding pool of voters with weakened party loyalties, created the conditions for the next realignment.

Much of this scenario we owe to the insights of others, as previously acknowledged. Our focus on the importance of the handling of the crisis by political leadership contributed to the realignment perspective, we think, in two ways. First, in emphasizing the role of leadership and the primarily reactive role of the electorate, we accounted for the fact that analysts always discover more electoral change, including electoral change of some duration, than they do realignments, and that many impressive electoral shifts that initially were hailed as realignments subsequently proved otherwise. Second, by making the connection between the behavior of voters and the institutions of government, we helped to draw attention to the ways in which changes in the behavior of institutions affect the progress of the realignment sequence. The excellent recent work of David Brady,[5] which argues that the insulation of the House of Representatives has considerably lessened the chances of realignment in the contemporary era, demonstrates the usefulness of this perspective.[6]

Over the last ten years, our views about the realignment process have been reinforced and challenged by the work of others that has appeared during that time.[7] In this Encore Edition, we have chosen to let the argument stand as we originally stated it, even though we, individually or collectively, might now wish that we had made some points differently. Our story ended, however, with the decay of the New Deal alignment. Although some of our data series extended into the 1970s, the nature of the analysis—indeed, we would argue, of the concept of realignment itself—requires some hindsight for a full interpretation. A new epilogue considers the events of the Reagan years, as well as the preceding two decades, in the light of the realignment perspective.

Jerome M. Clubb
William H. Flanigan
Nancy H. Zingale

NOTES

1. W. Dean Burnham, *Critical Elections and the Mainsprings of American Politics* (New York: W. W. Norton, 1970).

2. James Sundquist, *Dynamics of the Party System* (Washington, DC: Brookings Institution, 1973).

3. Paul A. Beck, "A Socialization Theory of Partisan Realignment," in Richard G. Niemi & Associates, *The Politics of Future Citizens* (San Francisco: Jossey-Bass, 1974), pp. 200–206.

4. V. O. Key, "A Theory of Critical Elections," *Journal of Politics* 17 (February 1955), pp. 3–18.

5. David Brady, *Critical Elections and Congressional Policy Making* (Stanford, CA: Stanford University Press, 1988).

6. At about the same time that *Partisan Realignment* appeared, Campbell and Trilling edited a volume of strong essays organized around the division between voters and leaders with one section on "elite behavioral change" and another on policy (Bruce Campbell and Richard Trilling, *Realignment in American Politics* [Austin: University of Texas Press, 1980]). Another impressive work that deals with political parties and public policy in the context of the realignment perspective is Richard McCormick's *The Party Period and Public Policy* (New York: Oxford University Press, 1986).

7. Among these are Russell Dalton, Scott Flanagan, and Paul A. Beck, *Electoral Change in Advanced Industrial Democracies* (Princeton: Princeton University Press, 1984); Peter F. Galderisi et al., eds., *The Politics of Realignment: Party Change in the Mountain West* (Boulder, CO: Westview Press, 1987); and Paul Kleppner, *Continuity and Change in Electoral Politics, 1893–1928* (Westport, CT: Greenwood Press, 1987).

ACKNOWLEDGMENTS

This study attempts to reconceptualize, expand, and test the prevailing view of American electoral history as characterized by sequences of realignments. Because our task is integrative as much as innovative, we have benefited, perhaps more than most scholars, from the work of numerous other researchers concerned with American politics in historical and contemporary perspective. We have attempted to acknowledge this indebtedness, albeit inadequately, in citations and textual references. The relevant literature, however, is both extensive and diverse, and we have undoubtedly overlooked important studies and failed in some instances to acknowledge work from which we have benefited. We apologize for such inadvertent omissions. We also regret any errors of interpretation of the work of others that we may have committed.

One intellectual debt deserves special mention. Walter Dean Burnham participated in the early stages of our research, and we owe special gratitude to him. Although he withdrew from the collaboration to accept a Fulbright Fellowship and because of other commitments, we continued to benefit from his insights and profound knowledge of American politics through numerous conversations and his many published works. He also read and commented extensively upon early drafts of several chapters. Readers will recognize that many of the ideas and interpretations underlying this book had their original genesis with him. While we owe a large debt to Dean, we have also departed from

7

his views in a variety of ways, and he should not be held responsible for the views and interpretations presented here.

We also owe a particular debt to a principle that has gained widespread acceptance in the social sciences during the past decade or more. This is simply the principle that original research data in the social sciences should be generally and readily accessible to the community of scholars. Our study is based upon data resources maintained and disseminated by the Inter-university Consortium for Political and Social Research, one of the major organizational expressions of this principle. Without the Consortium, this study could not have been carried out. Thus we owe a major debt of gratitude to the Consortium and to the numerous social scientists, academic administrators, and officers of research funding agencies in the United States and other countries who have seen the Consortium as a scientific resource worthy of maintenance and development.

One of the signal benefits of the principle of data sharing is the opportunity it provides for direct replication, testing, evaluation, modification, or extension of reported research findings. All data employed in this volume, along with several specialized data files created in the course of our research, are available from the Consortium. We hope that other scholars will employ these and other data to assess, refute, refine, or otherwise modify our findings. A second and equally important benefit of data sharing is the impetus it lends to cumulative research.

A very large number of individuals and organizations have contributed directly and indirectly to the research reported here. While these individuals and organizations bear no responsibility for our errors, they deserve no small measure of credit for whatever merits the present study may have. Our research and data analysis were made possible by awards from the National Science Foundation (Grants GS-28913, GS-42717, GS-28911, GS-42730, and GS-42733). Foundation support allowed us to draw upon the knowledge and intellectual and technical skills of several highly talented individuals. Erik W. Austin carried out much of the data management and analysis involved in the early phase of the project, and we benefited greatly from his knowledge of the substance and data of American political history. We also benefited, particularly during the earlier phases of the project, from the analytical skills of Michael W. Traugott. Santa A. Traugott contributed to the project in major ways, most visibly in our seventh chapter. Under a generous subsidy from the Center for Political Studies, Ruth Wasem skillfully carried out much of the detailed and demanding work involved in completion of our research. Donna Gotts was responsible for typing much of the manuscript both in early drafts and the final version. We are grateful for her skill, care, and patience.

Howard W. Allen, Paul Allen Beck, and Warren E. Miller read the entire manuscript, as did an anonymous reviewer for the publisher. Their detailed comments, criticisms, and suggestions saved us from a number of egregious errors. We could not follow all of their many suggestions, in some cases out of disagreement, but their efforts made this a better book. We are also grateful to Allan G. Bogue. Although he was unable to read the manuscript, our view of American political history and of the research process has benefited from our many contacts with him.

Acknowledgments are perhaps inevitably rather poor things. When we recall the numerous individuals and organizations that assisted us in one way or another, we realize our gratitude cannot be adequately expressed. We can only repeat that we are grateful for the assistance we have received. Without that assistance, this book could not have been written, and it is probably at best poor repayment.

Where collaborative works are concerned, it is sometimes the fashion among academics to attempt to assign primary responsibility to one or another of the authors. After a collaborative effort that has extended over more years than we care to count, we can only conclude that those who indulge in this pastime have never experienced genuine collaboration. The intellectual exchange involved in such an effort is both demanding and strenuous. It subjects ideas and notions to harsh tests, and it results in a product that is not the creation of a single individual. Indeed, we ourselves are no longer able to determine who should be blamed for what.

Ann Arbor   J.M.C.
Minneapolis   W.H.F.
St. Paul   N.H.Z.

INTRODUCTION

This study is concerned with partisanship and political leadership in the United States from the middle decades of the nineteenth century to the end of the 1970s. More specifically, we are concerned with the interrelations between voting behavior in the mass electorate and patterns of party control of the policy-making institutions of government. Our investigation is oriented by a view of American politics and political history which has emerged and gained widespread acceptance during the past two or more decades and which we call for convenience the "realignment perspective." Put briefly, the realignment perspective describes the political history of the United States as marked by repetitive sequences, or "party systems," each beginning with a "partisan realignment" which involved the appearance of a new electoral alignment which endured for a significant time and then deteriorated.

The realignment perspective is often couched quite narrowly in terms of the partisan voting behavior of the mass electorate, and, indeed, a major proportion of the empirical research on which the perspective is based is concerned with electoral behavior. Implicitly, however, the perspective is broader and conceptually more rich. Drawing heavily on the work of others, we will expand the discussion of the realignment perspective to link explicitly mass voting behavior with political leadership and to treat historical "realignment sequences" as marked by similar stages of control of government, elite behavior, and policy formation. In these respects, the realignment perspective is not confined to a few "critical elections" seen as dotting the American political past. Rather, this approach suggests a more comprehensive description of the political past which links together diverse aspects of the political and governmental system.

In our view, shifts in partisan control of government and policy action, as well as changes in the partisan behavior and attitudes of the electorate, are all seen as integral and necessary elements of the process of partisan realignment. Shifts in voting behavior in response to tension, crisis, and unsolved national problems give to one of the parties effective control of the agencies of government and an opportunity to take policy action addressed to those problems. Whether or not a new and lasting distribution of partisan loyalties is formed and whether the dominance of the temporarily advantaged party is perpetuated—whether or not, in other words, the process of partisan realignment is consummated—depends upon the degree to which this opportunity for effective policy action is fulfilled. In this view, the performance of government and of the political leadership is central to the realignment process. The formation of a new balance of partisan identifications within the electorate is seen not as an instantaneous response to crisis, but as a more gradual process coming in response to policy action that can be seen as effectively addressing national problems. The further deterioration of partisan alignments is similarly seen as the product of the interaction between the performance of political leadership and the behavior of the mass electorate.

This formulation of the realignment perspective rests upon several underlying and to some degree unexamined assumptions. These assumptions are by no means unique to our analysis, nor are they particularly controversial. It is necessary, however, to make them explicit both to elucidate our research concerns and to suggest the limitations of our efforts.

We view political parties and partisanship as primary mechanisms of political and governmental integration, of policy formation and implementation, and as sources of stability and change in mass polities. Parties can serve to aggregate and articulate

popular interests and needs and to translate these interests and
needs into effective demands upon government. Parties, in other
words, can organize mass participation in politics and link the
mass electorate to political and governmental elites. The capacity of the electorate to form lasting partisan loyalties provides
a stable base of support for partisan leaders in government and
works to constrain radical vacillations in public policy. In this
sense, the electorate constitutes a source of political and policy
stability. At the same time, the capacity of the electorate to
judge governmental action as inadequate and to reject the party
leadership considered responsible constitutes a source of political and policy change.

Political parties and partisanship, moreover, can work to link
together and organize leadership and elite groups and to provide
a basis for concerted, consistent, and responsible action. Parties
and partisanship also constitute mechanisms to link together
and organize governmental agencies both within particular levels
of government and across levels. In these terms, they constitute
mechanisms of vertical and horizontal political integration.
Hence they hold the potential for integrating governmental
activities at all levels and for the formation and implementation
of comprehensive and consistent public policy.

We view these functions and potentialities of political parties
as particularly important in a highly diffuse and decentralized
political system such as that of the United States. In the case of
the United States, the system of separate but overlapping
powers within all levels of government creates the strong potentiality for conflicting or ineffective action and for deadlock.
Much the same can be said of the arrangement of shared and
overlapping powers and jurisdictions between the local, state,
and national levels of government. Here again, the potentiality
is created for discordant and conflicting action and for what
amounts to vetoes at one level of government of policy actions
taken at another. At the electoral level, the very size and
diversity of the nation combined with a complex system of
territorial, "winner-take-all" representational districts impose
obstacles to the aggregation of popular needs and interests into

effective coalitions to demand action or to reject actions deemed inadequate. Whatever its other merits and advantages, such a system appears clearly biased against rapid, concerted, effective, and accountable governmental action. In the present view, the party system constitutes a primary mechanism to compensate for this bias.

A variety of objections to this general view can be raised. In particular, it might be objected that this view assigns too limited a role to the electorate as a source of political change and policy innovation. Indeed, we view the electorate as primarily passive and reactive in matters of governmental policy; policy innovation and promotion of specific policy directions are seen as largely emanating from political leadership. Through either positive approval or indifference, the electorate endorses policy actions by providing continuing electoral support for incumbent officeholders. On the other hand, the electorate's role in dictating policy directions is largely limited to generalized demands for change expressed primarily through rejection at the polls of partisan leaders in power. This view is intended as an explicit corrective to a tendency in much of the recent literature to treat the electorate as the primary driving force in American politics. Our view shifts the emphasis from the electorate and assigns greater weight to the performance of government and the political leadership.

The set of assumptions outlined above does not necessarily commit us to any particular position as to how well the political parties have performed historically the functions attributed to them. The realignment perspective and the evidence suggest, however, that they have performed these functions with reasonable effectiveness only during periods of partisan realignment. Only during these periods, it appears, have the weight and narrowed focus of national problems overcome, in relative terms, the obstacles to integrated and consistent policy action intrinsic to the national political system.

Our analysis also has a number of limitations. Several of these should be made explicit. Despite the obvious relevance, we have not examined matters of formal party organization. Such an examination would require extended data collection, organization, and analysis and would very significantly extend the scope of the present study. While we view research in this area as a pressing need, we doubt that the results of systematic empirical inquiry would seriously contradict our findings. The limitations of our discussions of the historical formation and content of public policy may be more serious. In this area, we have relied primarily, and somewhat impressionistically, upon traditional historical scholarship. Here again, systematic empirical inquiry in historical depth would require an innovative data collection and analysis effort of virtually monumental scope. While we have been forced to rule such an effort outside our purview, we recognize its results might modify our conclusions.

A further limitation of the present study must also be suggested. Our reformulation of the realignment perspective suggests processes that link electoral behavior to the behavior of members of Congress and to public policy. We have not, however, attempted empirical demonstration of the working of those processes. Rather, our analysis is limited to identifying parallel and coinciding patterns of change and stability in each of the political domains of concern. Our failure to examine these processes in empirical terms is in part a reflection of the characteristics of historical data. Effective examination of these linking processes would require systematic and representative data relevant to the political behavior and attitudes of individual members of the electorate. As is well known, data of this sort do not exist in any form for the period prior to the mid-1930s, while more satisfactory data begin only with the 1950s. Thus, we must rest our case primarily upon the rather striking coincidence of patterns of change in each of the political domains of concern and upon the plausibility of the linking processes postulated.

While we cannot examine effectively the attitudes and behavior of individual members of the electorate in historical contexts, we do make an assumption in this area which may seem to some a limitation of the study. We assume that the psychological mechanisms through which individuals form lasting attitudinal attachments to political parties—attachments which, in turn, influence their political behavior— have operated in essentially similar ways from at least the mid-nineteenth century to the present. We are aware, of course, of challenges to this view of individual political attitudes which argue it is time-bound, limited in its applicability primarily to the middle decades of the twentieth century, and of highly dubious applicability in the sharply differing circumstances of the nineteenth century. It is our view, however, that the social psychological model itself is applicable to individual behavior in differing eras, even though the various factors that influence behavior (group affiliations, partisanship, issue concerns, and so on) may vary in relative importance because of changing circumstances in the political environment.

Our intention in this volume, then, is to redirect attention away from the role of electoral change and toward the control of government and the role of political leadership in understanding the phenomenon of partisan realignment. Chapter 1 sets forth in more extended form our view of partisan realignment and the processes that underlie realignment sequences. In Chapters 2 and 3, using first traditional correlational techniques and then a technique based upon analysis of variance, we attempt to demonstrate that patterns of electoral change cannot by themselves account for the occurrence of partisan realignment. Chapter 4 examines indicators of partisan decay based on survey and aggregate voting data and makes a similar point about the inconclusiveness of mass electoral data in marking the deterioration of partisan alignment. Chapter 5 argues that an extended period of unified control of the branches of the federal government by one party is an essential ingredient of partisan realignment, offering the opportunity for concerted policy-making. Chapter 6 examines patterns of change in the control of government at the state level associated with realignment sequences. Chapter 7 addresses a similar point, in this case, change in the composition of Congress and in the partisan behavior of its members.

The effort in Chapter 8 is somewhat different. Here we first attempt briefly to summarize and evaluate the patterns of change observed in the preceding chapters in terms of the realignment perspective. We then draw upon examinations of the New Deal realignment—the one realignment for which data are relatively more diverse and rich—in an attempt to develop a detailed and plausible reconstruction of that realignment. This reconstruction is then applied to other realignments and to certain other periods and elections not usually seen as characterized by partisan realignment. The final chapter is concerned with longer-term patterns of change in American politics and in the American political environment. Our goal is to assess the nature and implications of that change. We also consider in this chapter recent predictions as to the fate of the American party system in the latter twentieth century. While we are unable to predict that fate, we do argue that the future may be more promising than it is sometimes made out to be.

From some points of view, a study placing partisanship and partisan processes clearly at center stage in the political drama may seem almost archaic. So much has been written recently of the deterioration and potential demise of political parties that they often seem to be little more than historical relics. Hence a study emphasizing the partisan connection might be seen as of no more than historical interest. It is clear, of course, that political parties—along with virtually all other political institutions in the United States—are under considerable strain. The outcome is by no means fully predictable, and the obstacles to revitalization of the parties and partisanship may be many. As we suggest in our final chapter, however, we see no reason to believe that the party system is on its way to inevitable extinction. But to stress the fate of political parties may misstate the problem. Parties, partisanship, and partisan processes are after all instrumentalities of political organization and government. The real issue lies, as it always has, in the capacity to use these instrumentalities to develop and implement realistic solutions to national problems.

Chapter 1

CRITICAL ELECTIONS, REALIGNMENTS,

AND PARTY SYSTEMS

It would be a serious exaggeration to suggest that what we will term the "realignment perspective" dominates the study of American political history. However, since the appearance of V. O. Key's seminal article in 1955, an extensive literature has appeared concerned in one way or another with critical elections, partisan realignments, party systems, and related political phenomena and processes.[1] The terminology of this perspective, at least, has penetrated the accounts of traditional historians, as well as the works of the more scientifically inclined of various disciplines, and it is also to be found in the writings of journalists and other political commentators. To a growing degree, moreover, political history is periodized, sometimes almost conventionally, in terms of party systems, or realignment eras. The realignment perspective, in short, has attained something of the status of an organizing or synthesizing framework for the study and discussion of the American political past.

Our task in this chapter is to develop a comprehensive and extended statement of the realignment perspective as a starting point for empirical investigation. Our effort is to state the perspective in a form that encompasses partisan control of the agencies of government, the behavior of partisan elites, and the policy products of government as well as the behavior and attitudes of the electorate. To do so, however, it is first necessary to consider relevant work in some detail both to identify elements of the realignment perspective that are often either left implicit or neglected and to suggest areas of needed research.

THE REALIGNMENT PERSPECTIVE

Discussions of the realignment phenomenon often and appropriately begin with V. O. Key's article, "A Theory of Critical Elections." Key identified one category of election which he described in an often quoted passage as "an election type in which the depth and intensity of electoral involvement are high, in which more or less profound readjustments occur in the relations of power within the community, and in which new and durable electoral groupings are formed."[2] Angus Campbell extended Key's conceptualization to include "maintaining" and "deviating" elections and later added "reinstating" elections to the scheme.[3] Gerald Pomper modified the classification to allow for realigning change that benefited the already dominant party, an election type he labeled "converting."[4]

Campbell's further contribution is less often noted. He explicitly linked this classification of elections to the social-psychological model of individual partisan attitudes and behavior developed in *The American Voter* and to the "normal vote" concept subsequently developed by Philip E. Converse.[5] In this way, he both extended the analytical utility of the classification and enriched its theoretical basis. It may be that a further and inadvertent consequence was to focus historical analyses even more narrowly upon realigning elections and periods to the relative neglect of other elections. While realigning elections shifted both the balance of partisan identifications within the electorate and partisan control of the agencies of government, maintaining, deviating, and reinstating elections did not. Hence the latter categories of elections could be seen as intrinsically less interesting and indeed less important than realigning elections.

Whatever its specific source, interest in critical elections and partisan realignment has led investigators in several directions. One endeavor has involved establishing the timing of realignments—that is, deciding which elections are critical—and has produced substantial disagreement. Virtually all analysts agree that sometime between 1920 and 1940 a realigning election took place, but each presidential election from 1924 to 1936 has been designated as *the* realigning election.[6] Similar disagreements surround the elections of the Civil War era and of the 1890s.[7] Much of this discussion has occurred without clear conceptualizations of the realignment process, clear ideas of realigning electoral change, or an effective means to assess and measure such change. We address the latter two issues in the following two chapters, while the first is in certain respects a central topic of our entire study.

One critical conceptual and empirical difficulty in research into historical electoral behavior, a source of disagreement among investigators, is the task of inferring the underlying distribution of partisan loyalties—and shifts in that distribution—on the basis of the actual vote. Realignments are seen as producing new patterns of partisan loyalties and as ushering in periods of relative electoral stability based upon a new distribution or alignment of underlying loyalties. As the classification of elections suggests, however, complete consistency in the partisan distribution of the actual vote is not a characteristic of periods of stability, and shifts in the actual vote in particular elections are not necessarily indications of lasting change in partisan identifications within the electorate. Change in the distribution of the vote, in other words, occurs both during supposedly stable periods as well as during realignments, and a critical task is to determine which of these changes in the actual vote are reflections of change in the underlying distribution of electoral loyalties.

To accomplish this task, a seemingly straightforward procedure has often been followed. Elections in which the distribution of the actual vote departs from the distribution of the vote in preceding elections but resembles the distribution in following elections are seen as realigning elections and as involving change in the basic partisan loyalties of the electorate. The implications of this operational definition of realigning electoral change introduce both theoretical and empirical tensions which are not as yet well reconciled. This definition implicitly identifies voting behavior with partisan attitudes and treats change in the former as a direct indication of change in the latter, despite recognition in other contexts that the partisan voting behavior of individuals often does not coincide with their partisan identifications. The implication of immediate conversion of electoral loyalties from identification with one party to identification with the other, which this procedure involves, is also at odds with other research suggesting the strength and enduring character of partisan identifications once formed.

In the hands of some investigators, this procedure has also involved an assumption of large-scale conversions of individual partisan loyalties during historical realignments. Increasingly, however, analysts have come to doubt on both theoretical and empirical grounds that realignments have involved such massive conversions of partisans from one party to the other. In the case of the New Deal, empirical evidence has been developed which suggests strongly that conversions of partisan identifications constituted a substantially smaller element in the realignment than is often suggested.[8] At a minimum, these conceptual difficulties, theoretical tensions, and conflicting views and findings seem to suggest that a more complex view of realignment is required.

Determination of the character and exact timing of historical realignments is complicated in other ways as well. The findings of various investigators indicate that realigning electoral change has not occurred historically only in the abrupt fashion suggested by the critical election formulation. Lasting electoral change has apparently also occurred over extended "critical periods," rather than in a single election, or over even more extended periods through a process that Key labeled "secular realignment."[9] Indeed, Key suggested that the gradual drift of particular population groups from one party to another could erode partisan alignments without ever causing a sharp break with past patterns.[10] And further complexities have also been encountered. The realignment perspective has been applied to regions, states, and occasionally communities as well as to the entire nation. One result has been the discovery that patterns of electoral stability and change are not identical at all levels, in all elections, or in all geographical areas. Thus here again, a different and more complex view of electoral change and of the realignment process seems clearly indicated.

Exploration of the realignment phenomenon has not, of course, been confined to empirical mapping of patterns of electoral change. In fact, a significant proportion of the literature is concerned with the causes of realignments and with the sources of the new patterns of partisan loyalties seen as their products. Certainly much of Key's work is in this category, as is the work of Samuel Lubell on the New Deal realignment.[11] James L. Sundquist, in a study of noteworthy historical depth, examined the various fates which may befall the political party system in the process of realignment and searched for causal factors in the nature of issue concerns, the character of the existing party leadership, and the nature of the existing partisan alignment. He considered realignment of the existing parties around a new issue dimension, absorption of a third party by the existing parties, and replacement of one or both of the major parties, as well as resolution of the precipitating crisis without realignment.[12]

With rather substantial agreement, scholars have treated realignments as the product of crisis or widespread tensions within society and have seen them as involving significant change in government and politics. In doing so, they call attention to

shifts in issue orientations accompanying realignments and to
their consequences for public policy and elite groups. Walter
Dean Burnham provided one of the striking statements of these
characteristics when he argued that realignments

> are themselves constituent acts: they arise from emergent tensions in
> society which, not adequately controlled by the organization or
> outputs of party politics as usual, escalate to a flashpoint; they are
> issue-oriented phenomena—centrally associated with these tensions
> and more or less leading to resolution adjustments; they result in
> significant transformations in the general shape of policy and they
> have relatively profound after effects on the roles played by institu-
> tional elites. They are involved with redefinitions of the universe of
> voters, political parties, and the broad boundaries of the politically
> possible.[13]

But these formulations leave a number of questions unan-
swered. Crises and tensions have been more common in American political history than partisan realignments, however
defined. Thus the question remains why such circumstances
sometimes produce realignments but at other times do not,
although Burnham, Paul Allen Beck, and others have suggested
partial answers to this general question in terms of gradual
erosion of partisan loyalties and generational change in the
composition of the electorate. A second area of uncertainty has
to do with the mechanisms relating these aspects of the realignment phenomenon to one another.

The rather substantial disruptions of the ranks of office-
holders that have resulted from realigning shifts in electoral
behavior obviously suggest one such mechanism, reconstitution
of the governing political elite. Research has shown change in
the composition of Congress and in the behavior of its members
accompanying realignments.[14] It is possible that much of the
literature on the presidency and the executive branch more
generally could be reinterpreted in the light of the realignment
perspective, but historically oriented work in this area has not
developed in such a fashion. Some analysis of the presidency
and the Supreme Court draws attention to the special problems

facing a president following realignments, but for the most part this literature is limited to Roosevelt and the New Deal.[15] In general, however, investigations of elite characteristics and behavior oriented by the realignment perspective are much less numerous than studies of electoral behavior.

Regardless of disagreement over the exact timing of realignments and some uncertainty as to their exact nature, causes, and consequences, numerous scholars have noted the regularity with which they have occurred. The regularity of their occurrence has been seen as rather neatly dividing the American political past into relatively discrete eras. Thus, Charles Sellers observed a repetitive "equilibrium cycle," and Burnham partitioned the course of American political history into a series of "party systems," each, except for the first, beginning with a partisan realignment and each, except for the latest, terminated by further realignment.[16] While Burnham noted continuities between party systems, he observed that "to a marked degree each is also a discrete entity, with characteristic patterns of voting behavior, of elite and institutional relationships, and of broad system-dominant decisions."[17]

Initially, emphasis was placed upon what were seen as the common and constant properties of these interrealignment eras. They were often treated as essentially "one-party" eras, marked by one party's relatively consistent dominance over the agencies of national government. Dominance over government by a single party, combined with relatively limited examination of electoral data, suggested that each of these eras was characterized by a standing, more or less stable balance of partisan strength in the electorate, which favored one of the parties. The politics of these eras, both at the electoral and the elite levels, were also seen as marked by a constant, dominant, and relatively well-defined pattern of issue concerns, although the empirical basis for this view is not well developed. In view of apparently common and constant properties, interrealignment eras could be taken as little more than periods of essential political stability.

But Sellers had described "cycles" in American two-party politics, roughly corresponding in time to Burnham's party systems, which were characterized by a period of ascendancy by one party followed by decline toward equilibrium between the parties.[18] More recently, examination in greater detail of the sequence of patterns during interrealignment periods, seen in the work of Burnham, Sundquist, and others, has provided a much more complex view of these eras.[19] Burnham has detected "mid-sequence realignments," which might better be termed adjustments, occurring roughly midway through each interrealignment era. In the case of the three most recent party systems, these midsequence adjustments were marked by strong but relatively transitory third-party movements—the Greenback Party in the latter 1870s, the Progressive and Socialist Parties in 1912 and 1914, and the Dixiecrats and Wallace Progressives in 1948.[20]

This more complex view has led to a tendency to divide interrealignment eras into relatively distinct subperiods. Each major historical realignment is seen as followed by a period of stability, a time of consolidation, with continuous dominance by the party advantaged by the realignment—the Democrats following the 1828 realignment, the Republicans during the Civil War and Reconstruction and again after the mid-1890s, then the Democrats following the New Deal realignment. During these phases, the majority party continued to control the presidency and to dominate Congress, although usually with levels of strength somewhat below those enjoyed during the realignment itself.

Perhaps alerted by the deterioration of the New Deal electoral coalition in the 1960s and 1970s, as documented by sample survey research, investigators have also tended to assign particular properties to the periods following midsequence adjustments. In general, the increasing tendency is to see these subperiods, which we label the "decay phases" of interrealignment periods, as times of growing political instability and of deterioration of the prevailing electoral alignments. Causal mechanisms underlying these patterns have been suggested in terms of the gradual disengagement of the partisan coalition created by the realignment, either as a consequence of the waning salience of the issues of realignment or the continuing reconstitution of the electorate by new voters who did not directly experience the earlier realignment.[21] Burnham also suggested that the emergence of third parties during these periods signaled decline toward another full-scale realignment.[22] These considerations are seen as providing at least partial explanations for both growing partisan instability during decay periods and for the periodicity of realignments.

These findings suggest a substantially more complex periodization of American political history. Interrealignment periods, in these terms, are no longer seen only as times of political stability. Thus the rather narrow preoccupation with the phenomenon of partisan realignment characteristic of the earlier literature has been somewhat alleviated. On the other hand, there is a continuing tendency to treat the decay phases of interrealignment periods as of little significance other than as preludes to the next partisan realignment.

The periodization of the political past provided by the realignment perspective is summarized chronologically in Table 1.1, which employs temporal boundaries approximating those which appear more or less conventionally in the literature. So depicted, the temporal boundaries of the several periods and subperiods may seem unduly precise. Indeed, it is almost certain that other investigators would contest some or all of the partitioning dates given here and would perhaps prefer to treat partisan realignments as occurring across relatively extended periods rather than in a single election. Without pausing to debate these issues, we can see that even in these schematic terms, the realignment perspective provides a superficially plausible chronological framework for describing the course of American political history.

As it has emerged in the recent literature, then, the realignment perspective has come to constitute a reasonably systematic and comprehensive view of the American political past. The perspective provides a typology of elections, and it parti-

TABLE 1.1   Electoral Sequences and Classification of Elections,
             1828 to the Present

Party System	Partisan Realignment	Stable Phase	Midsequence Adjustment	Decay Phase
II	1828	1830–1840	1842	1844–1858
III	1860	1862–1874	1876	1878–1894
IV	1896	1898–1910	1912	1914–1930
V	1932	1934–1946	1948	1950–

tions the political past into a relatively clearly demarcated pattern of repetitive periods and subperiods with particular characteristics. As the preceding discussion suggests, however, systematic empirical research oriented by this perspective has tended to focus most intensely upon the voting behavior of the mass electorate. While the perspective points directly to shifts in partisan control of government, to change in public policy, and to shifts in the issue content and orientation of politics which are seen as occurring in relation to electoral realignments, these characteristics are often left implicit and have been subjected less to systematic conceptualization and empirical investigation. In examining mass voting behavior, moreover, disproportionate attention has been focused upon the few historical realigning, or critical, elections. One consequence is that the empirical research has tended to involve intensive examination of limited series of elections, while comparison of extended series of elections has been less common. A second consequence also follows. The periods between realignments have received less attention than the realignments themselves with the result that much of American electoral history has suffered neglect.

Statements and conceptualizations of the general perspective have tended to share these characteristics. In such statements, the relation between electoral realignment, on the one hand, and partisan control of government and public policy, on the other, are recognized. On the whole, however, the more careful conceptualizations, like the more precise quantitative analyses, have tended to focus upon electoral behavior and the process of electoral realignment.

AN EXTENDED PERSPECTIVE

Our purpose in this section is to provide an extended and more consistent and comprehensive statement of the realignment perspective as a point of departure for the empirical investigation to follow in subsequent chapters. Our goal in doing so is to interrelate explicitly processes of electoral change and stability, the performance and policy products of government, and the behavior and performance of political leadership. As we move toward specifying the processes and mechanisms linking together these elements of the political and governmental system, our formulations, like the equivalent formulations of other investigators, become substantially less susceptible to direct support or falsification in terms of empirical historical evidence. Our purpose here, however, is to develop a reasonably coherent and intuitively plausible conceptualization of the realignment perspective, which is at least in some of its aspects subject to empirical assessment.[2 3]

Each of the major periods, or party systems, began with a partisan realignment which involved a shift in the distribution of the popular vote and gave to one of the parties dominance over the agencies of the national government and over an increased proportion of state governments. Shifts in the distribution of the vote came in response to national crises and major, widespread tension within society. As a consequence, the realignments also introduced a new set of issue concerns both at the governmental and the public levels, which were related to the crises and tensions producing the realignment. Control of the agencies of government allowed policy action within these areas to be seen as successfully coping with crises and reducing societal tension. The stable periods following realignments were marked by continued dominance by the party advantaged by realignment, both in terms of electoral strength and in terms of governmental control, although perhaps with the strength declining in both areas. During these periods, the issue concerns produced by crisis and realignment remained preeminent, and policy action in these issue areas continued.

The decay phases following and perhaps merging with these stable periods involved erosion of the electoral alignments produced by the realignments. The beginning of each of these periods was marked by a midsequence adjustment; and they involved at least temporary loss of governmental control by the dominant party and were marked by limited change in the distribution of partisan strength in the nation. The following periods were characterized by indications of greater volatility of the popular vote, by loss of consistent and effective control of government by the dominant party, by deviating elections, and by the appearance of third-party movements. During these periods, the centrality of the issues produced by crisis and realignment tended to decline, and the processes of policy-making worked less effectively, with an increasing propensity to avoid issues and to enter deadlock. These developments can be seen as reflecting increasing deterioration of the elite and popular coalitions produced by the earlier realignment.

These characteristics lead quite straightforwardly to expectations as to patterns of change and stability in indicators of historical political behavior. More precise expectations can be gained by specifying the mechanisms and processes underlying these characteristics. In doing so, however, we must also postulate aspects of past politics which are not subject to direct examination in terms of empirical historical data.

In this context, it is necessary to emphasize a more complex view of the process of partisan realignment than is often suggested by the literature. In this view, historical realignments are seen as involving several interrelated elements. Partisan realignments were initiated by shifts in the distribution of the popular vote in response to crisis conditions and widespread societal tension and dissatisfaction. It is likely that these initiating shifts in the popular vote involved little more than rejection of the party in power and of incumbent office-holders. The consequence, however, was to give the opposing party effective control of government and an opportunity to take policy action perceived as an effective response to crisis.[24]

The formation of a new distribution of electoral partisan loyalties, in this view, involved two steps. First, in response to crisis and as a reflection of widespread dissatisfaction, one party was rejected by the electorate. The second step involved endorsement and affirmation of the advantaged party in subsequent elections, apparently by somewhat different electoral majorities, as a response to governmental action perceived as alleviating crisis.[25] Governmental action perceived as alleviating crisis worked to reinforce new patterns of individual partisan voting behavior and produced a new distribution of attitudinal identifications with the parties. In this view, then, partisan realignment is seen as a process involving conceptually discrete but interrelated elements: electoral rejection of the party in power; capture of effective control of the elective agencies of government by the advantaged party; policy action by that party which could be seen as a response to crisis; and formation of a new distribution of partisan loyalties in the electorate.

Several implications follow from this general view of the realignment process. Electoral change, including lasting change in partisan voting behavior, is not the only component of partisan realignment, nor is it sufficient to account for realignment. Lasting electoral change may occur frequently and is not confined to periods designated as partisan realignments. Indeed, our research suggests that both long-term and short-term electoral change is a more constant property of American politics than much of the relevant literature would indicate. Only rarely, however, have patterns of electoral change combined to produce the major and unidirectional changes in partisan control over the agencies of government critical to historical realignments.

The surges in electoral strength going from one party to the other, which initiated realignments, appear from this perspective as deviating ones, perhaps involving little more than "throwing the rascals out." The central consideration is that these surges of strength could appear as mandates for governmental action; they produced the extraordinary margins of control of government that allowed the decisive and innovative policy actions often seen as characteristic of historical realignments. Policy action which appeared responsive to national problems and which could be perceived as alleviating crisis worked to convert temporary electoral strength into lasting partisan support and loyalty. Whether policy action was in fact responsible for the alleviation of crisis is another matter.

Obviously, we are not implying massive and "instantaneous" conversions of partisan loyalties from one party to the other. Change in voting behavior is conceptually distinguished from change in partisan attitudes. The formation of a new distribution of mass partisan attitudes is seen to be a more gradual process, coming in response to governmental performance and perhaps primarily involving mobilization and demobilization of segments of the potential electorate. This view treats control of government and governmental performance as central elements in the realignment process, and it places particular stress upon political and governmental leadership. Hence, it suggests that historical opportunities for full-scale partisan realignment have been more common than the actual occurrence. As we will argue, the fact that these opportunities did not consistently lead to realignment can be seen as the consequence of failure in the policy-making arena and of the intrusion of unforeseen and perhaps uncontrollable events.

This perspective also suggests processes underlying the characteristics of the periods following historical realignments. The combination of crisis, voting shifts, policy action, and popular response to policy action leads to the formation of new electoral alignments and new coalitions of voting groups. These new alignments and coalitions do not involve a complete break with past patterns of partisan loyalties. Indeed, there is reason to expect substantial continuity in individual partisan identifications from one realignment era to the next. Relatively small shifts, however, in the standing distribution of partisan strength within the electorate tend to work to the lasting advantage of one of the parties.

Realignment also leads to the formation of a dominant issue dimension or a limited set of tightly constrained issue dimensions, along which parties, individuals, and social and economic groups align themselves and toward which they direct their primary political attention. Thus one of the consequences of crisis and realignment is to suppress issue concerns that are not perceived as related to the crisis. Moreover, the same combination of crisis, voting shifts, policy action, and response to policy action creates a symbol (or set of symbols) which refers to crisis and which also alludes to perceived explanations for the crisis and to policies perceived as remedies. For example, the Great Depression, Herbert Hoover, Franklin Roosevelt, the New Deal, and social security are all elements of the symbol pattern produced during the realignment of the 1930s. Similarly, the symbols of the 1860s realignment include those of national union, secession, civil war, Lincoln, slavery, and the yeoman farmer, while those of the 1890s include symbols of business and industrial growth, national modernization, the infant industries, and the tariff.

Here again, realignments do not necessarily involve a sharp or complete break with the past. Rather, realignments apparently can work to reestablish, reinforce, and augment earlier symbol patterns. The realignment of the 1890s, with the restoration of Republican dominance in that decade, is a case in point. The realignment maintained much of the basic symbolic and issue content of the earlier Civil War realignment, while adding new elements related to the crisis, tensions, and policies of the 1890s. On the other hand, realignments shift the focus and add to the issue and symbolic content of politics. Moreover, 'the narrowing of the attention of the electorate to a limited range of issues, combined with shifts in electoral behavior, appears as a mandate for policy action and provides the conditions of united control over government, and the majorities, which permit the advantaged party to take action addressed to crisis and constituting a departure from previous policy patterns.

The symbol and issue patterns produced by partisan realignments work to sustain partisan loyalties during the years that follow. Their strength and endurance is related to the gravity of the realignment crisis and the perceived efficacy of remedial

policies. The stronger the realignment symbols, the greater the
probability of loyal party voting and the longer such loyalties
last following the realignment. But whatever the specific case,
the salience of realignment symbols and issues declines with the
passage of time, as do the stability and strength of the voter
alignments and coalitions produced by the realignment. It is this
process which underlies what we have called the decay phases of
interrealignment periods.

We can describe this process in different, more conventional
terms. The outcome of an election is the product of short-term
forces—that is, issues and conditions of all sorts, candidates'
personalities, campaign activities—and "long-term" forces, such
as party loyalty and other long-standing symbols and issues
which endure beyond a particular election. During a realignment, the dominant short-term forces are the realignment
symbols and issues; through the process of realignment, they
become dominant long-term forces. Over the years, however,
the realignment symbols decline in candidate and issue specif-
icity. Realignment issues become less salient and less controversial, and the positions of the parties with respect to them are
likely to become increasingly similar. As a consequence, the
capacity of realignment issues and symbols to dominate other
issues or candidate appeals also declines. With the passage of
time, new and current conditions lead to short-term forces
becoming increasingly potent in relation to the old issue and
symbol patterns. Since these new issues do not fit the issue
dimensions of the previous realignments, they often lead to
internal divisions within parties or provide the basis for third-
party activities.

This pattern of change is accompanied by the deterioration
of the partisan alignments and coalitions produced by the
realignment. The partisan orientations of individuals and groups
and the configuration of coalitions of voting groups are heavily
based upon and sustained by the symbols and issues associated
with the preceding partisan realignment. New issues and resurgent older issues cut across this pattern of realignment symbols
and issues; they frequently have the effect of politically acti-

vating, or reactivating, conflicting group affiliations and interests. For example, the nomination of a Catholic for president in
1960 had the effect of assigning (or reassigning) political relevance to the group differences between Catholics and Protes-
tants and worked to disrupt the partisan loyalties and partisan
coalitions that had resulted from the preceding realignment. In
other words, during the decay phase, short-term forces can
activate conflicting group affiliations and disrupt existing individual and group loyalties. As a consequence, individuals are
frequently confronted with politically conflicting group pressures; in the aggregate, these cross pressures lead to increased
variability in both partisan voting and turnout.

Just as the realignment symbol declines in strength as an
activator of partisan loyalties under the influence of short-term
forces, it becomes increasingly irrelevant to incoming members
of the electorate. In increasing numbers following realignment,
new voters enter the electorate who have not directly experienced the crisis and other circumstances of the realignment. As
a consequence of the natural attrition of the years, older voters
who were directly involved and who directly experienced the
events and circumstances of the realignment disappear from the
electorate. In other words, the electorate is increasingly composed of voters whose ties to the realignment are indirect and
relatively weak. Thus, during the decay phase, the tendency of
young voters to identify strongly with the parties gradually
diminishes, and the likelihood they will identify as independents increases. Like the increased proportion of individuals
under cross pressures, the greater proportion of independents
and weak partisans in the electorate leads in the aggregate to
greater variability in party support and levels of turnout, to
increase in split-ticket voting, and to greater susceptibility to
short-term forces.

The increasing importance of short-term forces and the
increasing electoral volatility characteristic of these periods do
not necessarily work to the advantage or disadvantage of either
of the parties. That is, they can work disproportionately to the
benefit of the minority or the majority party, or they can work

to the advantage of first one party and then the other. The point is that voting behavior becomes less consistent and partisan alignments less stable. Nor is electoral change limited to the effects of short-term forces or decline in the incidence and strength of partisan identifications. New voting groups appear with new partisan attachments, and secular realignment of particular groups occurs. But these patterns of change do not lead to dominance by either party; rather, they contribute to further derangement of the old alignment.

Electoral change is accompanied by parallel and related change in elite behavior and in the performance of government. The process of realignment creates new partisan elite coalitions with reasonably coherent issue orientations and policy goals. These coalitions work to provide at least a partial bridge between agencies of government, both at particular levels of government and from one level of government to the other. Thus they provide a basis for relatively integrated, coherent, and effective governmental action. During decay phases, elite coalitions are increasingly disrupted, and their issue and policy coherence diminished as new issues appear, as older issues temporarily suppressed by the circumstances of realignment regain salience, and as new leaders emerge.

As deterioration of electoral alignments continues, legislators and other elected officials are confronted with new, diverse, changing, and often conflicting constituency demands and interests. The process of realignment involves narrowing of electoral interests to a limited range of issues and results in relatively focused demand for governmental action addressed to those issues. As time passes following realignments, constituencies change in composition and issue orientations. As a consequence of the growing susceptibility of the electorate to new issues and short-term forces and as a consequence of the diminishing strength and incidence of partisan identifications during decay phases, officials are elected for increasingly diverse reasons, bases of electoral support become less dependable, and political parties as symbols have less and less common meaning both among voters and among leaders. But despite deterioration of the old alignment, political leaders are not fully free to abandon older issues and bases of support in order to embrace new issues in an effort to build new coalitions. The issues, symbols, and voter coalitions produced by the preceding realignment retain salience and importance for the electorate. To ignore them is to risk defeat at the polls.

These processes can lead to increasing incidence of deviating elections, to periodic loss of dominance over the agencies of government by the party advantaged by the preceding realignment, to divided partisan control of government, or, as in the latter nineteenth century, to the absence of a clear majority party. These conditions obviously diminished the capacity of either party to take consistent and effective policy action. But even when one party retains majority status and continues to hold consistent and united control of government, as in the 1920s, loss of internal coherence and unity diminishes its effectiveness as a mechanism of integrated policy formation and implementation.

These processes and patterns of change help to explain the characteristics of policy-making during the decay phases of interrealignment eras. In contrast to realignment periods, policy-making tends to be incremental rather than innovative, and the tendency to avoid issues increases. As the parties lose capacity to function as bridges between agencies of government and from one level of government to the other, the likelihood of coherent and consistent public policy diminishes, and discordant policy action increases. At the risk of overstating the case, the process of alignment decay can be seen as involving feedback and multiplier effects. The progressive decay of partisan alignments is accompanied by declining effectiveness of government, by increasing propensity for policy deadlock, and by failure to cope with new problems, tensions, and discontents within the polity. As a result, the propensity of the system to produce short-term forces and unresolved problems increases, and popular confidence in government and the parties declines, with temporal distance from the preceding realignment. It may follow as well that the likelihood of crisis of a magnitude sufficient to produce partisan realignment also increases with temporal distance from the preceding realignment.

This is not to say that deterioration of electoral alignments necessarily leads to a new realignment or that the issues gaining salience during decay phases necessarily anticipate the issues of a coming realignment. As electoral alignments deteriorate, the electorate becomes increasingly susceptible to realignment should a crisis of sufficient magnitude occur. This susceptibility has been indicated historically by increased incidence of third parties, by increasing variability in turnout and in the partisan distribution of the vote, by frequent deviating elections and conditions of divided partisan control over the presidency and Congress, and by increased incidence of split-ticket voting. These characteristics of decay phases reflect, in turn, growth of a pool of active or inactive voters whose attachments to the parties are weak or nonexistent and who are susceptible to realignment as a consequence of crisis, widespread tension, and dissatisfaction.

Historical interrealignment periods, except for the most recent, have terminated in crisis and a new realignment about 36 years after the preceding realignment, although we can neither specify the types of crisis that produce realignments nor argue that interrealignment periods are necessarily of any particular temporal length. With the passage of time, the electorate becomes sufficiently disengaged from the partisan divisions, issues, and symbols of the past to be susceptible to a realignment in partisan loyalties should crisis conditions, tensions, and dissatisfactions of sufficient magnitude develop. Various types of crisis, tension, and dissatisfaction can lead to realignment, and because of declining capacity of government during decay phases to address and resolve societal problems, the likelihood of such conditions may increase during these periods.

The probability that these conditions will produce realignment in any particular case is related both to the magnitude of crisis (in terms of the proportion of the population directly affected) and the temporal distance from the preceding realignment. Thus, the longer the erosion of the previous alignment has progressed, the less severe the crisis and tension needed to initiate a new realignment. Neither deterioration of electoral alignments nor crisis alone is sufficient to produce realignment, nor is the combination of the two. As we have argued above, policy action by government that can be popularly perceived as a meaningful and effective response to societal problems is a further and necessary component of the realignment process.

In terms of public policy and popular control of policy directions, the realignment perspective is a rather simple one. Much of the time, policy initiatives are at best incremental, often conflicting and ineffective, and electoral pressures are diffuse, erratic, and inconsistent. The realignment perspective suggests that "politics as usual," and the lack of policy direction and electoral intensity the phrase implies, are typical of the American political system. On the occasion of infrequent partisan realignments, public pressure on elected officials becomes much less ambiguous; during these periods, political parties reveal unaccustomed unity of purpose which bridges the diverse agencies and levels of government. These are periods when the public expresses strong preferences, and these views are translated more or less directly into governmental action by a newly dominant party. Historically, partisan realignments have occurred under conditions of national crisis—although not all crises have been accompanied by realignments—and have produced a level of political integration and articulation sufficient to allow effective and coordinated governmental response, albeit usually within a relatively limited and well-defined issue area. Partisan realignments can thus be seen as both the products of accumulated tensions and dysfunctions and as the means through which responses to these problems have occurred. But partisan realignments are rare. For the most part, the political and governmental system meanders along almost casually, and only intermittently is the direction of the system controlled firmly by a combination of electoral and leadership forces.

Although the formulation of the realignment perspective developed here is not ruthlessly parsimonious, the generalized manner in which it is presented may well provoke reservations.

It is stated as if it applied with complete consistency to a century and a half of American political history. This despite the massive social, economic, political, and institutional changes which have overtaken the nation during these years. Moreover, we encounter at a number of points significant empirical evidence that does not fully conform to even the extended realignment perspective sketched here.

In some degree, these deviations of empirical evidence from the realignment perspective appear explicable when historical patterns of change are taken into account. That is to say, when we specify even crudely what elements of change in the social, economic, and institutional environment of politics have occurred over the past 150 years, some of these deviations of empirical evidence from the realignment perspective appear plausibly reconciled. In other cases, however, this or other reconciliations are substantially less plausible. Hence doubts and questions arise at a number of points as to the adequacy of this general conceptual perspective. Whether these doubts and questions should be seen as products of measurement limitations imposed by the characteristics of historical data, as indications of the inadequacy of the realignment perspective either in general or as formulated here, or more simply as reflections of the inadequacies of the present research are matters to be left for subsequent investigation and evaluation. Readers may well wish for more definitive conclusions about the adequacy of this perspective and the complex patterns of relationships it involves, but the complexity and importance of the subject matter impose cautions which we are not inclined to resist.

Two further matters touched on above require additional stress. Political parties and partisan processes are central to the perspective developed and employed here, and the adequacy of the perspective and the following analysis is dependent upon the acceptability of the view of parties as basic elements of electoral behavior and policy-making. It is assumed that political parties are meaningful objects of identification for the bulk of the electorate, and that many voters are capable of using party labels to reward leaders with their votes when satisfied or to rebuke them by denying votes when dissatisfied. But the political party is also crucial for leaders as a basis for coordinating their policy-making activities within and between institutions at a given level of government, as well as a mechanism for coordinating, at least loosely, between levels of government.

Political parties are obviously not the only factor in the decision-making of either voters or political leaders, but parties are uniquely important to both. Political parties constitute an institutional device for organizing political and governmental action and for marshaling popular support behind policies and methods of implementation. Nothing about the realignment perspective argues that political parties will necessarily accomplish great feats, only that they have the capacity for coordinating policy-making and the ability to link mass preferences to policy-making. Of course, these capabilities may go unrealized.

The realignment perspective as developed here also places major stress upon the performance of government and upon political and governmental leadership. Students of politics almost invariably view political leaders as inadequate to the demands of the times, and while the judgment may be unduly harsh, it correctly focuses attention on leaders. The realignment perspective as presented above clearly views the political leadership as the active element in policy-making and the electorate as passive and reactive. The study of the mass public alone may yield accurate reflections of the behavior of leaders, but to a greater degree than heretofore, analytic attention must be focused on the leaders themselves. This volume cannot claim to be a major step in that respect; we hope it is a move in the right direction.

NOTES

1. The major landmark in this literature, of course, is V. O. Key, Jr., "A Theory of Critical Elections," *Journal of Politics* 17 (February 1955), pp. 3-18. Major works since 1955 are Walter Dean Burnham, "Party Systems and the Political Process," in

William Nisbet Chambers and Walter Dean Burnham (eds.), *The American Party Systems: Stages of Political Development* (New York: Oxford University Press, 1975) and *Critical Elections and the Mainsprings of American Politics* (New York: Norton, 1970); James L. Sundquist, *Dynamics of the Party System* (Washington, DC: Brookings Institution, 1973); Gerald Pomper, *Elections in America* (New York: Dodd, Mead, 1968). For a collection of major articles on the subject, see Jerome M. Clubb and Howard W. Allen (eds.), *Electoral Change and Stability in American Political History* (New York: Macmillan, 1971).

2. V. O. Key, Jr., "A Theory of Critical Elections," p. 4. A contemporary but relatively neglected work by Schattschneider outlined the major party systems and treated both 1896 and 1932 conceptually as critical elections. See E. E. Schattschneider, "United States: The Functional Approach to Party Government," in Sigmund Neumann (ed.), *Modern Political Parties* (Chicago: University of Chicago Press, 1956), pp. 194-215. A later version of many of the same points is more widely cited. E. E. Schattschneider, *The Semi-Sovereign People* (New York: Holt, Rinehart and Winston, 1960).

3. Angus Campbell, "A Classification of Presidential Elections," in Angus Campbell, Philip E. Converse, Warren E. Miller, and Donald E. Stokes, *Elections and the Political Order* (New York: John Wiley, 1966), pp. 63-77. For an earlier statement, see Angus Campbell, Philip E. Converse, Warren E. Miller, and Donald E. Stokes, *The American Voter* (New York: John Wiley, 1960), pp. 531-538.

4. Gerald Pomper, "Classification of Presidential Elections," *Journal of Politics* 29 (August 1967), pp. 535-566.

5. Campbell et al., *The American Voter*, pp. 523-538; Campbell, "A Classification of Presidential Elections," and Converse, "The Concept of a Normal Vote," both in Campbell et al., *Elections and the Political Order*, pp. 63-77 and 9-39 respectively.

6. For several possibilities, see Jerome M. Clubb and Howard W. Allen, "The Cities and the Election of 1928: Partisan Realignment?" *American Historical Review* 74 (April 1969), pp. 1205-1220. The election of 1924 is preferred by Allen J. Lichtman, "Critical Election Theory and the Reality of American Presidential Politics, 1916-1940," *American Historical Review* 81 (April 1976), pp. 317-348.

7. Most analysts mark the Civil War realignment at 1860, but Gerald Pomper uses 1864. See Pomper, "Classification of Presidential Elections." Walter Dean Burnham has used 1854; see Burnham, *Critical Elections*. There is more agreement on the date of 1896, although analysts who examine off-year elections mark the realignment at 1894. Again, see Burnham, *Critical Elections*.

8. See Philip E. Converse, "Public Opinion and Voting Behavior," in Fred I. Greenstein and Nelson W. Polsby (eds.), *Handbook of Political Science* Vol. 4, (Reading, MA: Addison Wesley, 1975), pp. 135-144; Kristi Andersen, "Generation, Partisan Shift and Realignment: A Look Back at the New Deal," in Norman H. Nie, Sidney Verba, and John R. Petrocik, *The Changing American Voter* (Cambridge, MA: Harvard University Press, 1976), pp. 74-95; Paul Allen Beck, "A Socialization Theory of Partisan Realignment," in Richard G. Niemi and Associates *The Politics of Future Citizens* (San Francisco: Jossey-Bass, 1974), pp. 199-119; and William Claggett, "The Development of Partisan Attachments in the American Electorate," Ph.D. dissertation, University of Minnesota, 1978.

9. See V. O. Key, Jr., "Secular Realignment and the Party System," *Journal of Politics* 21 (May 1959), pp. 198-210. The concept of a "critical period" is elaborated

in Duncan MacRae, Jr., and James A. Meldrum, "Critical Elections in Illinois: 1888-1958," *American Political Science Review* 54 (September 1960), pp. 669-683.

10. Such a formulation obviously can be amended to describe the gradual mobilization of formerly inactive political groups, which would then rearrange existing electoral coalitions and alignments. See V. O. Key, Jr., "Secular Realignment." During the last decade or so, considerable scholarly attention has been given to the assessment of gradual party realignment in the South, which apparently includes mobilization, inmigration and outmigration, as well as individual changes in identification. See, for example, Philip E. Converse, "On the Possibility of a Major Political Realignment in the South," in Campbell et al., *Elections and the Political Order,* pp. 212-242; Philip E. Converse, "Change in the American Electorate," in Angus Campbell and Philip E. Converse (eds.), *The Human Meaning of Social Change* (New York: Russell Sage, 1972), pp. 307-317; William C. Havard (ed.), *The Changing Politics of the South* (Baton Rouge: Louisiana State University Press, 1972); Bruce A. Campbell, "Patterns of Change in Partisan Loyalties of Native Southerners: 1952-1972," *Journal of Politics* 39 (August 1977), pp. 730-761; Paul Allen Beck, "Partisan Realignment in the Postwar South," *American Political Science Review* 71 (June 1977), pp. 477-496; Raymond E. Wolfinger and Robert S. Arseneau, "Partisan Change in the South," presented at the annual meeting of the American Political Science Association, 1974.

11. In many ways, Lubell's contributions to the early development of these analytic traditions were as important as Key's. See Samuel Lubell, *The Future of American Politics* (New York: Harper and Row, 1952).

12. Sundquist, *Dynamics of the Party System,* especially Ch. 2.

13. Burnham, *Critical Elections,* p. 10.

14. In addition to the work of Sundquist, *Dynamics of the Party System,* already cited, see David Brady, *Congressional Voting in a Partisan Era* (Lawrence: University Press of Kansas, 1973); David Brady, "Critical Elections, Congressional Parties and Clusters of Policy Changes: A Comparison of 1896 and 1932 Realignment Eras," presented at the annual meeting of the American Political Science Association, 1975; David W. Brady and Naomi B. Lynn, "Switched Seat Congressional Districts: Their Effect on Party Voting and Public Policy," *American Journal of Political Science* 17 (1973), pp. 523-543; Michael R. King and Lester G. Seligman, "Critical Elections, Congressional Recruitment and Public Policy," in Heinz Eulau and Morris Czudnowski (eds.), *Elite Recruitment in Democratic Politics* (New York: Halsted Press, 1976), pp. 263-299; H. Douglas Price, "The Congressional Career—Then and Now," in Nelson W. Polsby (ed.), *Congressional Behavior* (New York: Random House, 1971); Barbara Deckard Sinclair, "Party Realignment and the Transformation of the Political Agenda: The House of Representatives, 1925-1938," *American Political Science Review* 71 (1977), pp. 940-953; Barbara Sinclair, "From Party Voting to Regional Fragmentation: The House of Representatives, 1933-1956," *American Politics Quarterly* 6 (April 1978), pp. 125-146; Jerome M. Clubb and Santa A. Traugott, "Partisan Cleavage and Cohesion in the House of Representatives, 1861-1974," *Journal of Interdisciplinary History* (1977), pp. 375-401.

15. For an exception focusing on Jackson and Lincoln as well as Roosevelt, see Robert Scigliano, *The Supreme Court and the Presidency* (New York: Macmillan, 1971).

16. Charles Sellers, "The Equilibrium Cycle of Two-Party Politics," *Public Opinion Quarterly* 29 (Spring 1965), pp. 16-38; Burnham, "Party Systems and the Political Process."

17. Burnham, "Party Systems and the Political Process," p. 289.

18. Sellers, "The Equilibrium Cycle of Two-Party Politics."

19. See especially Sundquist, *Dynamics of the Party System*, and Burnham, *Critical Elections*.

20. Burnham, *Critical Elections*, p. 27 and passim.

21. Sundquist, *Dynamics of the Party System*; Beck, "A Socialization Theory of Partisan Realignment."

22. Burnham, *Critical Elections*, p. 27.

23. In formulating this perspective, we have particularly benefited from Burnham, *Critical Elections* and "Party Systems and the Political Process"; Gerald M. Pomper, *Elections in America: Control and Influence in Democratic Politics* (New York: Dodd Mead, 1970); and Sundquist, *Dynamics of the Party System*. It would be impossible to cite all the literature on political parties, elections, and government that might have influenced the content of this section. Many of the works already cited provide an overview of the realignment perspective, and we have attempted to utilize them. Some relevant works not previously cited are: V. O. Key, Jr., and Frank Munger, "Social Determinism and Electoral Decision: The Case of Indiana," in Eugene Burdick and Arthur J. Brodbeck (eds.), *American Voting Behavior* (New York: Macmillan, 1959), pp. 281-299; Paul Kleppner, *The Cross of Culture—A Social Analysis of Midwestern Politics, 1850-1900* (New York: Macmillan, 1970); Richard J. Jensen, *The Winning of the Midwest: Social and Political Conflict, 1888-1896* (Chicago: University of Chicago Press, 1971); Melvyn Hammarberg, *The Indiana Voter: The Historical Dynamics of Party Allegiance During the 1870's* (Chicago: University of Chicago Press, 1977); Ronald P. Formisano, *The Birth of Mass Political Parties: Michigan, 1827-1861* (Princeton, NJ: Princeton University Press, 1971); Samuel T. McSeveney, *The Politics of Depression: Political Behavior in the Northeast, 1893-1896* (New York: Oxford University Press, 1972); Richard J. Trilling, "Party Image, Party Identification and Partisan Realignment," unpublished; William L. Shade, *Social Change and the Electoral Process* (Gainesville: University of Florida Press, 1973); Michael P. Rogin and John L. Shover, *Political Change in California: Critical Elections and Social Movements, 1890-1966* (Westport, CT: Greenwood Publishing, 1970); Lee Benson, Joel H. Silbey, and Phyllis Field, "Toward a Theory of Stability and Change in American Voting Patterns: New York State, 1792-1970," in Joel H. Silbey, Allan G. Bogue, and William H. Flanigan (eds.), *The History of American Electoral Behavior* (Princeton, NJ: Princeton University Press, 1978); John L. Hammond, "Minor Parties and Electoral Realignments," *American Party Strength in the United States* (Charlottesville: University Press of Virginia, 1972); Ray M. Shortridge, "The Voter Realignment in the Midwest During the 1850s," *American Politics Quarterly* 4 (April 1976), pp. 193-222; Benjamin Ginsberg, "Critical Elections and the Substance of Party Conflict," *Midwest Journal of Political Science* 16 (November 1972), pp. 603-625; Dale Baum, "Know- Nothingism and the Republican Majority in Massachusetts: The Political Realignment of the 1850s," *Journal of American History* 64 (March 1978), pp. 959-986. For an earlier effort to state the perspective developed in this section, see Walter Dean Burnham, Jerome M. Clubb, and William H. Flanigan, "Partisan Realignment: A Systemic Perspective," prepared

for presentation at the Mathematical Social Science Board Conference on Historical Voting Behavior, Cornell University, 1973, and published in Silbev et al., *The History of American Electoral Behavior.* A perspective similar in some respects to the one developed in this book is provided by Paul Allen Beck, "The Electoral Cycle and Patterns of American Politics," *British Journal of Political Science* 9 (April 1979), pp. 129-156.

24. It would be a mistake to exaggerate the departure here from earlier work. Most analysts implicitly link electoral patterns with policy-making, but explicitly they conceptualize election returns as the realignment. In the closely related literature on competition, attention has been focused on control of government. See, for example, Joseph A. Schlesinger, "The Structure of Competition for Office in the American States," *Behavioral Science* 5 (1960), pp. 197-210, and "A Two- dimensional Scheme for Classifying the States According to Degree of Inter-party Competition," *American Political Science Review* 49 (1955), pp. 1120-1128; or, more recently, C. Anthony Broh and Mark S. Levine, "Patterns of Party Competition," *American Political Quarterly* 6 (July 1978), pp. 357-384.

25. It is hard to imagine any substantial investigation of this process of attitude formation without individual level data, and it would be odd to find circumstances in which aggregate data could effectively address these points. Some empirical evidence for these steps is in W. Phillips Shively, "A Reinterpretation of the New Deal Realignment—Based of All Things, on the *Literary Digest* Poll," *Public Opinion Quarterly* (1971-1972), pp. 621-624.

Chapter 2

IDENTIFYING REALIGNMENTS:

CORRELATIONAL ANALYSIS

Analysis of electoral change has been central to research involving the realignment perspective. Indeed, the identification of realignment periods has rested almost exclusively on the discovery of lasting changes in aggregate voting patterns. The electorate is conceptualized as having a relatively stable partisanship, a "normal vote" is Converse's term,[1] which, infrequently and dramatically, may be disrupted. Such a disruption results in a basic realignment of the partisan divisions in the electorate, producing a new alignment which endures with considerable stability until the next dramatic disruption.

This general point of view is illustrated well by the introduction to a collection of essays dealing with the history of American voting behavior. The editors, Silbey and McSeveney, sum-

marize the "pattern of political cycles" which forms the common
theoretical thread through their volume in this way:

> [The] stable periods are ended by short but intense periods of
> critical changes in partisan alignments. As a consequence of some
> violent social or economic experience, a number of groups in the
> electorate find their traditional voting habits no longer congenial.
> Many of them permanently change their partisan loyalties, resulting
> in a new distribution of party support in the electorate and the birth
> of a new electoral era.[2]

This view of stable electoral patterns punctuated by sharp
realignment dominates most of recent historical analysis and
many interpretations of contemporary electoral politics as well.

When stated in stark outline, such a formulation of electoral
history must provoke reservations. Several such qualifications
have already been alluded to in Chapter 1: Deviating elections
and midsequence adjustments mar the picture of stability; the
dramatic bursts of change may be gradual instead. Furthermore,
in studies of particular areas, various scholars have called attention to realigning change in connection with elections other
than those usually considered to be "critical elections." Shover
found evidence of realignment in California in connection with
the elections of 1916[3]; Sundquist refers to the "minor realignments" of the 1920s and the "aftershocks" of the New Deal in
Minnesota, Wisconsin, and elsewhere[4]; and Benson et al. have
noted in New York an electoral cycle involving substantially
more frequent realigning change than that observed by other
scholars.[5]

At the same time, evidence of great stability and continuity
in partisan voting behavior across realignments has also been
noted. In their analysis of voting in Indiana, for example, V.O.
Key and Frank Munger stressed the durability of partisan
attachments from the Civil War to 1948.[6] They found some
gradual, "secular" realignment in the New Deal years, but
mainly a pattern of stable partisanship with brief deviations.
While Indiana may be considered an extreme case of partisan
stability, other examples could be found in both the North and

South. Even so, it is probably accurate to suggest that most scholars, at least when speaking generally, would view American mass electoral politics as characterized historically by "stable periods . . . ended by short but intense periods of critical changes in partisan alignments."[7]

Viewed in this way, the assessment of changes in underlying partisan loyalty is crucially important to electoral analysts. As a consequence, most analysts of historical patterns have concentrated on the identification and timing of realigning elections and on describing the electoral alignments transformed by them. There is considerable agreement about the general timing of major realignments—the late 1820s, the latter 1850s and early 1860s, the middle 1890s, and the latter 1920s through the mid-1930s. Simply by looking at the vote for major party candidates for president since 1824, as represented in Figure 2.1, one can see how such general agreement came about. Obvious and lasting changes occurred in presidential voting in 1828 with the strong showing by Andrew Jackson, in 1860 following the emergence of the Republican party, in 1896 when the Republicans began an era of dominance after the close competition of the preceding decades, and in 1932 when the Democratic party escaped from minority status to hold the presidency for twenty years. Perhaps because these national data in Figure 2.1 are so simple and stark, it has been relatively easy for analysts to agree on the general timing of realignments, although attempts to pinpoint *the* critical election in these realignments and to interpret and explain the sources of the observed changes give rise to more argument.

THE CONVENTIONAL VIEW OF
ELECTORAL CHANGE

In addition to the general timing of the major realignments, there has been basic agreement on what form of electoral change constitutes a realignment and on the methodology to be employed in assessing such change. Almost universally, analysts have emphasized the differential shifting of social and geo-

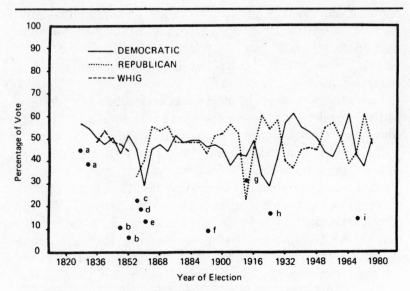

SOURCE: United States Historical Election Returns, Inter-university
Consortium for Political and Social Research

a	National Republican	f	People's
b	Free Soil	g	Bull Moose Progressive
c	American	h	Progressive
d	Southern	i	American Independent
e	Constitutional Union		

Figure 2.1: Partisan Division of the Presidential Vote, 1828-1976

graphical bases of support for the political parties as the sole
indication of a realignment. Conceptually, they have emphasized the movement of voters both toward and away from a
party. Attention has been focused on aspects of the crisis and
the political responses to it which rearrange the underlying
partisan loyalties by appealing to new support in some areas and
losing old supporters elsewhere.

The emphasis on differential changes in the discussion of
realignments can be seen most clearly in James Sundquist's
Dynamics of the Party System, where the "scenario" describing
the realignment of two existing parties draws on a diagram
similar to Figure 2.2.[8] This diagram, adapted by Sundquist

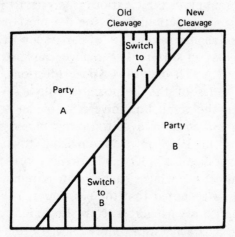

Old   New
Cleavage   Cleavage

Switch
to
A

Party

A

Party

B

Switch
to
B

Adapted from James L. Sundquist, *Dynamics of the Party System*
(Washington: Brookings Institution, 1973) p. 19.

Figure 2.2: Realignment of Two Existing Parties

from Schattschneider,[9] captures the prevailing meaning of
realigning electoral change quite appropriately. According to
Sundquist, the supporters of Party A and Party B are divided
along the "old cleavage" when a "new cleavage" cuts across
supporters of both parties. The new line of party cleavage cuts
across the old bases of party support, leading a segment of each
party to switch to the other party. Illustratively, at the top of
Figure 2.2, some former supporters of Party B switch to Party
A; there is a comparable switch from Party A to Party B. As a
result, according to the diagram, the parties remain the same in
size but have a somewhat different composition. Sundquist
realized that the diagram did not accurately represent electoral
reality and mentioned that point in a footnote, but the visual
image and the accompanying discussion give the impression of
compensating exchanges of supporters.[10] Of course, the fact
that the parties often do not remain the same size after such a
reshuffling is of critical importance since this changes the bal-

ance of power between the parties. But it is significant that the methodologies employed by various analysts to identify and interpret realigning elections have for the most part failed to take account of change in the *level* of party support.[11]

This emphasis on differential change can also be seen in Key's article, "A Theory of Critical Elections," where he plotted time series of the Democratic vote in New England towns.[12] When the trend lines diverged, like an "opening scissors," it was evidence of a shift in the underlying partisan cleavage. Thus, in 1928 in New England, towns that were heavily low income, Catholic, and foreign born moved in a Democratic direction while Yankee towns remained Republican. However, Key noted that the election of 1896 revealed a different pattern; towns across New England, regardless of socioeconomic characteristics, moved away from the Democratic Party, indicating a rather uniform rejection of the candidacy of William Jennings Bryan, a rejection which did not rearrange the basic partisan cleavages in the electorate. Key observed: "Perhaps the significant feature of the 1896 contest was that, at least in New England, it did not form a new division . . . the Republicans succeeded in drawing new support, in about the same degree, from all sorts of economic and social classes."[13] Other analysts have been quick to restore the emphasis on differential change in pointing out that the realignment of 1896 did indeed involve differential changes on the part of various population groups, but on a regional level.[14] As the North, East, and parts of the Midwest moved quite uniformly toward the Republican Party, the South and West became more Democratic, thus transforming the basis of geographical support of the two parties.

Both the substantive findings and their conceptual perspective led analysts to use quantitative techniques which assessed the presence of differential change occurring in the electorate. With escalating methodological sophistication, correlational analysis, or methods based on correlation, became the most widely used technique for demonstrating the same kind of divergent electoral behavior Key had sought to show with his trend lines. MacRae and Meldrum used factor analysis of the differential change in the Democratic vote in Illinois counties to identify the sources of partisan change during the "critical periods" of the 1890s and the New Deal.[15] Gerald Pomper used correlational techniques in several different ways both to identify realigning elections and to demonstrate the stability of the postrealignment electoral pattern.[16] In one analysis, he correlated the vote in successive elections, and in another, he correlated the vote by states in each election with an average vote in the four preceding elections, finding in some years sharp drops in the size of the correlation coefficients indicating changes in partisan patterns.[17]

As long as analysts focused on the reshuffling of electoral units, these statistical techniques served their conceptual purposes well enough. The broad conceptualization perhaps, and the specific techniques certainly, led analysts to ignore other forms of electoral change. And Pomper, in particular, makes it quite explicit that this is precisely his intention. Pomper explained correctly:

> Correlation analysis will indicate the relative degree of electoral continuity or change. If there is high geographical continuity between two elections, regardless of partisan victory or defeat, the correlation coefficient should be high. If there is change, even if the same party wins both elections considered, we should find a relatively low coefficient.[18]

Consequently, analysts have been able to assess breaks in electoral patterns as long as these changes were characterized by differential switching of geographical units.

The prevailing interpretations of electoral history reflect implicit agreement on three points: (1) Realignments occurred as dramatic bursts of change, disrupting a stable alignment but producing new stable electoral patterns; (2) realignments produced profound electoral reordering of population groups, considerably altering the bases of party support; and (3) major realignments occurred during or immediately preceding the Civil

War years, in the 1890s, and in the late 1920s or 1930s. Given a perspective that views all realigning change in American electoral history in the form of differential switching of partisans, one would expect to find dramatic breaks in correlations between elections at each of these periods. We do not intend to quarrel with the conclusion that these three time periods represent significant turning points in American electoral history. We will argue, however, that a reexamination of election data with basically the same techniques others have used does not lead unequivocally to this conclusion. The analysis presented in the remainder of this chapter, based upon the Democratic and Republican votes for president and for Congress from 1840 to the present, will show the following:

(1) Correlational analysis does not isolate 1896 and 1932 (or 1928) as realigning elections; using the criterion of a break in series of correlations between proximate elections, these elections appear to be deviating rather than realigning.

(2) Analysis of correlation matrices shows more stability *across* realignments than would be expected if realignments represent the formation of "new and durable electoral groupings."

Part, but only part, of the difference in our results from those of others is due to the more extensive data base that we have been able to employ. Use of the votes of both major parties--which are seldom mirror images of each other--and of congressional as well as presidential data shows that the important changes that occur in the electoral series for a single office and for one party are often peculiar to that series and fail to have the broader significance often attributed to them. Similarly, examination of the entire election series, rather than portions of it, demonstrates the long-term stability of electoral patterns.

More importantly, however, we will argue that correlational analysis does not reveal dramatic breaks in electoral patterns, because it captures only one type of change, missing other sorts of electoral shifts that have been at least as significant in producing the far-reaching political change we associate with major partisan realignments.

CORRELATION AS A TECHNIQUE
FOR MEASURING ELECTORAL CHANGE

As has been discussed above, realigning electoral change has usually been conceptualized as change in which some part of the electorate moves in one direction, another part in the opposite one. A realignment is seen as rearranging the electorate in terms of the relative strengths of the support that various elements give to one or the other party. Put another way, the relative ordering of units in terms of the support given to a party is changed.

Correlational approaches can be used to measure electoral change conceptualized in this way. Correlational techniques can assess the extent to which the units of analysis have remained in the same relative positions from one election to the next or assess the degree to which the units have been rearranged. The high, positive value for the correlation between, say, the Democratic percentages in two elections means that the units of analysis have remained in the same relative position in the two elections. (It does not necessarily mean, and in practice usually does not mean, that the Democratic percentages of the vote are the same in the two elections.) A low, positive value or a negative coefficient means that units have shifted differentially and perhaps have been completely rearranged.

Correlating a party's percentage of the vote in adjacent elections should reveal major breaks in electoral patterns. Correlations between elections with similar ordering of patterns of support for a party will yield a series of large, positive coefficients. A disruption of an orderly election series should be expected to take one of two forms. A single, deviating election would not be highly correlated with either the preceding election or the following election, so *two* coefficients in succession would have low values. A realigning election, on the other hand, would have little relationship with the preceding election but would be highly related to the next election, because a new pattern would be established. In the case of a realigning election, a *single* low value would interrupt the series of coefficients. (An erratic series would yield a string of low correlation coefficients.) Initially, we will use these rules to examine single series of correlations recognizing that a more elaborate examination is possible for matrices of correlations which we will take up subsequently.

Correlation coefficients have been calculated for presidential and for congressional voting in the nation, with states as the units of analysis. Series of correlations for the percentages of the total vote for Democrats and Republicans (and briefly Whigs) are shown in Table 2.1, and these series can be examined for indications of deviating and realigning elections. New states are added to the computations over the years as they enter the union, and the Confederate states are removed briefly during the Civil War period.[19] Consequently, there is a changing but usually growing set of states used as the basis for analysis.

Prevailing expectations are that evidence will be found of realigning elections during the Civil War era, in the 1890s, and around the New Deal for both parties. In other words, one would expect to find a single, low coefficient in a series of high values indicating the presence of an election not related to preceding elections and highly related to subsequent elections. The Republican presidential voting data for 1864 reveal this pattern for the correlations surrounding that election. The Republican vote in 1864 was not highly related to the party's vote in 1860, a correlation of .44, but the Republican vote in 1864 and 1868 revealed a strong correlation of .84. The Democratic pattern in the Civil War era suggests a deviating election in 1860. The Democratic vote, Douglas's support only, was negatively correlated with the party's showing in 1856, a correlation of -.49, and was almost totally unrelated to the Democratic vote in 1864, a correlation of -.05. The strong pattern of relationship between Democratic percentages in adjacent elections in evidence prior to 1860 began again with the 1864 election. The traditional Democratic vote was, of course, disrupted by the candidacy of Breckenridge in 1860. If his vote is combined with that of Douglas, the strength of relationship is restored to a moderately high, positive correlation of .67.

The interpretation suggesting that the Democratic vote in 1860 appears more as a temporary deviation than a realignment deserves some qualification. The Confederate states were not included in the analysis from 1864 until their individual readmissions to the union; thus the correlations are necessarily based on varying subsets of cases during these years. Nevertheless, the fact remains that correlational analysis alone reveals no evidence of realignment in the Democratic presidential vote during the Civil War period.

In the 1890s, the Democratic series shows a break suggesting that a realignment occured in the presidential vote in 1896. The correlation between the Democratic votes in 1892 and 1896 is a low .08, followed by a high correlation of .78 between the votes of 1896 and 1900. However, the Republican vote for president shows no such break; the correlations between 1892 and 1896 remain at .77. At best, the evidence of realignment in the 1890s, based on correlations, is ambiguous.

The evidence on the New Deal realignment indicates that 1928 was a slightly deviating election, since two moderately lower correlation coefficients, .76 and .78, for example, in the Democratic series, appear in succession in both presidential series. The evidence for 1932 is even more striking in what the correlation coefficients fail to show. By most accounts, 1932 was as dramatic a break as any in American electoral history, and, of course, the Democratic vote increased by 17%, yet there is barely a ripple in the two presidential series of correlations.

Several deviating elections are shown in the presidential data, and of course some of these disruptions are associated with third-party candidacies. The impact of Theodore Roosevelt in 1912 can be seen in a drop to .67 from .96 in the Republican series. Of course, Roosevelt's candidacy reduced the level of support for Taft more drastically than this drop indicates, because it was a relatively uniform effect throughout the nation with no massive differential switching. In 1948, Democratic voting shows the intrusion of Thurmond and Wallace. Truman's

TABLE 2.1 Correlations Between Adjacent Elections for President and Congress from 1840 to 1978 with States as Units of Analysis (Correlations are calculated between the indicated year and the preceding election.)

	President		Congress	
	Democratic	Republican	Democratic	Republican
1840		"Whig"		"Whig"
			.10	"-.37"
1844	.84	".84"	.04	".47"
			.58	".58"
1848	.79	".74"	.04	".80"
			.15	".58"
1852	.80	".60"	.47	".66"
			.31	
1856	.82		.51	.56
		D & B[a]	.68	.95
1860	-.49	(.67) .97	.16	.62
			.59	.80
1864	-.05	(.56) .44	.74	.33
			.40	.69
1868	.83	.84	.88	.89
			.42	.17
1872	.68	.69	.58	.44
			.54	.49
1876	.75	.76	.57	.73
			.71	.86
1880	.90	.90	.85	.80
			.67	.75
1884	.90	.88	.73	.63
			.79	.67
1888	.93	.94	.87	.84
		C & W[b]	.86	.83
1892	.77	(.80) .79	.83	.81
			.85	.94
1896	.08	(.75) .77	.41	.78
			.66	.80
1900	.78	.83	.89	.89
			.77	.93
1904	.86	.92	.84	.94
			.98	.91
1908	.94	.96	.90	.91
			.95	.95
1912	.95	.67	.95	.87
			.91	.88

TABLE 2.1 Correlations Between Adjacent Elections for President and Congress from 1840 to 1978 with States as Units of Analysis (Correlations are calculated between the indicated year and the preceding election.) (Cont)

| | President | | Congress | |
	Democratic	Republican	Democratic	Republican
1916	.92	.64	.86	.90
			.92	.88
1920	.90	.89	.93	.90
			.95	.83
1924	.97	.88	.93	.90
			.95	.95
1928	.76	.80	.97	.95
			.93	.92
1932	.78	.79	.91	.89
			.93	.92
1936	.93	.95	.95	.95
			.96	.95
1940	.93	.89	.92	.97
			.93	.97
1944	.99	.98	.97	.97
		T & Tᶜ	.97	.95
1948	−.38	(.94) .95	.97	.98
			.97	.98
1952	−.16	(.78) .77	.97	.97
			.96	.95
1956	.84	.78	.95	.95
			.93	.92
1960	.38	.60	.96	.96
			.89	.90
1964	.20	−.31	.84	.83
			.80	.82
1968	.82	−.38	.89	.90
			.90	.92
1972	.87	−.26	.77	.76
			.72	.74
1976	.08	−.01	.81	.79
			.68	.70

ᵃDouglas and Breckenridge vote combined.

ᵇCleveland and Weaver vote combined.

ᶜTruman and Thurmond vote combined. Adding Wallace has no appreciable impact on the correlation coefficients.

Source: Historical Archive, ICPSR.

vote alone was correlated with Roosevelt's 1944 vote at −.38, but when the Thurmond and Wallace votes are added to Truman's vote, the high correlations are restored. Beginning in 1964, the Republican presidential voting pattern became extremely volatile with four negative correlations in a row, examples of a succession of deviating elections.

The congressional series in Table 2.1 are even less supportive of conventional expectations about realigning change than the presidential data. Through the mid-nineteenth century, congressional election returns present an uneven pattern. There are many reasons for this pattern: erratic contesting of elections, changing practices in party labeling, numerous third parties, and the considerable variation in electoral laws from state to state. The congressional data portray 1896 as a deviating election, at least in Democratic voting, with 1896 correlated at .41 with 1894 and at .66 with 1898. Otherwise, most correlations in this era were over .8. During the 1920s and 1930s, neither series reveals a break during the New Deal period, even though there was a massive change in the composition of Congress. Over the last century, the congressional data for both Democrats and Republicans appear remarkably stable on the basis of these simple statistics.

The recent elections for both parties demonstrate the extent to which one series of data may be a poor guide to the patterns in other data. Both parties' congressional voting patterns remain stable, with correlation coefficients usually over .7 since 1960. Meanwhile, Democratic presidential voting patterns among states appeared to stabilize after 1964 for two elections but Republican presidential voting patterns shifted so frequently that each successive election since 1960 is negatively related to the preceding election.

By the simple standards applied here, realigning elections do not unambiguously appear at every point we expect them. A fuller analysis of these data, however, would also examine the correlations between elections widely separated in time. A matrix of correlations like Table 2.2 provides much more information than correlations between successive elections, and a

matrix should always be examined to check on patterns suggested by simpler data. The matrix in Table 2.2 can be read as
follows. The Democratic vote for President in 1896 is barely
related to the vote in 1892, with a correlation of .08, a finding
reported also in Table 2.1. By looking at a few elections back in
time (up the column in the table), it can be seen that the
association with 1884 is .61 and with 1880, .62, which reveals
that the break from these elections was not so dramatic. Looking beyond 1896 (across the columns in the table), the relationships are similar, with a correlation of .66 with 1908 and .53
with 1912, suggesting that 1896 was unlike the elections before
and after to about the same degree.

An election such as 1948 can be seen as quite unlike a long
series of elections both before and after in Democratic voting.
Or a very moderately deviating election like 1928 can be seen to
be somewhat less strongly associated with a series of elections
before and after in comparison with 1932. The differences in
correlation coefficients are not great, but they consistently
suggest a stronger relationship between the election of 1932 and
other elections—such as 1916, 1920, or 1940, 1944—than
between 1928 and these same elections. In sum, the evidence
provided by both the simple series of correlations and the more
complicated correlation matrices is uneven and unconvincing.
Breaks in the correlations at the expected times, if they appear
at all, are less substantial than we might have supposed, or
indicate a deviating election rather than a realignment, or occur
in only one of the four data series. If significant and long-lasting
changes in electoral patterns occurred during the Civil War, in
the 1890s and in 1932, we are hard pressed to demonstrate
them with correlational analysis.

IDENTIFYING ERAS OF ELECTORAL STABILITY
WITH CORRELATIONAL MATRICES

Matrices of correlations have also been used in the realignment literature to identify the period of electoral stability that
presumably follows an electoral realignment. A period of elec-

TABLE 2.2a Matrix of Correlation Coefficients between All Elections for the Democratic Vote for President from 1840 to 1976 with States as Units of Analysis

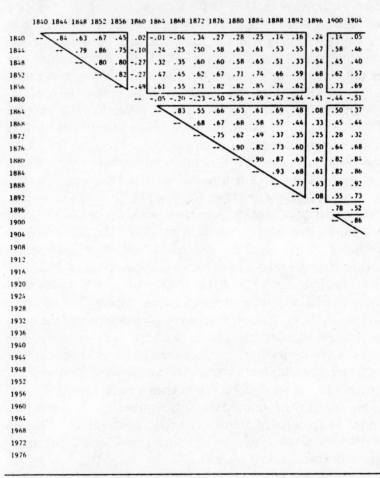

	1840	1844	1848	1852	1856	1860	1864	1868	1872	1876	1880	1884	1888	1892	1896	1900	1904
1840	--	.84	.63	.67	.45	.02	-.01	-.04	.34	.27	.28	.25	.14	.16	.24	.14	.05
1844		--	.79	.86	.75	-.10	.24	.25	?50	.58	.63	.61	.53	.55	.67	.58	.46
1848			--	.80	.80	-.27	.32	.35	.60	.60	.58	.65	.51	.33	.54	.45	.40
1852				--	.82	-.27	.47	.45	.62	.67	.71	.74	.66	.59	.68	.62	.57
1856					--	-.49	.61	.55	.71	.82	.82	.85	.74	.62	.80	.73	.69
1860						--	-.05	-.20	-.23	-.50	-.56	-.49	-.47	-.44	-.41	-.44	-.51
1864							--	.83	.55	.66	.63	.61	.69	.48	.08	.50	.37
1868								--	.68	.67	.68	.58	.57	.44	.33	.45	.44
1872									--	.75	.62	.49	.37	.35	.25	.28	.32
1876										--	.90	.82	.73	.60	.50	.64	.68
1880											--	.90	.87	.63	.62	.82	.84
1884												--	.93	.68	.61	.82	.86
1888													--	.77	.63	.89	.92
1892														--	.08	.55	.73
1896															--	.78	.52
1900																--	.86
1904																	--
1908																	
1912																	
1916																	
1920																	
1924																	
1928																	
1932																	
1936																	
1940																	
1944																	
1948																	
1952																	
1956																	
1960																	
1964																	
1968																	
1972																	
1976																	

SOURCE: United States Historical Election Data, Inter-university Consortium for Political and Social Research.

TABLE 2.2a (Continued)

1908	1912	1916	1920	1924	1928	1932	1936	1940	1944	1948	1952	1956	1960	1964	1968	1972	1976	
.13	.08	.10	.08	.07	-.01	.14	.16	.08	.03	-.13	.13	.18	-.00	-.25	-.18	-.17	.03	1840
.55	.49	.51	.51	.49	.34	.54	.54	.48	.46	-.27	.44	.44	-.23	-.57	-.56	-.57	.21	1844
.50	.45	.45	.48	.45	.11	.44	.45	.40	.34	.07	.30	.35	-.19	-.32	-.45	-.49	.09	1848
.64	.63	.61	.53	.58	.34	.65	.66	.59	.57	-.02	.45	.45	.02	-.41	-.44	-.51	.24	1852
.73	.73	.68	.72	.71	.36	.71	.76	.70	.66	-.04	.63	.63	-.06	-.57	-.75	-.73	.39	1856
-.50	-.57	-.52	-.56	-.59	-.31	-.44	-.52	-.61	-.55	.13	-.39	-.29	-.07	.33	.47	.33	-.41	1860
.30	.34	.13	.25	.22	.12	.05	.24	.45	.45	.08	.42	.20	.10	-.05	-.16	-.06	.05	1864
.39	.41	.35	.38	.37	.24	.34	.40	.38	.38	.01	.48	.35	.26	-.21	-.31	-.26	.26	1868
.25	.26	.19	.22	.29	.02	.26	.30	.26	.23	.28	.45	.36	.23	.10	-.27	-.23	.31	1872
.57	.65	.58	.65	.69	.44	.59	.65	.68	.66	-.01	.78	.69	.27	-.39	-.46	-.48	.55	1876
.77	.82	.76	.82	.82	.64	.73	.80	.83	.81	-.20	.72	.58	.25	-.50	-.55	-.57	.48	1880
.82	.87	.79	.85	.86	.71	.79	.82	.84	.82	-.21	.72	.62	.20	-.53	-.59	-.58	.53	1884
.88	.91	.87	.87	.88	.81	.84	.86	.91	.92	-.38	.78	.62	.26	-.63	-.59	-.58	.52	1888
.58	.64	.48	.59	.68	.58	.43	.49	.67	.70	-.21	.69	.38	.36	-.24	-.15	-.18	.62	1892
.66	.53	.74	.57	.48	.47	.67	.77	.61	.57	-.22	.30	.41	-.16	-.60	-.66	-.58	-.06	1896
.89	.85	.90	.85	.81	.79	.84	.88	.87	.85	-.33	.61	.55	.11	-.61	-.63	-.57	.32	1900
.94	.95	.89	.93	.96	.81	.80	.81	.91	.89	-.40	.71	.51	.21	-.59	-.58	-.60	.49	1904
--	.95	.94	.91	.91	.79	.86	.96	.87	.83	-.45	.58	.47	.00	-.68	-.67	-.64	.35	1908
	--	.92	.92	.93	.79	.86	.83	.88	.87	-.40	.65	.54	.12	-.64	-.63	-.60	.49	1912
		--	.90	.86	.80	.89	.90	.91	.89	-.42	.59	.52	.06	-.71	-.67	-.64	.30	1916
			--	.97	.77	.79	.81	.90	.87	-.37	.70	.55	.12	-.63	-.66	-.68	.43	1920
				--	.76	.79	.78	.89	.86	-.30	.73	.54	.18	-.56	-.60	-.64	.51	1924
					--	.78	.76	.80	.81	-.43	.57	.42	.22	-.50	-.38	-.37	.43	1928
						--	.93	.96	.84	-.29	.58	.64	.09	-.68	-.68	-.56	.43	1932
							--	.93	.91	-.32	.66	.66	.15	-.70	-.68	-.56	.36	1936
								--	.99	-.36	.78	.64	.27	-.65	-.60	-.55	.49	1940
									--	.38	.81	.66	.33	-.64	-.55	-.50	.51	1944
										--	.16	-.08	.17	.74	.39	.29	.04	1948
											--	.84	.57	-.44	-.33	-.29	.72	1952
												--	.38	-.49	-.42	-.26	.66	1956
													--	.17	.32	.31	.61	1960
														--	.82	.65	-.06	1964
															--	.82	-.02	1968
																--	.08	1972
																	--	1976

TABLE 2.2b Matrix of Correlation Coefficients between All Elections for the Republican Vote for President from 1856 to 1976 with States as Units of Analysis

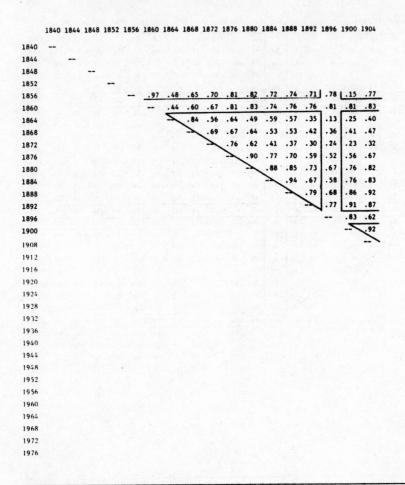

	1840	1844	1848	1852	1856	1860	1864	1868	1872	1876	1880	1884	1888	1892	1896	1900	1904
1840	--																
1844		--															
1848			--														
1852				--													
1856					--	.97	.48	.65	.70	.81	.82	.72	.74	.71	.78	.15	.77
1860						--	.44	.60	.67	.81	.83	.74	.76	.76	.81	.81	.83
1864							--	.84	.56	.64	.49	.59	.57	.35	.13	.25	.40
1868								--	.69	.67	.64	.53	.53	.42	.36	.41	.47
1872									--	.76	.62	.41	.37	.30	.24	.23	.32
1876										--	.90	.77	.70	.59	.52	.56	.67
1880											--	.88	.85	.73	.67	.76	.82
1884												--	.94	.67	.58	.76	.83
1888													--	.79	.68	.86	.92
1892														--	.77	.91	.87
1896															--	.83	.62
1900																--	.92
1908																	--
1912																	
1916																	
1920																	
1924																	
1928																	
1932																	
1936																	
1940																	
1944																	
1948																	
1952																	
1956																	
1960																	
1964																	
1968																	
1972																	
1976																	

SOURCE: United States Historical Election Data, Inter-university Consortium for Political and Social Research.

TABLE 2.2b (Continued)

1908	1912	1916	1920	1924	1928	1932	1936	1940	1944	1948	1952	1956	1960	1964	1968	1972	1976	
																		1840
																		1844
																		1848
																		1852
.75	.65	.67	.78	.75	.43	.70	.70	.72	.66	.67	.68	.68	.32	-.57	.46	-.67	.47	1856
.80	.63	.75	.85	.81	.51	.77	.73	.80	.73	.72	.68	.68	.36	-.61	.53	-.71	.46	1860
.30	.02	.09	.37	.21	.10	.08	.25	.43	.45	.17	.42	.21	.08	-.07	.05	-.05	.00	1864
.43	.32	.38	.41	.39	.28	.35	.38	.39	.36	.31	.49	.29	.41	-.27	.28	-.19	.24	1868
.25	.13	.20	.25	.29	.02	.24	.24	.23	.19	.18	.45	.13	.17	-.07	.15	-.19	.27	1872
.57	.42	.54	.67	.62	.44	.58	.61	.66	.64	.61	.77	.62	.47	-.42	.54	-.48	.51	1876
.78	.61	.73	.84	.76	.59	.74	.75	.79	.79	.75	.69	.68	.47	-.53	.57	-.56	.43	1880
.78	.55	.73	.85	.77	.72	.75	.77	.81	.83	.81	.71	.76	.48	-.51	.57	-.47	.50	1884
.89	.67	.86	.90	.86	.81	.86	.87	.88	.90	.90	.73	.79	.58	-.66	.65	-.56	.48	1888
.91	.69	.88	.82	.85	.63	.84	.85	.85	.85	.83	.63	.72	.52	-.74	.66	-.64	.38	1892
.74	.51	.79	.66	.72	.49	.71	.75	.64	.61	.65	.33	.56	.28	-.69	.27	-.56	-.02	1896
.97	.68	.94	.89	.88	.76	.86	.86	.87	.86	.88	.58	.76	.52	-.73	.58	-.64	.33	1900
.96	.63	.89	.93	.87	.81	.82	.80	.92	.91	.90	.72	.75	.62	-.67	.72	-.65	.47	1904
--	.67	.94	.92	.91	.77	.88	.86	.88	.88	.90	.60	.75	.53	-.75	.63	-.64	.35	1908
	--	.64	.60	.62	.49	.66	.63	.60	.59	.59	.37	.58	.32	-.59	.44	-.31	.36	1912
		--	.89	.91	.77	.90	.89	.89	.88	.88	.56	.73	.49	-.76	.56	-.67	.30	1916
			--	.88	.78	.83	.81	.92	.91	.90	.68	.80	.50	-.67	.64	-.66	.41	1920
				--	.80	.95	.92	.87	.86	.89	-.57	.77	.47	-.73	.52	-.59	.38	1924
					--	.79	.78	.83	.84	.87	.60	.77	.70	-.57	.64	-.39	.48	1928
						--	.95	.86	.85	.90	.57	.79	.51	-.74	.57	-.56	.41	1932
							--	.89	.89	.90	.62	.81	.57	-.72	.59	-.48	.37	1936
								--	.98	.95	.78	.83	.66	-.68	.74	-.59	.50	1940
									--	.95	.76	.83	.69	-.66	.76	-.53	.48	1944
										--	.77	.89	.68	-.68	.76	-.54	.55	1948
											--	.78	.75	-.38	.83	-.36	.72	1952
												--	.60	-.66	.70	-.45	.59	1956
													--	-.31	.85	-.09	.56	1960
														--	-.38	.69	.02	1964
															--	-.26	.71	1968
																--	-.01	1972
																	--	1976

toral stability would be characterized by a bloc of high, positive coefficients in a matrix like Table 2.2. In his work on realignments, Gerald Pomper employed this test of electoral stability for the postrealignment periods.[20] He found high correlations within blocs of elections from 1844-1860, from 1876-1888, from 1900-1920, and from 1932-1948.

In addition to the expectation that a cluster of elections will be highly and jointly interrelated following a realigning election, there is the further expectation that the bloc following a realigning election will *not* be highly related to the bloc of elections *preceding* the realignment. So far as we are aware, no analyst has examined United States electoral data for this property of relationships between blocs; yet it is a simple and necessary deduction from the idea that realignments disrupt old voting patterns and establish a new electoral alignment. Table 2.2 displays the correlations for blocs of years divided into sets representing conventional divisions into realignment eras.[21] The triangular blocs are postrealignment periods, and elections within the triangle are expected to be highly intercorrelated; that is, the correlation coefficients within the triangular bloc should be high. The rectangular blocs span realignments and the coefficients would be expected to be substantially lower in value if indeed a basic rearrangement of electoral patterns had occurred. The elections usually considered realigning are not included in any of the blocs in Table 2.2.

Pomper's work has shown that the elections following realignments are highly intercorrelated; Table 2.2 confirms his findings for both parties that blocs of elections following presumed realigning elections are indeed highly interrelated.[22] The table, however, indicates a high degree of relationship not only in the postrealignment periods but also across blocs, and thus across realignments. This is a striking finding about American electoral patterns: There is considerable stability in the relative ordering of states in their support of both parties in voting for the presidency and Congress, and this stability spans realignments.

TABLE 2.3 Average Correlations Within and Between Blocs of Three
Elections Surrounding 1896 and 1932

	Democratic Presidential Voting			
	1884–1892	1900–1908	1920–1928	1936–1944
1884–1892	.79	.78	.76	.78
1900–1908		.90	.86	.86
1920–1928			.83	.83
1936–1944				.94

	Republican Presidential Voting			
	1884–1892	1900–1908	1920–1928	1936–1944
1884–1892	.80	.86	.80	.85
1900–1908		.95	.86	.87
1920–1928			.82	.82
1936–1944				.94

It is cumbersome to assess the large number of correlation
coefficients in the blocs in Table 2.2. The stability over many
years is a sufficiently interesting property of voting behavior
that to establish a simpler method for examining before-realign-
ment and after-realignment patterns is worthwhile. A reasonable
and simple way to examine this property is provided by the
average correlations among blocs of three elections before and
after each realigning election. Table 2.3 displays the average
correlations within and between the blocs surrounding 1896
and 1932. For example, while the average correlation within the
bloc of Roosevelt elections from 1936 to 1944 is .94, the
average correlation of these elections with the elections of 1920
to 1928 (from which the New Deal era was supposedly a
dramatic break) is still .83. Looking further back to the post-
Reconstruction elections from 1884 to 1892, the average correlation with the New Deal elections remains a substantial .78.
The same pattern emerges in the Republican vote for President,
the average correlations among the same three eras being .94
within 1936 to 1944, .82 between those years and the 1920s,
and .85 between the New Deal elections and the average for the
period 1884 to 1892. Similarly, the average correlation among

the Democratic presidential votes in the post-1896 realignment era is .90, while the average correlation of these elections with the prerealignment period is .78. The comparable Republican averages are .95 and .86.

Nothing comparable to Table 2.2 has been presented here for congressional voting, because it is much too large; each matrix would contain over 1800 entries. The full matrix would show that congressional voting for both parties over the past century is as stable as presidential voting.[23] Also a comparison of a few congressional elections before and after each realignment shows patterns of stability similar to the presidential data in Table 2.3.[24]

These strong correlations over long periods of time would support the interpretation that American electoral history has been characterized by stable voting patterns, and that the few disruptions that have occurred have been temporary. Indeed, if we search these data for permanent "breaks" in the patterns as a means to identify realignments, we are forced to conclude that the best candidates are the elections of 1876 and 1964. The full matrix of correlations in Table 2.2 clearly implies that almost a hundred years of elections represent a basic stability which is occasionally disrupted but to which voters quickly return. The high degree of stability over long periods of time should also be taken as evidence against secular realigning change that would have rearranged electoral units gradually. Viewing similar stability across a ninety-year period of Indiana electoral history, V. O. Key referred to the "standing decision" of voters. On the basis of the correlations displayed here, a similar statement might be made about American electoral history as a whole.

The conventional realignment perspective suggests that long-term stability in underlying partisanship is interrupted by dramatic shifts in loyalty. The realignment shift is followed by another long period of stability, but the postrealignment pattern should not be highly related to the stable bloc of elections before the realignment. In short, we have found too much stability in voting patterns to give much support to the notion of realignments as dramatic disruptions in past loyalties. In terms of the shifts of support for the parties among the states, a number of elections appear to be deviating, temporarily disruptive but no more. From the perspective of conventional analysis of realigning change, there have not been dramatic, lasting shifts in national voting patterns.

Few would be willing to accept this interpretation, however faithful to the data it may be. As analysts of national election data have observed frequently, the strong correlations reflect the consistent and overwhelmingly Democratic behavior of the South and the nearly as consistent Republican support in sections of the North. These regional differences in underlying partisanship contribute to high correlations in the nation as a whole. About half of the variance in the national data over the years can be accounted for by the differences among the regions.[25] The breakdown of these long-standing regional patterns in voting for president in the 1960s is reflected in the negative correlations in the matrix of Table 2.2. These considerations imply that examining correlations within regions might lead to substantially different results. It is of course possible that within regions, the national realignments cause dramatic switches in the electoral behavior of smaller units, yet this is obscured in the national analysis of states. The following section presents a similar correlational analysis of the Democratic vote within six regions, using counties as the units of analysis.

A REGIONAL ANALYSIS
OF THE DEMOCRATIC VOTE FOR PRESIDENT

Introducing regional controls in this correlational analysis (using counties as the units of analysis) does not pose any unusual problems, although within some regions, analysis is delayed until a sizable number of counties are available and until county boundaries have a reasonable degree of stability. It is necessary to use counties rather than states in the analysis in order to have enough units within regions; at the same time, no units smaller than counties are available for such extensive analysis.

The expectations for regional patterns of correlations based upon the realignment perspective could vary considerably. One could argue that national patterns of basic stability should extend to lower levels of analysis. Thus the regional series would be essentially similar to those for the nation. On the other hand, one could anticipate variation in patterns from region to region if the main national patterns were the product of diverse patterns of regional change. The actual data on regions, with counties as units of analysis, offer evidence on a complex mix of both patterns.

Again, in order to reduce the quantity of data printed here, only correlations between successive elections in Democratic presidential voting within the regions will be presented. Table 2.4 shows correlations between successive elections for six regions with the Democratic vote for president. [26] If all the regional data were essentially the same as the national pattern, they would require no commentary. There are, however, various regional patterns and none precisely like the national pattern. Overall, the regional series of correlations suggest high levels of stability and occasional temporary disruptions, but there are several instances of lasting breaks in electoral patterns and a few periods of continuing erratic voting.

Like the national data, the regional correlational analysis suggests that 1860 produced a temporary deviation (two successive low correlations) in the Democratic vote for president in the Northeast, and to a lesser degree in the border states. The limited availability of alternatives to Douglas in northeastern states led to uneven departures from normal Democratic voting in 1860. For example, in Rhode Island, with no alternatives to Douglas and Lincoln, the Democratic vote increased 5% over 1856, while in Connecticut it dropped over 20% since Breckenridge nearly matched Douglas's vote. No change is evidenced in the correlations for the Midwest during this period, while the voting patterns in the southern, western and Plains states cannot be assessed. [27]

TABLE 2.4 Correlations Between Adjacent Elections with the
Democratic Vote for President from 1844 to 1976 with
Counties as Units of Analysis. (Correlations are calculated
between the indicated year and the preceding election.)

	Northeast	Midwest	Plains[a]	South	Border	West[a]
1844	.97	.88		.90	.90	
1848	.69	.95		.92	-.14	
1852	.72	.86		.83	.00	
1856	.74	.73		.74	.72	
1860	-.37	.81	.80	.01	.37	
1864	.01	.73	.65		-.17	
1868	.98	.93	.68		.79	
1872	.92	.57	.57		.18	
1876	.93	.58	.70	.46	.71	
1880	.96	.91	.84	.69	.87	.80
1884	.95	.93	.70	.85	.85	.82
1888	.97	.87	.83	.79	.94	.80
1892	.98	.93	.63	.47	.93	.60
1896	.78	.45	.23	.51	.75	-.39
1900	.87	.69	.27	.75	.94	-.36
1904	.88	.94	.25	.80	.95	.18
1908	.90	.96	.63	.90	.97	.60
1912	.88	.93	.83	.77	.95	.66
1916	.83	.77	.51	.36	.96	.48
1920	.83	.76	.69	.36	.96	.56
1924	.80	.91	.81	.82	.91	.54
1928	.38	.34	-.19	.67	.82	.22
1932	.75	.77	.82	.67	.71	.66
1936	.77	.57	.42	.91	.39	.56
1940	.89	.84	.73	.93	.99	.57
1944	.96	.96	.96	.95	.99	.92
1948	.92	.45	.87	.02	.99	.81
1952	.94	.49	-.09	.65	.53	.78
1956	.96	.92	.96	.94	.93	.82
1960	.81	.83	.96	.80	.84	.80
1964	.83	.76	.96	.32	.91	.78
1968	.94	.89	-.29	.74	.86	.91
1972	.90	.56	-.06	.69	.84	.88
1976	.86	.53	.78	.29	.74	.82

[a]In the Plains states and the West, analysis was delayed until at least 100 counties
were in existence.

Since the 1890s realignment was alleged to be a differential shifting of regions, there might be little evidence of shifting within the regions, and generally that is our finding. A very modest drop in the correlations appears at 1896 in the Northeast and the border states, suggesting a slight realignment in these regions. Somewhat larger declines in the coefficients occurred in the Midwest and South, but the patterns indicate deviating elections—in the Midwest in 1896, in the South in 1892—rather than realignment. The greatest disruptions occurred in the Plains states and the West, but these take the form of long series of low correlations, indicative of erratic voting patterns, not a sharp and durable realignment.

The regional data for the 1932 realignment presents a more interesting contrast to the national patterns. Considerable change occurred in the elections surrounding 1932—seldom *in* 1932—but this change took different forms in different regions. In the Northeast, the election of 1928 appears to have been a realignment, its correlation with 1924 dropping to .38, but its correlation with 1932 returning to a reasonably high .75. In other words, the 1928 Democratic vote in northeastern counties was not related to the vote in 1924 to a high degree, but it was fairly strongly associated with the 1932 vote for Roosevelt. Thus it appears that a new pattern in presidential voting was established which has endured to the present.

The Midwest revealed an almost identical break in 1928, with correlations of .34 with 1924 and .77 with 1932. This pattern is complicated, however, by another drop in the correlation between 1932 and 1936, followed by a longer era of relative stability. This same pattern appears in the Plains states. Probably, this indicates that the more enduring change in presidential voting in the Midwest and the Plains states came in 1936 in response to Roosevelt's first term rather than earlier, as in the Northeast.

Other patterns occurred in the other regions. In the South, 1928 appears to have been a deviating election, returning to normality in 1932. In contrast, the border states evidenced no change in 1928, but appear to have undergone a realignment in

1936, a single correlation dropping to .39 between 1936 and 1932, then returning to extremely high levels thereafter. The West continued its erratic pattern of voting throughout the 1930s; its series of correlations finally stabilized in 1940.

Other regional variations are also apparent. The election of 1916 produced a temporary disruption in voting patterns in the South, Midwest, and Plains states, as did 1948 in the Midwest. Regional realignments seem to have occurred in 1872 in the border states and in 1952 in both the Plains states and the border states. The election of 1964, as we might expect, suggests realignment in the South, but the roots of this change lie as far back as 1948, which appears as a substantial break from previous patterns.

This regional analysis somewhat complicates but does not basically change the conclusions drawn from the national analysis. Based on correlational evidence, a high degree of stability is found in the most populous regions of the nation over the past century. The disruptions that occurred were as likely to be deviating as realigning. Only in the New Deal era does realigning change, nonexistent in the national data, appear in the regional analysis. Even there, however, the evidence of change appears in elections before or after, rather than in, the election which converted the minority party into a winning party. Examination of correlational data not shown here—the regional correlations for the Republican presidential vote, as well as the matrices of correlations of the presidential vote in both parties and the series of correlations of the congressional vote in each party—confirms this overall impression of stability, with occasional but usually temporary interruptions.

It is important to place the interpretation of these correlations in proper perspective. The correlations reveal that the *ordering* of county percentages of the presidential and congressional vote was highly stable from the 1840s to the 1960s with a few dramatic breaks. The high degree of stability across these occasional breaks, shown in the correlation matrices, suggests that substantial differential shifts, if they occurred, were neither lasting enough nor large enough to change the relative order of the states from one era to the next. This is interesting evidence bearing upon one form of stability in American electoral behavior, but it is highly unsupportive of the realignment perspective.

To put this interpretation differently, in American voting behavior over the years, differential shifts in the vote have not been lasting; characteristically, units quickly returned to their prior order. To press the point, the differential shifting of the realignment conceptualization as measured by correlations does not appear to capture permanent changes in electoral behavior. As suggested above, the problems are not that correlations are inappropriate for analyzing election data, but that the conceptualization of realignments has overemphasized differential change and neglected across-the-board shifts in the level of party support. The prevailing conceptualization of electoral change led to the use of correlational analysis, but on second thought this is unsatisfactory on both conceptual and empirical grounds. In the next chapter, we will make the simple corrective step of adding across-the-board change to the analysis.

NOTES

1. Philip E. Converse, "The Concept of the Normal Vote," in Angus Campbell, Philip E. Converse, Warren E. Miller, and Donald E. Stokes, *Elections and the Political Order* (New York: John Wiley, 1966) pp. 9-39.

2. Joel H. Silbey and Samuel T. McSeveney (eds.), *Voters, Parties, and Elections* (Lexington, MA: Xerox College Publishing, 1972), p. 2.

3. John L. Shover, "The Progressives and the Working Class Vote in California," *Labor History* 10 (1969), pp. 584-601.

4. James L. Sundquist, *Dyanmics of the Party System*, (Washington, DC: Brookings Institution, 1973), Ch. 9, 11, 12.

5. Lee Benson, Joel Silbey, and Phyllis Field, "Toward a Theory of Stability and Change in American Voting Patterns: New York State, 1792-1970," in Joel Silbey, Allan Bogue, and William Flanigan, *The History of American Electoral Behavior* (Princeton, NJ: Princeton University Press, 1978).

6. V. O. Key, Jr., and Frank Munger, "Social Determinism and Electoral Decision: The Case of Indiana," in Eugene Burdick and Arthur Brodbeck (eds.), *American Voting Behavior* (New York: Macmillan, 1959).

7. Silbey and McSeveney, *Voters, Parties and Elections*, p. 2.

8. Sundquist, *Dynamics of the Party System*, p. 19.

9. E. E. Schattschneider, *The Semisovereign People* (New York: Holt, Rinehart and Winston, 1960), pp. 62-77.

10. Sundquist points out in various footnotes that the diagram is misleading, because it does not accurately reflect the different amount of support for each party. See Sundquist, *Dynamics of the Party System*, pp. 72, 146, 199.

11. As we will discuss at greater length in a subsequent chapter, many of these analyses also fail to consider possible change in the composition of the total electorate which may result from the mobilization of new or formerly inactive members of the electorate or from the demobilization of formerly active voters.

12. V. O. Key, Jr., "A Theory of Critical Elections," *Journal of Politics* 17 (1955), pp. 3-18.

13. Key, "A Theory of Critical Elections," p. 12.

14. Walter Dean Burnham, *Critical Elections and the Mainsprings of American Politics* (New York: Norton, 1970); Gerald Pomper, "Classification of Presidential Elections," *Journal of Politics* 29 (1967), pp. 535-661; Schattschneider, *The Semisovereign People*. More detailed analysis of the early 1890s within regions complicates this overall pattern considerably. See especially Samuel McSeveney, *The Politics of Depression* (New York: Oxford University Press, 1972); Paul Kleppner, *The Cross of Culture* (New York: Macmillan, 1970); Paul Kleppner, *The Third Electoral System, 1853-1892* (Chapel Hill: University of North Carolina Press, 1979); and Richard Jensen, *The Winning of the Midwest* (Chicago: The University of Chicago Press, 1971).

15. Duncan MacRae, Jr., and James Meldrum, "Critical Elections in Illinois: 1888-1958," *American Political Science Review* 54 (1960), pp. 669-683. This highly innovative analysis used an "interaction" or residual term as the basic data for direct factor analysis of two matrices that are cross products of the raw data. The interaction term cancels out all the variations in voting associated with levels of support and leaves only residual change, i.e., the data used reflect the departures from a unit's normal behavior in a particular race corrected for the average departure of all units in that race.

16. Pomper in "Classification of Presidential Elections," p. 549, clearly justifies the use of correlational analysis as ignoring changes in the level of support and capturing only the discontinuity in state patterns.

17. Awkwardly for Pomper's analysis, 1932 does not appear to be much of a disruption with these two indicators.

18. Pomper, "Classification of Presidential Elections," p. 540.

19. The calculations use every state for which there are percentages in both years. In other words, "pairwise deletion" is followed. The two most common reasons for omitting a state in the correlational analysis are late entry into the union and the disruptions of the Civil War years. In a few instances, states have simply not reported results; some southern states do not report election returns for uncontested congressional races. Notice that congressional district results are aggregated to a single state total.

20. Pomper, "Classification of Presidential Elections." See also Allan Lichtman, "Critical Election Theory and the Reality of American Presidential Politics, 1916-1940," *American Historical Review* 81 (April 1976), pp. 317-348.

21. As in the computation for Table 2.1, all correlations are based on pairwise deletions of states. This means that correlations between elections early in the period and more recent elections are based on the smaller number of states in the union at the earlier date. The varying set of states used for computation throughout the matrix is not ideal, but it is preferable to elimination of a state from the entire matrix, through listwise deletion, if it is missing at any election.

22. Pomper, "Classification of Presidential Elections," pp. 544-547.

23. These correlation matrices for congressional voting are available from the Inter-university Consortium for Political and Social Research.

24. For example, Democratic voting for Congress using average correlations for sets of five elections are as follows:

	1884-1892	1900-1908	1920-1928	1936-1944
1884-1892	.77	.77	.75	.74
1900-1908		.85	.86	.83
1920-1928			.89	.90
1936-1944				.86

25. Over the years and on the average, the differences between regions account for about half the variation in county electoral behavior. However, there is considerable change in the capacity of regional differences to account for county behavior, ranging from high values of about two-thirds explained by regions through the many years during which the South was extremely pro-Democratic to recent elections in which regions account for only about one-third of the total variation.

26. The states were assigned to regions as follows. Alaska and Hawaii are not included, nor is Washington, D.C. *Northeast:* Connecticut; Maine; Massachusetts; New Hampshire; New Jersey; New York; Pennsylvania; Rhode Island; Vermont. *Midwest:* Illinois; Indiana; Michigan; Ohio; Wisconsin. *Plains:* Iowa; Kansas; Minnesota; Nebraska; North Dakota; South Dakota. *South:* Alabama; Arkansas; Florida; Georgia; Louisiana; Mississippi; North Carolina; South Carolina; Tennessee; Texas; Virginia. *Border:* Delaware; Kentucky; Maryland; Missouri; Oklahoma; West Virginia. *West:* Arizona; California; Colorado; Idaho; Montana; Nevada; New Mexico; Oregon; Utah; Washington; Wyoming.

27. The Civil War years create missing data problems for the South; in the Plains and West, too few counties are available for analysis in this period.

Chapter 3

IDENTIFYING REALIGNMENTS: A REASSESSMENT

The preceding chapter raises questions about the standard view of American electoral history as characterized by prolonged periods of partisan stability punctuated by periodic critical realignments. On the basis of correlational analysis alone, the electoral patterns appear to be more stable and the disruptions less intense and of shorter duration than most discussions of partisan realignments would suggest. It might be concluded, on the basis of the evidence offered thus far, that the occurrence and reoccurrence of partisan realignments has been overstated, and that periods usually identified as realignments did not in fact involve significant, lasting breaks in electoral patterns. Rather than draw that conclusion, we will offer instead two potential remedies: first, an enriched analytic conceptualization of electoral change, and second, the translation of the conceptualization into an appropriate measurement technique. The following conceptualization of electoral change departs somewhat from the familiar schemes in the literature but should be

viewed as a modification of earlier work rather than a fundamentally different approach.

Implicit in Key's original article on critical elections, but not
elaborated upon, is the distinction between two different patterns of change in aggregate electorates both of which can result
in lasting rearrangements of partisan divisions.[1] One type of
change, discussed at length in Chapter 2, is "differential"
change, in which the aggregate vote in some units shifts toward
one of the parties, while in other units shifts are toward the
opposing party. In other words, electoral forces impact differentially upon the various electoral units—states, counties, or
others—and the result is change in the relative ordering of units
in terms of their support for the parties. This pattern of change
involves shifts in the sources of electoral support for the parties,
although if the shifts for and against the parties are counter-
balancing, change in the total vote received by the parties does
not result.

The other type of change is "across-the-board" change in
which there is a generally similar increase (or decrease) in the
vote received by the parties in all or most electoral subunits. In
this pattern of change, electoral forces have a similar impact
upon all or most units. The result is an increase (or decrease) in
the total vote received by the parties, but the ordering of units
in terms of support for the parties does not change. In some
senses of the word, this pattern of change does not involve
disruption of the prevailing alignment of units, although the
relative electoral strength of the parties overall is modified.
Across-the-board change implies that in each subunit there is a
similar average increase or decrease of support for a party, while
differential change means that the electorates in some subunits
increase support while others decrease, or, more generally, that
units change their level of support by differing amounts.

In Figure 3.1 across-the-board change is illustrated and compared with an illustration of differential change (Figure 3.2). In
the diagram illustrating differential change, the new alignment
cuts across the old, and some supporters of both parties switch
to the opposing party. In contrast, across-the-board change

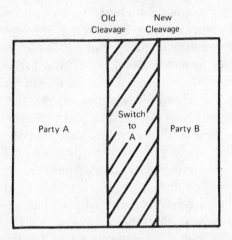

Figure 3.1: Diagram of Across-the-Board Electoral Change

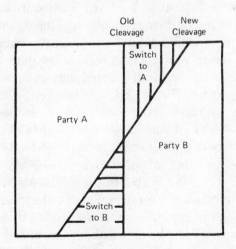

Figure 3.2: Diagram of Differential Electoral Change

results in a new alignment in which Party A gains new adherents
without losing former adherents to the opposition, Party B.
This new alignment might have stemmed from charges of corruption or mismanagement by Party B, issues which, if salient,
are only likely to move voters away from Party B without any
countermovements in favor of that party. On the other hand, in
the diagram illustrating differential change, the new alignment
rests on an issue which affects different voters in different ways;
for example, clear and contrasting stands by the parties on the
abortion issue would push some supporters of Party B toward
Party A, while winning others away from Party A.

We have argued that previous analyses of electoral change
have tended to neglect across-the-board change and have concentrated only on differential change. Certainly, across-the-
board change appears less interesting and dramatic in a diagram,
since it leaves the supporters of one party undisturbed and only
divides the supporters of the other party. On the other hand,
this pattern of across-the-board electoral change may more
accurately describe most actual shifts in American electoral
behavior. Furthermore, it is, of course, this form of change that
leads to shifts in the balance of power between the parties.

Correlation coefficients and related techniques capture only
the differential type of change in which subunits move dissimi-
larly. Change in which all subunits move in the same direction
by similar amounts would yield high correlation coefficients
and thus produce no break in a correlation matrix to be identified as realignment. Figure 3.3, for example, illustrates this
situation. The aggregate vote for Party A in each subunit
increases by 20% in Election 2 as compared with Election 1, yet
the vote for Party A in the two elections is perfectly correlated.
If the relative ordering of subunits remains the same from
election to election, the correlation coefficients will be high,
even though a substantial proportion of the electorate may have
changed their voting behavior, as demonstrated by Figure 3.3.[2]

One might argue that the across-the-board change illustrated
in Figure 3.1 does not represent a rearrangement of the partisan
cleavages in the electorate, since there is a uniform shift on the

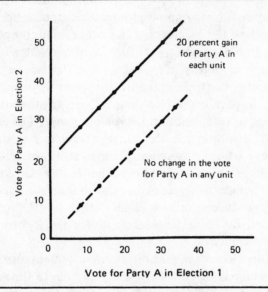

Figure 3.3: Diagram of Correlation of the Vote in Two Elections for a Set of Units

part of all subgroups toward the advantaged party. Certainly the stock in trade of political analysts is the dissimilar reactions of various demographic and other groups to the programs and candidates offered by the parties. Analysts of aggregate voting behavior in particular have not found elections characterized by uniform change to be of much interest. Once it is discovered that everybody liked Ike—or disliked Goldwater or McGovern— and the vote in all subunits increased or decreased by a similar amount, analytic attention shifts away from the voters to the sources of universal appeal or lack thereof of the candidates. Little insight can be gained from studying the characteristics of the voting units, since all reacted more or less the same regardless of their differing demographic or socioeconomic characteristics. In contrast, an election like 1960, when the issue of Kennedy's Catholicism cut across the existing partisan cleavage, offers more opportunities to explain the behavior of voters or voting units by focusing on the characteristics of the voters themselves.

Across-the-board change may not result in basic change in the configuration of demographic groups which make up the coalitions supporting the parties. On the other hand, it does involve change in the proportion of such groups that support the parties, and it obviously may mean the difference between one party or another controlling the institutions of government with consequent impact on public policy. Nor do students of electoral politics, in fact, ignore this type of change. The election of 1932 involved a dramatic shift in the level of support for the Democratic party. Consequently, analysts have usually considered 1932 as an example par excellence of a partisan realignment even though the large, across-the-board electoral change in that year produces only a slight ripple in the correlation matrices used by these same analysts for the identification of electoral realignments.

The distinction between differential and across-the-board electoral change is of course an analytic one. In the real world, we would expect the two kinds of change to occur jointly. A party's stand on an issue will attract some supporters and repel others, but will do so unequally. There is some reshuffling of the party's base of support, but also a net gain or loss in the number of supporters, as in Figure 3.4. There is no doubt that analysts of electoral realignments have had this situation in mind in discussing the major historical realignments—in 1896 the Democrats gained in the South and West, while the Republicans gained enough more in the Northeast and Midwest to provide a secure majority nationally; the New Deal involved a reshuffling of party supporters along class lines, with the Democrats gaining a numerical advantage in the process. The distinction has never been stated clearly, however, and as a result, the methodologies selected to analyze electoral change and to identify realignments have generally not been sensitive to across-the-board change.[3] Since, as we will see, across-the-board change is typically of far greater magnitude in American elections than differential change, this omission has serious ramifications for the interpretation of historical realignments. In the remainder of this chapter, we will operationalize this conceptualization of

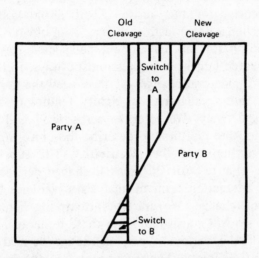

Figure 3.4: **Diagram of Combined Across-the-Board and Differential Electoral Change**

electoral change in such a way as to allow measurement of both differential and across-the-board change on a common scale.

TECHNIQUE OF ANALYSIS

The conceptualization of electoral change used here (and at least implied by most other analysts of electoral history) demands the ability to distinguish and measure the relative amount of four types of electoral change:

	Temporary	Lasting
Across-the-Board	Deviating Surge	Realigning Surge
Differential	Deviating Interactive Change	Realigning Interactive Change

The distinction between across-the-board and differential change was discussed extensively in the preceding section. The other dimension in the above classification, distinguishing temporary change from lasting change, is an obvious and necessary distinction for the realignment perspective, but one that has been treated largely in impressionistic ways. In labeling the four types of electoral change, we have used the familiar terms "deviating" and "realigning" to signify temporary and lasting changes respectively. We refer to across-the-board change as "surge," adopting the term to describe the uniform movement across all segments of the electorate.[4] The substitution of "interactive change" for differential change derives from our use of the interaction term in analysis of variance to measure this type of change. We are not attempting here to create jargon, but we will consistently use these terms to refer to the estimates of the various types of change derived from our measurement technique. The reader may think of these terms as the operational indicators for the concepts outlined above. It should be stressed that this conceptualization distinguishes different types of electoral change, not types of elections. Thus any particular election might be characterized by any or all of these types of changes. Indeed, it might be expected that most or all elections would be characterized by all four types in varying magnitudes. The analytical task is to distinguish among the four types.

To measure these four types of electoral change, we have developed a technique based on analysis of variance. This technique is discussed extensively elsewhere, and only a summary of the approach need be presented here.[5]

The basic data analyzed are the percentages of the vote for a particular political party in a set of geographical subunits (e.g., states within the nation or counties within a state) over a series of elections.[6] Below is a hypothetical array of vote percentages for Party X in three states over five elections, which we will use to illustrate our operationalization of the concept of electoral change:

		Election					
		1	2	3	4	5	State Means
	1	45%	35%	50%	40%	55%	45%
State	2	50%	40%	55%	50%	55%	50%
	3	55%	45%	60%	60%	55%	55%

	Election						
Means (or percentage of vote in nation as a whole)	50%	40%	55%	50%	55%	Grand Mean
							50%

We define electoral change as movement away from expected voting patterns; thus, a first requirement is some estimation of the expected vote. The expected voting pattern of the electorate is operationalized as the grand mean of the array (which is also the mean vote of the nation as a whole over the series of elections). The expected voting pattern of a state is operationalized as its mean vote over the set of elections.

If the actual vote in an election does not deviate from these expected voting patterns (as in Election 1, where the vote of each state and of the entire nation equals its respective mean), we would say that no change had occurred. Election 2, on the other hand, is an illustration of the kind of change which we have defined as across-the-board change or surge. Each state moved away from its expected vote by the same amount: -10%. We can measure this amount of surge very simply by taking the difference between the election mean and the grand mean (40% -50% = -10%). Election 3 evidences a similar type of electoral change, except that it is a lesser amount in a positive direction, but it can be measured in parallel fashion (55% - 50% = +5%).

Using the terminology of analysis of variance more explicitly, we can say something more about Elections 2 and 3. Taking the actual vote for each state in either election, we can say that the deviation of this percentage from the expected vote of the entire nation (the grand mean) is completely accounted for by the difference between the state's expected vote and that of the nation *and* by the difference between the nation's actual vote in that election (the election mean) and the nation's expected vote. Put another way, once we take into account the fact that the state normally votes differently from the nation as a whole and that the entire nation departed from its expected vote in this particular election, there is nothing about the behavior of the state which remains to be explained. Or arithmetically, we can say:

State Vote – Grand Mean = (State Mean – Grand Mean) + (Election Mean – Grand Mean)

or,

35% – 50% = (45% – 50%) + (40% – 50%)
using State 1 in Election 2.

The reader can verify that the same holds true for each state observation in Elections 2 and 3. Notice, however, that this is not the case in Election 4, which demonstrates the kind of departure from the expected vote that we have conceptualized as "interactive." After taking account of the difference among the state means and of the amount of surge (which happens to be 0%), we find that there is residual variation in two of the three state observations.

State 1: (40% – 50%) = (45% – 50%) + (50% – 50%) + (– 5% Residual)
State 3: (60% – 50%) = (55% – 50%) + (50% – 50%) + (+5% Residual)

State 1 has voted 5% less for Party X than we would anticipate given the expected vote of the state and given the behavior of the nation as a whole in this election; at the same time, State 3 has voted 5% more for Party X than would be predicted. In the language of analysis of variance, we would say that the "interaction" of the state with Election 4 has produced this residual deviation from the grand mean, state mean, and election mean. Put another way, this is nonuniform change from expected voting patterns. We have labeled it interactive change, since it is measured by the interaction term in the analysis of variance model. Since the positive and negative residuals will always sum to zero, one can also think of these departures from expected voting patterns as compensating changes. More formally this term is:

$$\text{Residual} = (\text{State Vote} - \text{Election Mean} - \text{State Mean} + \text{Grand Mean})$$

or

$$\text{Residual for State 1 in Election 4} = (40\% - 50\% - 45\% + 50\%) = -5\%.$$

To find the interactive change for the entire unit in Election 4, we ignore signs, sum the residuals across all states, and take the average amount.

$$\text{Interactive Change} = \frac{\Sigma \left| \text{State Vote} - \text{Election Mean} - \text{State Mean} + \text{Grand Mean} \right|}{\text{Number of States}}$$

Election 5 in our example combines both types of change, and we measure each in the same way as in the pure cases:

Surge = Election Mean − Grand Mean = 55% − 50% = +5%
State 1 Residual = (55% − 55% − 45% + 50%) = +5%
State 2 Residual = (55% − 55% − 50% + 50%) = 0%
State 3 Residual = (55% − 55% − 55% + 50%) = −5%
Interactive Change = 3.3%[7]

Although not indicated in this hypothetical and simplified example, the vote percentages that form the basic data in the analysis are weighted according to the number of votes cast. Thus changes in large population areas are appropriately weighted more heavily to reflect the larger number of votes involved than comparable changes in subunits of smaller size.

This procedure also establishes a set of criteria for discriminating between short-term, "deviating" change on the one hand, and long-term, "realigning" change on the other. In terms of this procedure, an election that is unlike both the elections that precede it *and* those that follow it is said to reveal temporary or deviating change; elections that are unlike those that precede but are like those that follow are seen as realigning and mark the establishment of a new pattern.[8]

The amount of change in voting patterns is thus classified as "deviating surge" or "realigning surge," "deviating interactive change" or "realigning interactive change." The numerical results have a straightforward interpretation as percentage point changes. For example, a deviating surge of -4.3 in Party X's vote means that all subunits moved an average of -4.3 percentage points away from the expected vote and that this change was temporary. Similarly, a deviating interactive change of 1.8 would mean that the subunits temporarily moved in different directions from their own expected votes and from the behavior of the unit as a whole by an average of 1.8 percentage points. (Since these movements are increases in the vote for some subunits and decreases in others, no sign is attached to interactive changes.) Realigning surge and realigning interactive changes are interpreted similarly except that the changes are lasting. A realigning surge of 3.5, for example, represents a 3.5 percentage point increase in the expected vote for Party X and thus establishes a new expected vote. Realigning interactive change of 2.6 would mean an average change of 2.6 percentage points in the expected votes of the subunits, some of these being increases, the others decreases.

Some caveats are in order where the use of the technique is concerned. The operationalization of the expected vote as a mean across a series of elections requires that some arbitrary decisions be made about which elections to include in the calculation of these means. We have chosen to use moving cross sections of four elections. In large part, using a moving average to represent the "expected vote" of the unit and subunits was decided upon to eliminate arbitrary cutting points between cross sections. The number of elections in the cross sections, however, remains arbitrary, and this decision obviously affects the results of the analysis. Had we used three or five elections in a set instead of four, the results would be marginally different. In effect, we are arbitrarily saying that the fluctuations in the actual vote over a twelve-year period average out to an approximation of the underlying partisanship of the electorate. Obviously, others may argue with this decision in favor of eight years, or sixteen years, or other time spans.

Again as a consequence of using means to represent the expected votes of subunits in the analysis, there is a time lag in the calculation of the interactive change components for new states (or other subunits) entering the nation. The interaction term measures the extent to which a subunit departs from its own expected vote as well as from the expected vote of the unit as a whole, and from the average behavior of the entire unit in the particular election. In order to make this calculation, the subunit has to have been in existence long enough for its expected vote to be estimated—by the rules used here, for four elections. As a result, a state does not begin to contribute to the summation of interactive change immediately upon its entrance into the union. As is noted below, this fact is particularly troublesome in the analysis of the electoral patterns of the 1890s. Several of the western states entered the union too recently to be included in the calculation of interactive change for the 1890s, even though those states were characterized by patterns of voting changes different from those of the rest of the nation. Similar problems are not encountered in the calculation of surge, since that calculation depends only on the grand mean and the election means which have been calculated independently of subunit data.[9]

There is an analogous problem at the beginning of the historical series. Using this technique, the magnitude of the various types of changes cannot be calculated until an expected vote (grand mean) for the nation is established. Thus we have no estimates of electoral change for the Democratic Party before 1836, even though the election data series begins in 1824. This is an even greater problem in analyzing the Republican vote, since we cannot estimate the amounts of electoral change until after the Civil War realignment is presumed to have occurred.[10]

A somewhat different problem appears at the end of the historical period. We cannot ascertain if a realignment has taken place in the most recent three elections, because we are unable to calculate a "postelection" grand mean and test whether the results of the election are more like the preceding pattern or the succeeding one. Note that this is really a conceptual rather than a methodological problem, though one often ignored by "instant analysts": If a realignment is defined as lasting change in the expected vote, one must wait a while to find out if the observed change does indeed last. We can measure the amounts of interactive and surge change in the three most recent elections relative to the expected vote established in the last identified realignment, but we cannot distinguish deviating from realigning change in these years.

As we turn to the application of this technique to American voting patterns, it should be reiterated that the data employed are votes and the changes measured are changes in behavior, not in attitudes. It is often tempting to infer the latter from the former, but it is a temptation that should be resisted. Our observations about electoral change must be in terms of changes in the percentages of votes cast, not in percentages of voters who thought of themselves as partisans of one or the other party.

NATIONAL ELECTORAL CHANGE

This conceptualization and its operationalization in the form of the analysis of variance technique allows comprehensive assessment of the magnitude and nature of electoral change from 1840, in the case of the Democrats, and 1868, in the case of the Republicans, to the present. In the following pages, patterns of electoral change in the presidential and congressional vote for the two parties are examined from a national perspective, with states as units of analysis. In a subsequent section, the same technique is employed to gain a regional perspective, with counties as units of analysis. While these perspectives provide an improved view of the process of realignment, they also call into question aspects of prevailing interpretations of electoral history.

Table 3.1 presents estimates of national realigning and deviating surge and interactive change in the Democratic and Republican presidential and congressional vote. The distinction between across-the-board surge and interactive change, and the capacity to measure both types of change on a common scale, permits observations about the characteristics of the major realignment periods which could not be made on the basis of correlational analysis. In particular, the capacity to measure across-the-board surge corrects one of the anomalies that appeared in the correlation matrices discussed in Chapter 2. In Table 3.1, the election of 1932 clearly appears as the most impressive realignment for both parties during the entire period considered. The truly major across-the-board electoral change in that year suggested by the table is in keeping with the generally accepted view that this period was marked by general, large-scale, and lasting shifts in electoral behavior, a view not supported by the correlational analysis discussed above.

On the other hand, the data series provide little evidence of lasting interactive change during these years. The elections of the period were characterized by interactive change, but change of this form appears to have been mostly temporary, or deviating, in nature. In other words, the realignment of the 1930s did not seriously disrupt the ordering of states in terms of their relative support for the parties; those states that constituted the primary bastions of Republican strength before the realignment remained the principal sources of Republican strength during the years that followed, but Republican strength in these as in other states was sharply reduced. The same pattern was apparently also characteristic of the Democratic vote but with the opposite effect. In this sense, the prevailing electoral alignment of earlier years was not disrupted in the 1930s; instead, it continued into the years that followed, an element of continuity also suggested by the results of the correlational analysis.

TABLE 3.1a Estimates of Realigning and Deviating Surge and Interaction in Voting for President from 1836 to 1976, with States as Units of Analysis

| | Democratic Vote for President | | | | Republican Vote for President | | | |
| | Surge | | Interaction | | Surge | | Interaction | |
Election Year	Deviating	Realigning	Deviating	Realigning	Deviating	Realigning	Deviating	Realigning
1836	1.18		4.01	5.65				
1840	-.57	-3.61	2.50					
1844	2.17	-5.59	1.80					
1848	.71		5.62					
1852	8.88		2.15					
1856	3.50		3.76					
1860	-13.09		12.04	2.80				
1864	2.56		3.10	1.65				
1868	-.32	6.09	1.77		-.07		1.83	
1872	-3.65		2.92		2.62		2.93	
1876	1.94	1.45	2.71		-.17	-4.68	2.50	
1880	-.85		2.21		.22		2.45	
1884	-.60		1.97		.19		1.91	
1888	-.49		1.84		-.24		1.85	
1892	-1.81		3.90		-3.87		2.75	
1896	-.71		5.60		-1.66	5.16	3.69	
1900	-1.78		2.06		-1.00		1.74	
1904	-6.21		3.79	1.14	3.75		4.19	
1908	-.00		1.86		-1.09		1.73	

TABLE 3.1a   Estimates of Realigning and Deviating Surge and Interaction in Voting for President from 1836 to 1976, with States as Units of Analysis (Cont)

Election Year	Democratic Vote for President				Republican Vote for President			
	Surge		Interaction		Surge		Interaction	
	Deviating	Realigning	Deviating	Realigning	Deviating	Realigning	Deviating	Realigning
1912	.02		1.59		−22.53		5.79	
1916	6.31		3.27		1.80		3.27	
1920	−6.18	−1.77	3.59		7.31	7.73	3.79	
1924	−11.44		5.19		1.03		4.17	
1928	.49		4.37	1.92	5.06		5.23	
1932	.86	16.28	3.26		−2.07	−11.33	3.04	
1936	4.22		2.37		−5.17		1.97	1.20
1940	−1.87		2.86		3.06		1.56	
1944	−3.21		2.02		4.18		1.31	
1948	3.25	−8.20	3.10	1.15	1.93		2.18	
1952	−2.06		2.01		4.98	2.47	2.19	1.26
1956	−4.47		2.29		7.22		3.46	
1960	1.98	1.30	2.60		−.59		1.84	
1964	13.24		2.82	2.06	−9.16	−2.45	3.79	1.16
1968	−5.03	a	2.52	a	−4.14	a	4.25	a
1972	−10.19	a	2.20	a	12.99	a	3.64	a
1976	2.24	a	5.00	a	.31	a	2.56	a

aEstimates of realigning change are not possible for these years given the characteristics of the technique, which depend on four subsequent elections to determine whether or not change is lasting.

TABLE 3.1b Estimates of Realigning and Deviating Surge and Interaction in Voting for Congress from 1838 to 1978, with States as Units of Analysis

| Election Year | Democratic Vote for Congress | | | | Republican Vote for Congress | | | |
| | Surge | | Interaction | | Surge | | Interaction | |
	Deviating	Realigning	Deviating	Realigning	Deviating	Realigning	Deviating	Realigning
1838	2.51		4.50					
1840	1.52		4.10					
1842	1.77		4.29					
1844	-.55		4.93					
1846	.51		1.65					
1848	1.23	-5.13	5.52	4.61				
1850	2.13		7.84					
1852	6.70		5.73					
1854	-13.76		14.35					
1856	.92	2.05	7.39					
1858	3.21		4.91					
1860	-6.57		8.47					
1862	1.08	1.17	4.43	1.95				
1864	-4.95		5.58					
1866	.54		3.46					
1868	.08	1.02	2.74		1.53		2.81	
1870	.10		2.80		-3.15		2.14	
1872	-1.37		3.36		.03	-7.08	2.54	
1874	.46		6.30		.09		3.39	
1876	3.59	1.40	4.94	2.22	3.21		2.51	
1878	-5.71		5.32		-4.08		3.76	

TABLE 3.1b Estimates of Realigning and Deviating Surge and Interaction in Voting for Congress from 1838 to 1978, with States as Units of Analysis (Cont)

Election Year	Democratic Vote for Congress				Republican Vote for Congress			
	Surge		Interaction		Surge		Interaction	
	Deviating	Realigning	Deviating	Realigning	Deviating	Realigning	Deviating	Realigning
1880	-1.33		3.05		1.67		4.39	
1882	2.48		4.40		-3.48		5.11	
1884	2.25		2.92		1.18		4.75	
1886	-.82		4.87		1.40		3.83	
1888	-.46		3.60		.58	2.32	3.60	
1890	3.66		4.39		-4.18		4.00	
1892	-1.38		5.14		-4.62		3.98	
1894	-5.75	-3.48	3.47		1.34		3.34	1.10
1896	-.01	1.20	7.21		1.47		4.70	
1898	1.96		5.05	1.22	1.13		2.11	
1900	1.87		3.82		4.27		1.91	
1902	1.42		4.07		2.81		2.43	
1904	-2.39	-1.57	3.74		5.97		2.81	
1906	-1.17		4.03		.55		4.08	
1908	3.02		3.05		-.11		2.41	
1910	2.10		3.85	1.71	1.82	-6.08	3.56	
1912	1.09		4.64		-12.43		6.15	
1914	.02	-2.58	3.41		-4.83		4.73	
1916	2.50		5.10		-1.39		5.98	
1918	1.32		2.61		2.61		3.72	1.87
1920	-4.75		3.98		3.20	7.00	3.99	

TABLE 3.1b Estimates of Realigning and Deviating Surge and Interaction in Voting for Congress from 1838 to 1978, with States as Units of Analysis (Cont)

Election Year	Democratic Vote for Congress				Republican Vote for Congress			
	Surge		Interaction		Surge		Interaction	
	Deviating	Realigning	Deviating	Realigning	Deviating	Realigning	Deviating	Realigning
1922	2.69		4.24		−.96	−2.00	2.86	
1924	−1.49		4.31		5.60		4.39	
1926	−.29		4.58		5.21		4.30	
1928	1.40		4.07		5.23		3.99	
1930	4.00		4.24		1.38		4.45	
1932	3.12	8.80	4.04	1.55	−2.49	−5.14	3.60	1.99
1934	1.71		1.92		−3.68		2.65	
1936	3.68		2.44		−4.81		2.15	
1938	.27	−2.58	2.26		1.78		2.17	
1940	1.28		2.72		1.19		2.65	
1942	−2.85		2.20		1.43	3.85	2.73	
1944	3.15		3.16		−1.12		2.78	
1946	−3.85		2.66		4.96		1.88	
1948	−.58	2.79	3.97		−2.80	−1.50	2.09	
1950	−3.00		2.24		1.19		1.68	
1952	−3.05		2.54		2.44		2.57	
1954	−1.08	4.62	2.44	1.35	−.64		2.35	1.66
1956	−2.51		3.57		.93		3.73	
1958	1.58		3.13		−2.03	−1.52	3.27	
1960	1.40		1.92		−.61		1.61	

TABLE 3.1b Estimates of Realigning and Deviating Surge and Interaction in Voting for Congress from 1838 to 1978, with States as Units of Analysis (Cont)

Election Year	Democratic Vote for Congress				Republican Vote for Congress			
	Surge		Interaction		Surge		Interaction	
	Deviating	Realigning	Deviating	Realigning	Deviating	Realigning	Deviating	Realigning
1962	-1.43		3.09		2.39		2.74	
1964	4.30		3.49		-2.51	-1.04	3.98	
1966	-2.21		2.94		3.61		2.70	1.08
1968	-2.42	a	2.53	a	3.42	a	3.98	a
1970	-.33	a	3.35	a	-.09	a	2.39	a
1972	-1.27	a	3.48	a	1.94	a	2.94	a
1974	3.78	a	3.11	a	-4.01	a	2.62	a
1976	2.33	a	3.57	a	-2.36	a	3.05	a
1978	.04	a	3.20	a	-.12	a	3.31	a

aEstimates of realigning change are not possible for these years given the characteristics of the technique, which depend on seven subsequent elections to determine whether or not change is lasting.

It is true, of course, that indications of interactive realigning change of limited magnitude appear in the case of the Democratic vote in the presidential election of 1928, in the Republican presidential vote in 1936, and in the congressional vote for both parties in 1932. The asymmetry in the timing of interactive change in the presidential vote for the two parties is in accord, moreover, with widely held views of the shifts in voting behavior that took place during the period and conforms closely to the evidence provided by the regional correlational analysis in Chapter 2 above. The candidacy of Al Smith in 1928 has often been seen as a first step by the immigrant stock, urban working class into what would be the New Deal coalition.[11] W. Phillips Shively has also argued that the movement of major segments of the middle class into the Republican fold in the course of the realignment of the 1930s came only after the character of New Deal policies became apparent—in other words, in 1936.[12] It is clear, however, that interactive change, signifying rearrangement of geographically defined population groupings, was miniscule indeed compared with the across-the-board shifts that occurred during these years. It was this enormous across-the-board shift toward the Democrats and away from the Republicans, which appears to have come quite uniformly from all areas of the nation, that provided the Democrats with the opportunity to take the policy initiatives associated with the New Deal.

Characteristics of the 1896 realignment also appear more clearly once the concept of across-the-board electoral change is made explicit and subjected to measurement. Evidence of a realigning surge toward the Republicans can be observed in the presidential vote in 1896 (Table 3.1), and a similar Democratic loss can be seen in the congressional vote in 1894. The election of 1896 apparently was also marked by significant interactive change, but change of this nature was temporary, or deviating, in character. This pattern very closely parallels the results of correlational analysis presented in Tables 2.1 and 2.2 above. In that analysis, 1896 appears only as a momentary disruption in a continuing pattern of relative partisan strength extending from the 1850s to the 1950s. In short, both analyses suggest that the ordering of states in terms of the relative strength of the two parties tended to remain constant after 1896. In this sense, it is possible to speak of the prevailing alignment as persisting across the 1896 realignment. On the other hand, the data in Table 3.1 show that the balance of partisan strength in the nation shifted toward the Republicans, a change not revealed in the correlational analysis of Chapter 2.

Neither of these analytical approaches fully captures the patterns of electoral change characteristic of the elections of the 1890s. Compared with 1892 and earlier elections, the Democratic presidential vote rose sharply in the western and Plains states, and William Jennings Bryan carried many of these states.[13] In part, this shift toward the Democrats in 1896 was a reflection of the Populist incursion in 1892. In Colorado, Idaho, Kansas, North Dakota, and Wyoming, the Populists displaced the Democratic ticket entirely, and in still other states, the Populist candidate apparently cut into both the Democratic and Republican vote. These increases in the Democratic vote in 1896 reflected in part the absorption by the party of the Populist movement.

These Democratic gains in the West in 1896 are not clearly apparent from Table 3.1. In 1896 many of the larger and more heavily populated states remained relatively stable in terms of the partisan distribution of the vote, while large changes were concentrated in the western and less populous states. Since the data employed in Table 3.1 are weighted in terms of the magnitude of the total vote in each state, the less populous states contribute to the calculation of surge and interactive change only in proportion to the size of their electorates. This is an appropriate reduction on several grounds, most notably that it more accurately reflects the net proportion of the electorate that actually changed its voting behavior. On the other hand, the dramatic shifting of a few geographically concentrated states, even if they contained few voters, may have significance for the development of regional cleavages and for the policy initiatives available to elites in control at the state level. In this sense, the analysis may underplay change that is politically relevant in a federal system.

The lessening of the impact of the western states on the calculation of interactive change is exacerbated by their late entrance into the union. Idaho, Montana, North and South Dakota, Utah, and Washington were not admitted as states until the late 1880s and early 1890s. As a consequence, and as noted above, interactive voting shifts in these states during the 1890s are not reflected in Table 3.1. It was, of course, in these states among others of the West and Plains that the Populist movement was strongest and the shift toward Bryan in 1896 was most pronounced. As a result, the analytical technique underestimates the magnitude of interactive change that occurred in 1896, though it does not affect the estimate of surge.

Even with these methodological difficulties in mind, the evidence strongly suggests that the interactive changes in the Democratic presidential vote in 1896 were deviating rather than realigning. If realigning change in the Democratic vote occurred, it appears to have been later, in 1904. We might, then, offer an interpretation of the realignment of this period that differs somewhat from standard renditions. Apparently the election of 1896 involved a temporary shift toward the Democrats in states of the Plains and West, a shift which is underestimated in Table 3.1 and in Tables 2.1 and 2.2 above, and a more lasting movement toward the Republicans in the states of the northeastern quadrant of the nation. The evidence of realigning change appearing in the election of 1904 marks the return of the West and the Plains to the Republican fold and the consolidation of the new Republican alignment.[14]

The analytical approach employed here allows only a limited view of the patterns of electoral change characteristic of the 1850s and 1860s. Since the Republican party appeared only in the 1850s, measurement of change in the vote for that party can begin only with the election of 1872. For earlier years, analysis is confined to the Democratic vote. Even in the case of the Democratic vote, moreover, southern secession and the subsequent return of the southern states to the union add elements of obscurity to the analysis.[15]

It is obvious, of course, that the years surrounding the Civil War were marked by major change in electoral partisan loyalties. The demise of the Whig Party and the appearance of the new Republican Party were elements of that change, and southern secession marked the total disruption of the nation. As Table 3.1 suggests, the Democratic presidential vote and to a lesser degree the congressional vote in 1860 involved substantial deviating electoral change of both interactive and across-the-board form. Realigning change in the presidential vote in 1860, however, was only moderate and was even less pronounced in 1864. The congressional Democratic vote was characterized in 1862 by negligible realigning change. The magnitude of presidential and congressional Democratic realigning electoral change in these years fell well short of that of the latter 1840s and earlier 1850s, which apparently marked the shift of the southern states into the Democratic camp.

The limited magnitude of interactive change reflected in Table 3.1 reinforces a suspicion derived from the correlation matrices presented above. The major historical realignments might usefully be interpreted as relatively brief disruptions of a basic ordering of states that has persisted with a high degree of continuity over the years. The measure of interactive change employed in Table 3.1 captures the same type of change as is indicated by a break in a correlation matrix, although the analysis of variance technique allows measurement of the relative magnitudes of this type of change and includes an explicit criterion for distinguishing deviating from realigning changes. While a considerable amount of interactive change is exhibited in Table 3.1, it is almost entirely deviating in nature. It appears, in short, that all elections are characterized by some departure from expected voting patterns, but these departures do not reflect lasting change in underlying voting patterns. The election of 1896 is a notable case in point. That election evidences deviating interactive change of larger than usual magnitude but no interactive realigning change. This characteristic again closely parallels the findings based on correlational analysis presented in Tables 2.1 and 2.2. There the election of 1896 also appears as little more than a momentary disruption in a continuing pattern of relative partisan strength stretching from the 1850s to the 1950s.

The failure to identify realigning interactive change in association with major realignments is contrary to expectations derived from other investigations of historical voting patterns. Realignments are usually seen as producing differential shifts in voting patterns and new and enduring voting alignments of states or other geographical units. Both correlations and analysis of variance, however, indicate little in the way of lasting, interactive electoral change or, in other words, little in the way of reordering of the states in terms of their relative electoral support for the parties.

It is conceivable, of course, that differential shifts in voting alignments have been gradual, that the interactive change associated with realignments occurred gradually over the years, and that only realigning across-the-board change occurred abruptly. While the simple correlations between elections temporally distant from each other are high enough to cast doubt on this possibility (see Table 2.2 above), the analysis of variance procedure allows a further test. By dropping intervening elections, the latter procedure can be employed to examine blocs of elections distant from each other in time in order to assess the magnitude of realigning interaction across long time periods. Table 3.2, which displays the results of this test, reinforces the impression of a stable and persistent partisan alignment of the states which has endured through much of American electoral history. The several comparisons displayed in Table 3.2 reflect only low levels of realigning interaction and force the conclusion that lasting, differential change has not occurred over lengthy time spans any more significantly than at realignments.

A further test of the proposition that states have maintained substantially the same relative ordering over a century and a quarter can be made by using estimates of the expected vote for each state. Estimates of the expected votes for each of the states can be derived as a by-product of the analysis of variance procedure introduced in this chapter. This indicator of the expected vote is simply a moving average of the actual vote for

TABLE 3.2 Interactive Realignment in Democratic Presidential
           Voting for States

Comparison from . . .	to . . . 1876–1888	1896–1908	1932–1944
1840–1856	2.40	.0	2.50
1876–1888			1.10
1896–1908			.0

a party corrected for sharp and lasting shifts in the average, i.e.,
corrected for electoral realignments. Thus it provides estimates
of the voting pattern established by a realignment, estimates
which will change gradually in response to deterioration of the
partisan alignment, or sharply in response to abrupt shifts in
voting patterns.[16]

To test whether states have maintained their same relative
ordering over a long time period, the earliest estimate of the
expected vote for each state can be linked to its equivalent
expected vote for the post-New Deal period. In this analysis, the
expected vote estimates for each state are based on the Democratic vote in presidential elections. The year of the earliest
estimate differs from state to state depending upon admission
to the union; for over half the states, the estimates were derived
from the pre-Civil War years. For all states, the expected Democratic vote in 1944 was used for the post-New Deal period. The
relationship between these two sets of expected votes is displayed in Figure 3.5 where the vertical axis is the post-New Deal
expected vote, and the horizontal axis is the earliest expected
division of the vote.

As can be seen, there is a fairly strong relationship between
these two estimates of expected vote strength; the slope is 1.13
with a correlation coefficient of .69. The extremely strong and
consistent pro-Democratic voting of the southern states
strengthens the relationship overall, while the behavior of the
other states is somewhat less orderly. Although not the same
form of evidence as introduced in Chapter 2, this strong relationship reinforces the findings based on the correlation matri-

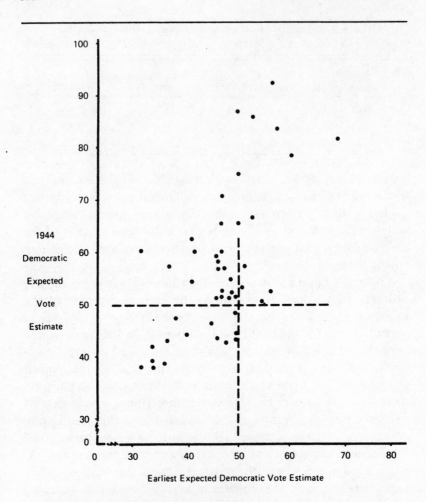

Earliest Expected Democratic Vote Estimate

a. Estimates are percentages based on expected votes drawn from the analysis
   of variance technique described in the text.

Figure 3.5: Expected Vote Estimates by States for Earliest Period and for 1944 Based
on Democratic Vote for President[a]

ces presented there. At the same time, the fact that most of the
states lie above the diagonal indicates that across-the-board
change in the states generally favored the Democratic party.

As we have seen, patterns of electoral change during the three
periods usually identified as major electoral realignments

emerge more clearly once the concept of across-the-board change is introduced and an appropriate measurement procedure is employed. At the same time, far more indications of realigning change appear than can seemingly be tolerated by any simple view of American electoral history as characterized by prolonged periods of stability punctuated by occasional electoral upheavals. In fact, introduction of the concept of across-the-board change, along with use of an appropriate measurement procedure, results in identification of more, not fewer, indications of realigning change. During four periods in particular, there are indications of surge or interactive realigning change in two or more of the data series displayed in Table 3.1: the Democratic vote for both president and Congress in 1848; the Democratic presidential and congressional vote in 1876 and the Republican presidential vote in 1876; the Republican presidential and congressional vote and the Democratic presidential vote in 1920; and the presidential vote for both parties in 1948 and 1952 and the Democratic and Republican congressional vote in 1954. These clusters of lasting electoral change have also been noted by others, and the term midsequence adjustments has been applied to them, since each appears approximately midway in historical realignment cycles.

But there are additional indications of electoral realignment as well. Indications of realigning change of small or moderate magnitude appear in one or the other of the data series in the Democratic presidential vote in 1904; in the Republican congressional vote in 1888, 1910, 1916, and 1942; and in 1856, 1880, 1906, 1910, and 1914 in the Democratic congressional series. Even if we ignore realigning change of small magnitude, evidence remains of considerable lasting electoral change at times other than those usually seen as periods of major realignment.

Superficially at least, these analytical findings appear paradoxical. There is evidence, on the one hand, of a highly durable alignment that persisted across more than a century of American electoral history. The evidence suggests that, in general, those states that supported one or the other of the parties most strongly in relation to other states during one period also supported the same party most strongly during other periods. Lasting shifts in electoral support for the parties did occur, but usually took the form of surges toward one or the other of the parties that did not disrupt the underlying alignment. On the other hand, the evidence, viewed from a different perspective, suggests substantial electoral instability. Lasting -shifts in the relative strength of the parties were frequent—more frequent than discussions of the realignment phenomenon usually suggest.

REGIONAL ELECTORAL CHANGE

There are a variety of obvious questions concerning the national electoral patterns discussed above and in the preceding chapter. One question has to do with whether these patterns were characteristic of all areas of the nation or were limited to only a few areas instead. Did some realignments involve substantial shifts in electoral strength in all areas and affect both parties and contests for all offices? Were others of more limited scope and impact? Another and in some respects more fundamental question concerns whether or to what extent the evidence of national electoral patterns above is little more than the artifact of an aggregation process that sums individual vote decisions to the state level. To what extent, in other words, are the above findings consistent with evidence developed at a different level of analysis? The weighting of subunits also may allow differential patterns to emerge in the regional analysis. Significant changes in less populous areas, like the Plains states, may have been overwhelmed by changes in the heavily populated Northeast in the national analysis.

To address these and related questions, we have shifted our perspective from that of the nation as a whole to that of the regions of the nation and our level of analysis from the states to the counties. Table 3.3 presents the results of a regional analysis, based on counties, of the Democratic and Republican presidential and congressional vote using the same analysis procedures as were applied to the states.[17] For the sake of simplicity, and to conserve space, only realigning change, both surge and interactive, is displayed in the table. Realigning change in magnitudes in excess of 5% is highlighted.

A striking similarity between the results of the regional analysis based on counties presented in Table 3.3 and those of the national analysis based on states presented in Table 3.1 is the infrequent incidence and the limited magnitude of interactive realigning change. At first glance, this similarity is surprising. Counties are smaller, and presumably more homogeneous geographical units than states. Thus one might have expected that the differential impact of political forces upon the behavior of specific population groups would produce a greater incidence and magnitude of interactive change in the analysis based on counties than in the national analysis. In other words, the process of aggregation to the state level, and the greater heterogeneity of the states, would mask or cancel out the differential shifts in the electoral behavior of specific population groups. Thus differential behavior would be more readily observable at the county level and would be reflected in indications of greater interactive realigning change.

In fact, of course, the relative absence of interactive realigning change is in conformity with widely accepted interpretations of historical realignments. Both the realignments of the Civil War years and of the 1890s are usually seen as regional in character. That is, political forces in these years are usually seen as exerting an essentially similar effect upon all or most population groups within particular regions. The indications provided by Table 3.3 of across-the-board regional shifts toward one or the other of the parties during the Civil War years and the 1890s are in keeping with this general interpretation.

The absence of evidence of regional interactive electoral change in 1932, along with the uniformity of across-the-board regional shifts toward the Democrats and away from the Republicans, is—again, at first glance—somewhat more surprising. The realignment of the 1930s is frequently interpreted as working to polarize the electorate along class, economic, and rural-urban lines. It could be expected that realignment of this sort would be reflected in indications of substantial interactive electoral change among county units.

In fact, the data require a somewhat more complex interpretation, but one that is also in keeping with widely accepted views of the pattern of electoral change during these years. The indications of across-the-board shifts toward the Democrats in 1932 can be seen as reflections of the pervasive impact of the Great Depression and can be taken as a product of the shift of voters throughout the nation into the ranks of the Democratic Party. Although not displayed in Table 3.3, there is also evi-

TABLE 3.3a   Estimates of Realigning Surge and Interaction
              Based on Democratic and Republican Voting
              for President from 1856 to 1964 for Regions
              Using Counties as Units of Analysis[a]

	Democratic Vote for President												Republican Vote for President											
	Surge						Interaction							Surge						Interaction					
Year	E	M	P	S	B	W	E	M	P	S	B	W	Year	E	M	P	S	B	W	E	M	P	S	B	W
1856	-4	-3																							
1860			[-17]	-2	-4	4																			
1864	[7]	[-7]						3	3	1	[6]	1													
1868			[23]	[10]	[6]					[6]															
1872				-1	-1						[5]														
1876	1	4	3	[11]	2	1	3				2		1876	-3	-4		[-9]								
1880		-3							1				1880					-4							
1884		2											1884			2									[7]
1888			1	[-4]									1888		[-3]					1					
1892		[-3]	1		[-3]				2				1892		-4		-2					1			
1896	[-6]	[-6]	4		2				2				1896	[5]	[5]	2	3			1			2		4
1900			-4										1900												
1904		[5]					1	2	3		4		1904							1					
1908	3	-1		[6]									1908												
1912													1912	-2	-2	-2		1							2
1916													1916												
1920	-2	-3		-3									1920	[7]	[8]	[8]	[7]	[5]	[10]						
1924													1924			-4.		1							
1928							2	4	3				1928					1	1	1					
1932	[14]	[17]	[18]	[12]	[10]	[-3]						1	1932	[-12]	[-12]	[-10]	[-9]	[-8]	[-20]						
1936									2				1936							1					
1940													1940	[6]	[9]					2	2	4		2	
1944				[-7]									1944				[7]	[13]							3
1948	[-3]	[-3]		[-20]	[-11]							3	1948												
1952		[-12]					2	[8]					1952			[17]				1					
1956			[-8]	-1									1956												
1960	[8]	[6]			2								1960	[-8]						2					
1964		2					3						1964		-4	[-5]		-2							

a. For a listing of the states in each region see footnote 26, page 76.

TABLE 3.3b   Congress from 1854 to 1966

| | Democratic Vote for Congress | | | | | | | | | | | | | Republican Vote for Congress | | | | | | | | | | | | |
| | Surge | | | | | | Interaction | | | | | | | Surge | | | | | | Interaction | | | | | |
Year	E	M	P	S	B	W	E	M	P	S	B	W	Year	E	M	P	S	B	W	E	M	P	S	B	W
1854	-1	-1		13	2																				
1856			2		2			5																		
1858	6								5																	
1860	-6						3																			
1862	1			-14	-26								1862	-1				17								
1864													1864								1					
1866			-3				5					12	1866	8	9		13	21		1	2		7		3
1868				17									1868												
1870			30										1870				-1						4		
1872	-4	-1				1				2			1872					-2							
1874	6		-4		1			6		2			1874	-2	-3	-4									
1876			3	12									1876				-1	3							
1878			1		-5		2						1878			-3	-14					2	3		
1880													1880												
1882	4	2	-1				4	4		2	2		1882				-3								
1884	-1						1						1884	3											
1886			-2										1886										2		
1888	-4			-5									1888				11								
1890			2				1						1890	-1						3					
1892								3	2				1892		-4	-2			2						
1894	-3	-4	-2	-2	-10		3						1894	4	7										
1896							3						1896			2							4		
1898			1										1898	-2											
1900	4					2							1900	5	2		1								
1902		11	12	10		2				4			1902	-2		4		1							
1904					3								1904												
1906	-2			2									1906												
1908													1908				-4								
1910		-1											1910	-4	-4										
1912		-3	2										1912	-2	-2										
1914				-6					5				1914				-5		1						
1916							3						1916	2		4									
1918						3							1918	9	9		6					5			
1920													1920	9		4			2						
1922	7	3	4		1								1922	-4		-3	-3	2	2						
1924		4		2		1	3						1924												
1926					3								1926												
1928													1928			2									
1930	10												1930												
1932	4		6	4	4	14				3			1932	-7	-7	-6	-8	-4				2			
1934					1	2							1934			-3	4	2	2	2					
1936													1936			2									
1938	-2	-5											1938	4							2				
1940			-6										1940												
1942		-3	-1	-3			2						1942	5	7	4									
1944			3				4						1944			7		3			1				
1946													1946		4										
1948	3	2	3										1948	-2	-4	-3									
1950		-2											1950												
1952						2							1952						2						
1954			10			6							1954			6				4					
1956					1								1956	-2											
1958	4	1											1958	-6											
1960			-1										1960		1										
1962			-15	1									1962			14	-2								
1964	1		2										1964	-1											
1966		-1											1966	-3											

dence of substantial deviating interactive change in 1932 and in immediately following and preceding elections. The evidence is consistent with the view that the election of 1932 involved a temporary movement of voters in areas more affluent and more traditionally Republican toward the Democrats as a consequence of the collapse of the national economy. As the direction of New Deal policies was established, and with a measure of economic recovery, these voters tended, it is argued, to return to their earlier voting patterns and partisan loyalties.[18]

In still other respects, the data presented in Table 3.3 are in conformity with our expectations and in keeping with widely accepted interpretations of the three major historical realignments. In general, indications of realigning change at the regional level coincide with those observed at the national level. Moreover, indications of realignment, particularly in the case of the 1890s, appear more clearly from a regional perspective than from that of the nation. Apparently, the use of states as units of analysis tends to mask indications of realigning electoral change in these years.

The pattern of electoral change during the Civil War years also appears more clearly from the regional perspective. As at the national level, electoral change during these years seems to be largely interpretable in terms of southern secession, occupation, and Reconstruction. Realigning change in the Democratic presidential vote was largely concentrated in the South and the border states—first reflecting the decline in the Democratic vote in 1860 accompanying the Douglas-Breckenridge split in the party followed by secession, then by resurgence in the Democratic vote as southern states were readmitted to the union, and by further increase as Reconstruction governments in southern states were terminated. The Democratic congressional series is more erratic during this period, but it shows increases in Democratic strength in the South as the southern Whigs floundered. The drop in Democratic strength in the South and border states in 1862 is again attributable to secession, while the realigning surge in the Democrats' favor in subsequent years can be seen as a product of readmission and later the end of Reconstruction. Of course, one dramatic form of realignment not reflected in this type of analysis is the emergence of the Republican Party, which was the last major change in the party system in American history.

The regional analysis of the presidential vote during the 1890s appears as would be expected given usually accepted interpretations of the period. The evidence presented in Table 3.3 suggests that the Northeast and Midwest regions experienced realigning surges toward the Republicans in 1896, while the West and Plains became marginally more Democratic. This latter shift, however, was quite small and probably better interpreted as recovery from the Populist intrusions into Democratic strength in 1892 in these regions. The congressional series suggests a shift away from the Democrats in most regions in 1894, presumably in response initially to the Depression of 1893 and perpetuated in subsequent elections by disaffection with the Populist alliance. Here again, however, while indications of lasting electoral change are clear, the realignment of 1896 appears substantially less impressive than might have been expected.

The election of 1932 provides the clearest example of national realignment. Evidence of realigning change is remarkably uniform for all regions of the nation. The results of the analysis of presidential voting returns in Table 3.3 provides evidence of a pronounced realigning surge toward the Democrats in 1932 in all regions and a corresponding, lasting drop in Republican strength. The congressional series is slightly less uniform. The Midwest, it appears, shifted toward the Democrats in 1930, while in the already heavily Democratic southern and border states, the party made only marginal additional gains. In the northeastern states, as well, Democratic gains in the congressional elections of the early 1930s were apparently relatively limited. The data suggest, instead, a more substantial shift toward the Democratic party in the congressional elections of 1922. But despite these qualifications, the shift in the congressional vote toward the Democrats, with the corresponding drop in the Republican congressional vote, appears highly pervasive and substantial. Here again, the early 1930s appear as the prototype of a national partisan realignment.

The results presented in Table 3.3 suggest still other aspects and complexities of the New Deal realignment. The data provide evidence that the presidential election of 1928 was characterized by small amounts of interactive realigning change, particularly in the Northeast, Midwest, and Plains. Although not paralleled by indications of equivalent change in the congressional vote, these shifts could be taken as evidence of an "Al Smith uprising" that preceded the "Roosevelt revolution" of the early 1930s.[19] There is also evidence of further realigning change of varying magnitude during the late 1930s and the early 1940s. These indications, characteristic of both the presidential and the congressional series, obviously suggest recession of the Democratic tide and perhaps the consummation of polarization of the national electorate along class lines.[20]

A regional analytical perspective, then, does provide evidence of lasting change in the relative electoral strength of the parties during each of the three periods usually described as major partisan realignments. In both the Civil War years and the 1890s, however, that perspective suggests very complex patterns of electoral change combining regional changes of varied magnitudes. Only in the case of the election of 1932 is there evidence of the pattern of sharp, large-scale, and pervasive change that is usually considered an attribute of historical realignments.

This perspective, moreover, also provides evidence of realigning change during a variety of elections in addition to those usually considered realigning. We have noted the indications of lasting electoral change during the late 1860s and the 1870s that probably reflected the return of the Democratic South to full participation in national elections as well as the recovery by the party of legitimacy in the North. Both the presidential and congressional series also provide evidence of lasting electoral change in the course of the progressive years. As in the national analysis, the presidential election of 1920 and to a somewhat lesser degree the congressional elections of 1918 and 1920 stand out as realigning. The presidential vote in all regions and the congressional vote in most regions show a substantial shift toward the Republican Party. These shifts, however, are not paralleled by Democratic losses. To some degree, this is an analytical product of the third-party vote for Theodore Roosevelt in 1912 and of third-party activity during the progressive years more generally. The analytical effect of these factors is to depress the Republican expected vote prior to 1920 (1918 in the case of the congressional expected vote) without affecting the Democratic expected vote. Thus the shifts toward the Republicans in 1918 and 1920 are without parallel deficits for the Democrats. Despite these qualifications, these two elections appear as a sharp, relatively pervasive, and lasting recovery of Republican strength after the losses of the progressive period.

And still other indications of realigning change appear as well. The most recent decades are marked by impressive indications of lasting change in the presidential vote. Most notably in the South, but in other regions as well, the Democrats experienced significant and lasting losses in 1948 reflecting initially the Dixiecrat bolt and, subsequently, disaffection with northern liberal Democratic candidates. Indications of further realigning change appear in association with each of the following presidential elections through that of 1964. Outside the South, Democratic losses in those years were not in general accompanied by equivalent Republican gains. Moreover, as Table 3.3 suggests, the frequent realigning change characteristic of the presidential vote during those years is in marked contrast to the high degree of partisan stability of the congressional vote during the same period. In the following chapter, we will suggest that these characteristics of the vote can be taken as reflections of increased independent voting in presidential contests, of weakening partisan ties, and of the deterioration of the partisan alignment that had emerged in the New Deal years.

Taken in total, examination of regional voting patterns suggests findings that are in keeping with the national patterns observed in the preceding section. There is no indication that the national patterns described there are merely statistical artifacts of the process of aggregating individual voting decisions to the state level. At the same time, the regional perspective allows more detailed assessment of the nature and pattern of electoral change during historical realignments. To a considerable degree, these assessments support the findings and interpretations of other investigators.

In critical ways, however, the present findings also depart from other depictions of the realignment process as it occurred historically. As at the national level, a regional perspective yields little in the way of evidence of the massive reshuffling of voters that is often understood as an attribute of historical realignments. In terms of the analytical techniques employed here, historical realignments appear primarily as surges for or against the parties. These surges did not disturb the ordering of the counties within the various regions in terms of their support for the parties. Thus it is possible to speak, as at the national level, of alignments within regions that persisted over extended periods.

A second departure lies in the nature and magnitude of the historical realignments. The Civil War realignment appears as a relatively transitory phenomenon when one compares Democratic voting in the 1840s with the 1870s. With the end of Reconstruction, there was a return to the closely competitive conditions nationwide of the pre-Civil War years, albeit with a change in one of the major partisan protagonists. Although apparently of more lasting electoral consequence, the realignment of the 1890s appears more diffuse, involving more moderate electoral change than is usually suggested in scholarly accounts. Only the realignment of the 1930s involved the sharp, massive, pervasive, and lasting electoral change that is often taken as a general characteristic of historical realignments.

A third departure concerns what might be termed an over-abundance of realigning change. From the present analytical perspective, lasting electoral changes were clearly not confined to the several periods and elections usually identified as realignments. In fact, such change has been a virtually constant property of the historical political system. Moreover, a further classification of certain elections as midsequence adjustments will not account for this overabundance of realigning change.

It is obvious that investigators would not have been led to identify particular periods and elections as national partisan realignments solely by the examination of voting patterns. Indeed, there are only a few examples of anything approaching comprehensive analysis of presidential voting, and little in the way of comprehensive examination in national scope and in historical depth of the congressional vote much less the vote for other lesser offices—has been attempted. The present examination clearly suggests that voting patterns alone do not serve to identify the Civil War era, the 1890s, and the 1930s as national "critical" realignments; nor do voting patterns alone serve to distinguish these periods fully from other periods and elections of comparable electoral change. In identifying these periods as the major national realignments, investigators have obviously relied upon other evidence in addition to electoral change, including lasting shifts in partisan control of government and in the directions of national policy. But they have done so neither explicitly nor systematically, allowing the standard "definition" of realignment to stand as "a lasting change in the partisan division of the electorate." In Chapters 5 through 7, we will return to the task of explicitly incorporating such other factors into the discussion of partisan realignment.

NOTES

1. V.O. Key, Jr., "A Theory of Critical Elections," *Journal of Politics* 17 (February 1955), pp. 3-18.

2. The use of intercepts might seem a straightforward means of measuring this type of change without departing from the regression model; unfortunately, once we leave the pure case of across-the-board change, the intercept moves in response to both the amount of change from one election to the next and the strength of the correlation between the votes in the two elections. Thus the intercept does not distinguish across-the-board change from differential change, and its interpretation is ambiguous.

3. There are exceptions. Burnham's use of the discontinuity variable may be viewed as an attempt to capture shifts in the level of partisan support; however, its purpose focuses more on verifying the occurrence of a shift than on measuring its magnitude. Walter Dean Burnham, *Critical Elections and the Mainsprings of American Politics* (New York: Norton, 1970), Ch. 2.

4. In Angus Campbell, "Surge and Decline: A Study of Electoral Change," *Public Opinion Quarterly* 24 (Fall 1960), pp. 397-418, the term "surge" is used in a somewhat different way to describe the movement of peripheral voters toward a popular candidate.

5. William H. Flanigan and Nancy H. Zingale, "The Measurement of Electoral Change," *Political Methodology* 1 (Summer 1974), pp. 49-82; Nancy H. Zingale, "Electoral Stability and Change: The Case of Minnesota, 1857-1966," Ph.D. dissertation, University of Minnesota, 1971. For a similar approach, see John L. McCarthy and John W. Tukey, "Exploratory Analysis of Aggregate Voting Behavior: Presidential Elections in New Hampshire, 1896-1972," *Social Science History* 2 (Spring 1978), pp. 292-331.

6. In standard analysis of variance terminology, this is a two-way analysis of variance (election by subunit) with interaction and one observation per cell, yielding the following formulation:

Total variation = Election Sum of squares + Subunit sum of squares + Interaction sum of squares

or

$$\sum_{i=1}^{I} \sum_{j=1}^{J} (X_{ij} - \overline{X}..)^2 = I \sum_{j=1}^{J} (\overline{X}._j - \overline{X}..)^2 +$$

$$J \sum_{i=1}^{I} (\overline{X}_i. - \overline{X}..)^2 +$$

$$\sum_{i=1}^{I} \sum_{j=1}^{J} (X_{ij} - \overline{X}._j - \overline{X}_i. + \overline{X}..)^2$$

where X_{ij} is the vote percentage in the ith subunit in the jth election. (In an analysis of variance design with one observation per cell, there is no within subclass variation, hence no error term in the formulation.) Basically, surge is measured by the election sum of squares and interactive change by the interaction sum of squares, but we have made a number of modifications. Since we are interested in the amount of change in each election, not in the entire set, we do not sum either term across elections. Second, because the magnitude of the sum of squares is directly affected by the number of categories in the factors in the design, greater electoral changes would be noted in the modern era simply as a function of increasing numbers of subunits—either states or counties. Therefore, we have standardized results by dividing both election and interaction term by the number of subunits. Additionally, the squaring of deviations from the mean in the calculation of the sums of squares emphasizes extreme deviations. We see no substantive reason for wishing to retain this over-emphasis; therefore we have ignored signs rather than squaring the election and interaction terms before their summation.

7. It should be noted that State 3 does not actually increase its vote for Party X by the 5% implied by the amount of surge measured for Election 5, nor does it actually depart from its own expected vote by the –5% implied by its residual. The more precise interpretation of State 3's behavior is the following: It failed by 5% to increase its vote for Party X by the same amount as the nation as a whole. Put another way, as the other subunits were moving toward Party X by an average amount of 5%, State 3 did not depart from its expected vote at all.

8. The specific rules for making these determinations are outlined in Flanigan and Zingale, "The Measurement of Electoral Change," pp. 61-64.

9. One might argue that a conceptual problem exists in these cases, however, since for purposes of calculating surge, we are using the first votes of a subunit as an indication of that subunit's expected vote rather than averaging a series of election returns.

10. It is worth noting that these same general difficulties are encountered in the use of matrices of correlation coefficients to investigate electoral patterns, although the fact is often neglected.

11. See, for example, Key, "A Theory of Critical Elections," and Samuel Lubell, *The Future of American Politics* (New York: Harper and Row, 1952).

12. W. Phillips Shively, "A Reinterpretation of the New Deal Realignment," *Public Opinion Quarterly* 75 (1971-1972), pp. 621-624.

13. This pattern of change is reflected in simple change scores calculated for pairs of adjacent elections. See, for example, Gerald Pomper, "Classification of Presidential Elections," *Journal of Politics* 29 (1967), pp. 547-549; Walter Dean Burnham, Jerome M. Clubb, and William H. Flanigan, "Partisan Realignment, a Systemic Perspective," in Joel H. Silbey, Allan G. Bogue, and William H. Flanigan (eds.), *The History of American Electoral Behavior* (Princeton, NJ: Princeton University Press, 1978), pp. 54-57.

14. This pattern of change is further elucidated in the analysis of regional electoral change presented in a subsequent section.

15. Again, the estimates of interactive change are affected for a longer period than the actual absence of the southern states from the union, due to the inability to calculate expected votes for the southern states for the elections immediately before and after secession. The estimates of surge are not similarly affected.

16. Conceptually, this expected vote is of course similar to Philip Converse's normal vote. See "The Concept of a Normal Vote," in Angus Campbell, Philip E. Converse, Warren E. Miller, and Donald E. Stokes, *Elections and the Political Order* (New York: John Wiley, 1966), pp. 9-39. Operationally, they are very different; our estimates are based upon aggregate data of voting behavior, not upon the individual reports of partisan identification and voting behavior that Converse is able to use.

17. The regional divisions are the same as those employed in Chapter 2. (see note 26 in the preceding chapter.)

18. For variations of this argument, see Shively, "A Reinterpretation of the New Deal Realignment"; Philip Converse, "Public Opinion and Voting Behavior," in Fred J. Greenstein and Nelson W. Polsby (eds.), *Handbook of Political Science, Vol. 4* (Reading, MA: Addison-Wesley, 1975), pp. 140-144; and James L. Sundquist, *Dynamics of the Party System,* (Washington, DC: Brookings Institution, 1973), pp. 208-211.

19. The major partisans of the 1928 realignment generally based their assertions on data limited to these regions. See, for example, Key, "A Theory of Critical Elections," for which the data base was a set of New England towns, and Lubell, *The Future of American Politics,* p. 34, who used as evidence the vote gain for Democrats in the nation's twelve largest cities.

20. See Shively, "A Reinterpretation of the New Deal Realignment," and Sundquist, *Dynamics of the Party System,* for similar observations.

Chapter 4

THE DETERIORATION OF ELECTORAL ALIGNMENTS

The analysis discussed in the preceding chapter indicates that electoral change during the historical periods usually identified as realignments was not in every case either as sharp or as pervasive, nor was lasting change as narrowly confined to a few periods, as the literature suggests. Although these periods were marked by both deviating and realigning electoral change, which shifted the balance of partisan strength within the electorate toward one or the other of the parties, these shifts did not involve the massive reshuffling of the electorate that some formulations of the realignment perspective describe. Moreover, indications of substantial continuity of the alignment of electoral forces across virtually the whole sweep of American electoral history can be observed.

If electoral patterns do not, by themselves, clearly and unequivocally point to the occurrence of partisan realignment, similar questions might also be raised about the decay phase of the realignment sequence. The realignment perspective outlined in Chapter 1 emphasizes the apparent deterioration of the partisan alignment following a period of postrealignment stability. Indeed, in many respects, it is the notion of the decay phase that gives the realignment perspective its dynamic quality, providing the link between the prior realignment and the creation of the conditions allowing the next realignment to occur. As with the conventional conceptualization of partisan realignment, the idea of the deterioration of the prevailing alignment relies heavily for both theory and data on the behavior of the electorate. In this chapter, we will examine the evidence for the occurrence of such decay periods following the partisan realignments of the 1860s, the 1890s, and the 1930s.

In several writings, Walter Dean Burnham has called attention to the disintegration of the bases of partisanship since 1896, a disintegration temporarily halted by the New Deal realignment and its aftermath, but which now continues onward.[1] This has led to the current view in David Broder's phrase, that "the party's over," that the detachment from partisan loyalties on the part of the electorate is so far advanced that the functions which political parties have traditionally performed will either be taken over by other institutions or will not be performed.[2] On the other hand, observation of other periods indicates that similar decay may have followed each partisan realignment, suggesting that a shorter cycle of realignment and decay, followed by another realignment, may also exist. Approximately a decade and a half after each of the major realignments—in the 1840s, in the latter 1870s, in the second decade of the twentieth century, and in the late 1940s and early 1950s, the dominant party suffered decline in strength, defeat at the polls, and loss of unified control of the elective agencies of the state and national governments. These midsequence adjustments are viewed as ushering in periods of greater electoral instability and continued deterioration of the prevailing partisan alignments.

A number of investigators have noted this recurring cycle of realignment and decay and have suggested underlying processes as the source of these sequences.[3] Partisan realignments, precipitated by some apparent crisis, are seen as focusing public

attention on a narrow set of issues upon which the political
parties take relatively clear and differentiated stands. As time
passes, the salience of the realignment issue begins to fade; new
issues arise that cut across the existing party cleavage and cause
defections from party loyalty in voting. Third parties crop up to
capitalize on issue concerns that the major parties fail to meet.
A second factor seen as contributing to the decay of the
previous alignment is the accumulation of new entrants into the
electorate who lack the firm partisan attachments of preceding
generations who had experienced the realignment crisis first-
hand. Paul Allen Beck has suggested an explanation for the
observation that realignments seem to occur at forty-year inter-
vals. The generation experiencing a realignment will have well-
developed and intense partisan loyalties, loyalties they transmit
to their children through vivid and emotion-laden political discussion. The succeeding generation, however, will receive its
partisan socialization thirdhand, from parents who are partisan
but who never directly experienced the events that were the
basis for their loyalty. The partisanship of this third generation
is thus substantially weaker, and these relatively detached individuals may be candidates for conversion in a subsequent
realignment.[4] Others have suggested the presence of a large pool
of apolitical or nonmobilized people, such as immigrants or the
children of immigrants or newly enfranchised groups, as a
characteristic of the period antecedent to a realignment.[5] However created, a pool of voters or potential voters, without strong
partisan attachments and therefore available for capture by one
or the other of the parties, has often been seen as a precondition for realignment. Only when a substantial portion of the
electorate is relatively free of partisan loyalties can a crisis
become the catalyst that results in the restructuring of the
partisan cleavages in the electorate.

Much of the attention to the deterioration of partisan alignments has grown out of consideration of the political trends of
the last fifteen years, widely regarded as evidence of the decay
of the New Deal alignment. We will first discuss this evidence
from the recent past, much of it originally presented by others,

and almost all of it based upon survey data. We will then turn to the more hazardous task of demonstrating the occurrence of similar decay in the other realignment sequences for which survey data are unavailable.

DETERIORATION OF THE
NEW DEAL ALIGNMENT

In broad and impressionistic terms, the roots of the deterioration of the New Deal alignment seem to be found as early as 1946. In that year, the majority Democratic party lost control of Congress and in 1948 experienced division on the left and right. Despite a narrow victory in 1948, control of Congress was lost in 1950 and of the presidency two years later. The departure of the South from the Democratic Party in presidential voting since 1948 is widely regarded as symptomatic of the break-up of the New Deal coalition. The years since the late 1950s have been dotted with protest movements and other indications of popular discontent, although increased legal obstacles have tended to prevent the expression of protest and discontent through third-party activity. Even so, during these years, the majority Democratic party has been plagued with internal divisions. The discontent and efforts of George Wallace and his supporters in the 1960s and 1970s seemed to perpetuate, although in aggravated form, the unrest produced by social issues centering upon race that first appeared in the candidacy of Strom Thurmond. At the opposite end of the Democratic spectrum, the disturbances of the "New Left" and the dissatisfaction with the party and its policies on the part of formerly loyal liberal elements seemed to reflect in some ways continuation of the liberal disenchantment that led to the candidacy of Henry Wallace in 1948. There were indications, as well, that the Republican party since the 1940s has suffered from similar internal divisions. The acrimonious convention of 1964 was visible evidence of the split between Goldwater conservatives and Rockefeller liberals, a split which continued in muted form in 1968 and which, with different standard bearers, led to primary challenges of an incumbent, if unelected, Republican president in 1976.

The sophisticated collections of survey research data amassed since the early 1950s allow detailed examination at the individual level of the dynamics and correlates of the political behavior that has produced this apparent disarray. The opportunity is of considerable importance. If these richer indicators provide evidence of the deterioration of the New Deal alignment and of the processes involved in that deterioration, then we are perhaps entitled to place greater confidence in similar patterns to be found using the more inadequate and less reliable indicators that are available for earlier periods. Certainly, the patterns and relationships observed for the more recent years can aid in the interpretation of the more fragmentary indicators for earlier years.

The most compelling evidence for the current deterioration of the New Deal alignment lies in the increase in the proportion of the electorate that has apparently become detached from partisan ties. This evidence takes a variety of forms, and much of it is by now well known. The most straightforward and most widely reported piece of evidence was the impressive rise in the proportion of independents in the electorate. Following twenty or so years of documented stability in partisan identification, the percentage of independents increased from 23% to 36% between 1964 and 1974 and continued at this high level through 1976. Half of this increase occurred among those independents who indicated that they did not feel "closer" to either party, a group that grew from 8% to 14% during this period.[6] The independents who indicate some preference for one or the other of the parties increased from 15% to 22% of the electorate. The consequent decline in partisans came more heavily from the Democrats; however, because of the numerical advantage of the Democrats, both parties lost similar proportions of their respective strengths over this period. A related change, though not a logically necessary one, was a decline in the number of strong partisans relative to those with only weak attachment to the parties. Between 1952 and 1976, the proportion of the electorate calling themselves strong Democrats dropped from 22% to 15%, that of strong Republicans from 13% to 9%. The proportions of weak Democrats and Republicans remained constant at 25% and 14% respectively. Thus detachment of party loyalties took the form of both rejection of party identification for some and a weaker loyalty for others who nonetheless considered themselves partisans.

Most of the increase in independents has been concentrated in the younger cohorts of the electorate. Although the youngest age groups have always been the most independent, the current crop of young eligible voters is more heavily independent than those of the past, and these voters are remaining independent longer. In Table 4.1 we can see that between 1952 and 1972 the proportion of independents among twenty- and thirty-year-olds almost doubled while the proportions of strong Democrats (but not strong Republicans) dropped precipitously. The proportion of independents has been further increased by the expansion of the electorate to include eighteen- to twenty-year-olds, a heavily independent group.

Beck has constructed an interesting socialization theory of realignment on this fact of increasing independence among the young.[7] In a period of dealignment, Beck argues, the issues of the old realignment crisis are not as salient to the new generation of voters, with consequent slippage in the efficiency with which parental identifications are transmitted to their offspring. Intriguing as the idea is, Beck has offered little data to support it, and Table 4.2 raises some doubts about the validity of the theory as a general explanation of the realignment phenomenon. Table 4.2 shows the rate of "successful transmission" of party identification among respondents in 1952 and 1976, that is, the proportion of respondents who are of the same party as their parents when both parents shared a party affiliation. These data have some rather obvious flaws: They are based on a sample of offspring, not parents; and they rely on testimony of adults about their parents' attitudes in the sometimes distant past. Still, the data are illuminating. As Beck would predict, the rate of successful transmission of partisan-

TABLE 4.1   The Distribution of Party Identification by Age, 1952
and 1972

1952	18–19	20–29	30–39	40–49	50–59	60–69	Over 70
			Current Age				
Strong Democrats		22%	19%	20%	26%	22%	26%
Weak Democrats		27	32	25	21	18	16
Independent Democrats		10	11	12	8	8	6
Independents		5	5	6	4	7	6
Independent Republicans		13	7	6	4	6	7
Weak Republicans		12	15	15	14	12	12
Strong Republicans		8	7	12	20	22	20
Apolitical		5	4	4	3	4	7
Total		102%	100%	100%	100%	99%	100%
n =		279	394	338	264	192	122

1972	18–19	20–29	30–39	40–49	50–59	60–69	Over 70
Strong Democrats	6%	9%	11%	17%	18%	17%	21%
Weak Democrats	30	25	26	27	27	27	23
Independent Democrats	18	17	12	8	9	8	3
Independents	18	16	14	13	9	9	7
Independent Republicans	11	16	13	10	7	8	6
Weak Republicans	13	10	16	13	18	12	18
Strong Republicans	4	6	8	12	11	18	19
Apolitical	1	2	1	1	1	2	3
Total	101%	101%	101%	101%	100%	101%	100%
n =	80	529	360	392	312	274	231

Source: Survey Research Center/Center for Political Studies

ship is noticeably higher in 1952 than it is in 1976, a decade or
more into a dealigning period. And, when a control for age is
introduced, the younger age groups, those who came of age
after World War II, were less likely to receive parental identifications than those who came of age during the New Deal. The
difficulty occurs in generalizing this pattern to other dealigning

TABLE 4.2 The Transmission of Parental Party Identification, 1952 and 1976

1952

Year of Coming of Age Politically:	1944–1952	1934–1943	1924–1933	1914–1923	1904–1913	Before 1913	Total
Current Age:	20–29	30–39	40–49	50–59	60–69	Over 70	
Both Parents Are:							
Democrats	70[a]	75	72	72	73	76	73
Republicans	56	58	62	65	70	64	63

1976

Year of Coming of Age Politically:	1968–1976	1958–1967	1948–1957	1938–1947	1928–1937	Before 1928	Total
Current Age:	20–29	30–39	40–49	50–59	60–69	Over 70	
Both Parents Are:							
Democrats	57[a]	54	55	62	66	74	60
Republicans	44	53	46	62	63	80	56

[a]Entries are the percentages of successful transmissions of parental party identification.
Source: Survey Research Center/Center for Political Studies

periods. The 1952 data and the data for those seventy and over in 1976 both show very high levels of transmission for respondents coming of age in the two decades prior to the New Deal, that is, during the decay of the 1896 alignment.[8] Therefore, whatever the correctness of this formulation as an explanation for the current detachment of the young from partisan preferences, some caution must be exercised in assuming that a similar phenomenon occurred after each of the historical realignments.

The realignment perspective might also be taken to suggest that due to the increase in issues unassociated with the previous realignment crisis, older age groups would also experience some decline in the numbers of partisan identifiers and in the strength of partisanship during a dealignment period. This idea has generated considerable controversy, since it runs counter to an equally plausible hypothesis that partisan identifications are strengthened through reinforcement over the course of a lifetime. Some rather sophisticated data analysis has been brought to bear on this question of the relative strength of life cycle, generational and period effects on changing partisanship,[9] and we do not propose to enter that debate here. However, if we look back at Table 4.1, a comparison of the age cohorts in their twenties, thirties, and forties in 1952 with their counterparts twenty years later in their forties, fifties, and sixties, shows little support for the notion that these groups have become more independent or less strongly partisan over time. While there are fewer strong Democrats in these age cohorts in 1972 than in 1952, the proportion of strong Republicans has increased, and the proportion of independents is little changed, although there are fewer "leaning Democrats" and more pure independents. Indeed, if one were to think of the seven-point party identification scale as a monotonic continuum,[10] the most parsimonious description of the changes in these cohorts over the twenty years would be a shift toward the Republicans of roughly four percentage points at each step along the continuum. The result survives a control for region, so it is not simply an effect of possible growing Republicanism in the South.

While a decline in partisan attitudes among older age groups may still be open to question, there is no doubt that partisans of all ages are behaving less loyally. This decline in loyalty among partisans can be seen in the increasing rate of defection from party candidates in voting for president and Congress. Table 4.3 shows the percentage of partisans who voted for the candidate of another party in presidential and congressional elections from 1952 to 1976, in the nation as a whole and in the South and Nonsouth. This table suggests that the years from 1952 through 1976 were marked by a moderate increase in voting defections. Of course, these defections have come at the expense of both parties, and in any given election, a party benefited by short term forces may have experienced few defections. Relatively few Republicans, for example, abandoned Eisenhower in 1952 or 1956 or Nixon in 1972, but defections from the Democratic ticket in these years were substantially larger. Similarly, Democrats overwhelmingly supported Johnson in 1964, but Republicans defected from Goldwater in larger numbers. As Table 4.3 shows, partisan defection was more pronounced in the South during these years. Even so, an increased rate of defection was characteristic of elections for both offices in both regions from 1952 through 1976, with the greatest increase coming between 1964 and 1968, coinciding with the rise in the proportion of independents.

The election of 1976 has been interpreted as a "reinstating" election, in which party loyalties reemerged as a paramount factor in determining vote choice, perhaps in response to the salience of economic issues and their continued association with the New Deal alignment. The data in Table 4.3 do not dispute this interpretation, although it should be observed that the drop in the defection rate occurs only in the presidential series and the drop is much greater in the South, where presumably a native son running as the Democratic candidate had an important effect.

As could be expected, the incidence of "split-ticket" voting also increased during these years. The proportion of respondents who indicated that they did not vote a "straight ticket" in

TABLE 4.3 Percentage of Party Identifiers[a] Defecting, 1952-1976

	Nation		Nonsouth		South	
	President	Congress	President	Congress	President	Congress
1952	15	13	15	14	29	6
1956	16	9	14	9	25	7
1960	14	11	9	7	24	9
1964	16	15	17	15	16	14
1968	23	18	19	18	34	18
1972	27	18	22	18	38	17
1976	17	21	17	21	17	22

[a]Strong and weak partisans are included here. The findings would be changed little by adding leaners.
Source: Survey Research Center/Center for Political Studies election studies.

state and local elections from 1952 through 1972 is given in Table 4.4. Taken in total, the table conveys an impression of a very substantial increase in ticket splitting. As might be expected, at each election the incidence of ticket splitting was greatest among independents and smallest among those who indicated they usually thought of themselves as "strong" Republicans or Democrats. Nevertheless, the frequency of ticket splitting among strong and weak identifiers of both parties more than doubled across this period. Independents, with somewhat higher rates to begin with, had somewhat lower rates of increase. In all cases the greatest increases occurred in the early 1960s.

The greater volatility in electoral behavior is a product of both weakened party loyalties and responsiveness to issues that do not correspond to the old partisan alignment. This latter phenomenon has been documented in a variety of ways. Trilling has found a decline in the use of New Deal symbols and issues in the candidate and party evaluations of respondents in the Survey Research Center and Center for Political Studies surveys since 1952.[11] Perhaps the most extensive treatment of this facet of the current dealignment is the analysis of Nie et al. in *The Changing American Voter.*[12] They argue that the role of issues in determining vote choice has increased significantly relative to party identification since 1964. Although their primary concern

TABLE 4.4 Ticket Splitting for State and Local Offices, 1952–1972

	Strong Democrats	Weak Democrats	Independent Democrats	Independents	Independent Republicans	Weak Republicans	Strong Republicans
1952	14	31	44	45	35	28	15
1956	16	28	42	57	44	31	17
1960	13	26	44	35	49	32	21
1964	20	47	63	47	67	56	29
1968	28	57	68	76	57	51	26
1972	35	63	72	73	70	60	40

Figures are the percentage of each category reporting splitting their tickets for state and local offices. A comparable question was not asked in 1976.

Source: Survey Research Center/Center for Political Studies election studies.

is in showing the issue orientation of the American voter in the recent era, their data are also consistent with an interpretation of voter response to salient issues that do not fit the old New Deal alignment. The independent contribution of issues to explaining vote choice can increase only if these issues cut across, rather than reinforce, existing partisan cleavages.[13]

This line of thought helps to explain some seemingly contradictory evidence presented by Ladd and Hadley.[14] Using many old Gallup and Survey Research Center studies for most years since the mid-1930s, they examine the relationship between "New Deal issues" and party identification from the mid-1930s to the early 1970s. Given the difficulty in finding comparable policy questions in many unrelated surveys over a long time period, only a rough assessment was possible of the changing relationship between party preference and stands on the New Deal-related issues of social welfare and domestic economic policy. However, their basic finding is simple enough: There is no clear tendency for the relationship between party identification and issue positions to decline from the 1930s onward. Indeed, as other analysts have also noted, the relationship strengthens sharply around 1964.[15] On the other hand, we would argue that the essential point is not a presumed deterioration in the relationship between the parties and the issues of the old realignment—in fact, we should expect that *if* voters select a party, it will be on the basis of those issues on which the parties take discernible stands. Rather, the critical characteristic of the decay period is that fewer voters adopt a party preference because they fail to see the relevance of these old issues, or, if they are partisan, these issues are not invariably the salient ones on which they base their current votes.

Several scholars have noted the increased salience of a racial dimension in political attitudes beginning in 1964 and the tenuousness of the relationship between these issues and traditional party loyalties in the white South and the working-class North.[16] Similarly, Miller and Levitin see evidence of the appearance in the early 1970s of a "New Politics" dimension consisting of attitudes toward Vietnam, race, law and order, and the counter culture.[17] Attitudes on these issues appear to be virtually independent of partisanship, but rather highly related to age. By 1974, the so-called Silent Minority of conservatives had dwindled to a very small number, while the New Liberals gained many new adherents particularly among the young. Indeed, by this time, the New Politics issues seem to have become for the most part generational or life-style issues that less frequently have political overtones. In 1972 these issues cut across and disrupted the existing partisan division in the electorate, but they appear not to provide a basis for the lasting realignment of those loyalties.

In a somewhat different vein, Ladd and Hadley, as well as Nie et al., argue that the social group basis of the New Deal coalition is disintegrating.[18] While this argument has several facets—for example, the departure of the white South from the Democratic presidential party the most interesting aspect is the evidence suggesting a disengagement along generational lines of the class basis of partisanship in the North. To put it succinctly, the children of the middle class appear to be considerably more liberal and less Republican than their parents. Ladd and Hadley, particularly, develop the thesis that the intelligentsia of a post-industrial society is a profoundly different political animal than the entrepreneurs of previous generations, despite our tendency to treat them both analytically as "middle class."[19] As a result, class becomes less of a determinant of political tendencies than it was at the height of the New Deal era.

The data for the years from the early 1950s to the mid-1970s have also allowed exploration of another issue pertinent to formulations bearing upon the decay phase of electoral sequences. These concern the change in attitudes toward political and governmental leaders and institutions. It was hypothesized in Chapter 1, and other investigators have taken the same view, that these historical periods have been marked by relatively ineffective government, by continuing and unmet national problems and tensions, and, as a consequence, by decline in popular confidence in the capacities of government and political leaders.

Decline in confidence and trust in government and political leaders after 1952, and particularly from the mid-1960s onward, has been richly documented in the literature.[20] Of course, the decline in confidence and trust was not confined to political and governmental leaders and institutions; rather, trust and confidence in most American institutions and centers of authority reached low levels by the early 1970s.[21] It is also clear that measures of confidence and trust in government and political officials have fluctuated sharply in relation to particular events and developments, and indeed to which party is in office.[22] Thus the middle months of the Ford administration were marked by a significant but transitory restoration of trust and confidence. The termination of involvement in Vietnam and the early months of the Carter administration were marked by similar fluctuations, prior to the rather steady decline that marked the second and third years of his term. Despite these fluctuations, the fact remains that decline in trust and confidence has been an undeniable characteristic of the latter 1960s and 1970s.

Considering this evidence collectively, it seems clear that the factors assumed by the realignment perspective to be indicators of the deterioration of the old partisan alignment and necessary preconditions for the occurrence of a realignment are present in the period since 1964: growth in the pool of voters, particularly new voters, without firm partisan attachments; a weakening in the intensity of the loyalty of partisans to their party, if not in attitude, at least in behavior at the polls; the appearance of short-term issues independent of traditional party stands; and a general malaise affecting attitudes toward political leaders and institutions.

One important qualification about these data should be made. The decline in party loyalty and the increase in political independence have not affected all population groups the same way, even taking into account the differences that age makes. In particular, at least for part of the time period under consideration, black voters have moved against the tide, becoming more rather than less partisan. Paul Abramson has shown that between 1960 and 1964, a significant increase in partisan strength among blacks occurred, these new partisans coming from the ranks of the previously apolitical.[23] During the same period, white voters had a stable or declining level of partisanship. This observation does not refute the primary contention that this was in general a period of weakening party attachments; rather, it serves to underline the point made in earlier chapters that the realignment process may affect various subgroups of the population differently and may occur at somewhat different times in different areas of the country. Indeed, the politicization of blacks in the early 1960s has most of the earmarks of a realignment: the mobilization of a previously uninvolved segment of the eligible electorate, with these new voters coming into the electorate overwhelmingly on the side of one party in response to a perceived crisis about which the parties take distinctive stands.

DETERIORATION OF HISTORICAL ALIGNMENTS

In our view, the past decade illustrates well the processes that lead to the deterioration of an existing alignment and create an electorate capable of realignment; that is, an electorate with a sufficiently large pool of potential converts should a crisis occur which advantages one political party. Indeed, most of the theorizing by other scholars as well as ourselves about the processes of individual political change underlying the decay periods of realignment sequences has been prompted by observation of current trends.[24] Verification of these views requires examination of other historical periods of presumed alignment decay for the occurrence of similar processes. Impressionistically, deterioration of the existing electoral alignment also seems to have occurred in each of the other historical sequences following what has been termed a midsequence adjustment in the early 1840s, the latter 1870s, the second decade of the twentieth century, as well as the late 1940s and early 1950s. These adjustments mark a recession of the strength attained by the dominant party in the preceding realignment, the first crack in a heretofore stable alignment. In each historical period, events clearly reflected development of divisions within the majority parties, as well as growth of popular dissatisfaction with the alternatives provided by the parties. Division within the majority Republican party was indicated by the Liberal Republican bolt in 1872, and perhaps only the bizarre Democratic nomination of Horace Greeley as their presidential candidate saved the Republicans from defeat at the polls. Democratic victories in the congressional elections of 1874 provided further evidence of the decline in Republican strength. Democratic victories in the congressional election of 1910, the "Bull Moose" revolt in 1912, the minority victory of Woodrow Wilson in that year, and Democratic majorities in both Houses of Congress that followed were equally clear indications of divisions among Republicans and recovery of Democratic electoral support. These patterns parallel the post New Deal decline in Democratic strength evidenced by Republican victories in House and Senate in 1946, internal divisions on the left and right in the Democratic party in 1948, and the Democrats' loss of the presidency in 1952.

The cast of politics following these midsequence adjustments was distinctly different than during the preceding years. With the exception of the decade of the 1920s, these elections were followed by periods of narrow and unstable majorities, by frequent deviating elections, by conditions of divided control of government, and by further realigning change. However, the change.in voting during these years did not reestablish either the electoral strength of the majority party or unified and effective control of government by that party, but contributed instead to further derangement and destabilization of the partisan coalitions produced by the earlier realignment.

Substantial, though relatively unsystematic evidence suggests that these periods were marked by significant popular dissatisfaction with the course of political events, with the performance of government and political leaders, and with the alternative provided by the political parties. Numerous writers have detailed the litany of third-party and "protest" movements of the years from the 1870s through the mid-1890s including the Liberal Republicans, Grangers and the Greenback Party, "Mugwumps" and Knights of Labor, Prohibitionists, the Farmers Alliances, and the Populists. Although such movements did not always find expression in electoral behavior, they can be taken as signifying the dissatisfaction of segments of the nation. It may also be that these developments can be taken as indications of decline in trust and confidence, to use terms that have become popular in the 1970s, in government and political leaders, parties, and institutions.

The decades of the 1840s and 1850s were marked by characteristics that were at least superficially similar to those of the 1870s, the 1880s, and the early 1890s. In this case, however, because of the unstable and formative nature of the party system, systematic data are scanty and interpretation more risky. Even so, the numerous reform movements that dot these two decades, ranging from utopian and health movements through educational reform and crusades for female rights to abolitionism, could all be taken as indications of a widespread feeling of dissatisfaction with government, the parties, and other normal political channels as means to solve problems and to secure redress of grievances. Similar evidence is, of course, provided by the third-party movements of these years. The Free Soil, Liberty, and American parties were each movements of some magnitude lasting for significant periods. Taken individually and cumulatively, they can be seen as indicative of interests that the Democratic and Whig parties did not represent and reflections of the failures of the parties and government to satisfactorily resolve the divisions that increasingly plagued the nation. The most obvious and convincing indication of deterioration of earlier partisan divisions and arrangements and of ineffective government is to be found, of course, in the formation of the Republican party and the lingering demise of the Whigs.

At first glance, the 1920s stand out as an exception to this general and recurring pattern of events. Republican dominance was disrupted in the elections of 1910 and in the three national elections that followed, and the progressive revolt was an obvious indication of division within the party. The elections surrounding 1920, however, involved apparent restoration of Republican electoral dominance in an even stronger form than was characteristic of the early years of the century. Even so, the events of the period provide at least suggestive evidence of popular dissatisfaction. That evidence includes the shifts in voting behavior and the third-party movements that Sundquist has described as the "minor realignments of the 1920s."[25] The LaFollette Progressives in 1924, the Farmer-Labor movements in the upper Midwest and the far West which in a few states displaced the Democratic party, the southern rejection of the Democratic presidential candidate in 1928 and the Al Smith incursion in northern cities in the same year all suggest electoral instability and the presence of substantial political disaffection.

Unfortunately, indicators equivalent to the survey data presented in the preceding section do not exist for the most part for these earlier periods. Through the third decade of the twentieth century, there are no data at the individual level that bear upon mass voting behavior and political attitudes, with the exception of a very few, scattered, and relatively miniscule finds such as county poll books. And even these occasional caches of individual level data rarely allow direct examination of the link between attitudes and behavior.[26]

For the period preceding the New Deal realignment, roughly the 1920s, several scholars have sought to reconstruct individual level data from the recall information contained in Survey Research Center and Center for Political Studies surveys of the 1950s to the 1970s.[27] In discussing the decay period of the 1920s, we will draw upon this survey-based analysis, particularly the very interesting work of Kristi Andersen.

Aside from this, however, we are forced to rely upon aggregate data to find indicators analogous to those in the preceding section. Fluctuations in popular participation in elections; long-term shifts in the electoral strength of the parties; fluctuation of measures of split-ticket voting and in the relation between the distribution of the votes for the various offices, particularly the vote for president and Congress; the relative volatility of the popular vote as reflected in the magnitude and incidence of "deviating" electoral change; and the vote for minor parties and their candidates will be used to show the general deterioration of the existing electoral alignments. Invariably, each individual indicator is an imperfect measure of the processes of electoral decay, as we shall take pains to discuss as they are presented. Taken separately, any of these indicators could be disregarded or its evidence explained away. However, a variety of such measures, all showing a general direction of change, albeit each imperfectly, would collectively lend weight to the argument. Although the individual data presented in the preceding section are far more direct measures of the electoral processes at work during a dealignment, finding parallel trends in aggregate indicators in each period gives credence to the conclusion that similar processes of partisan deterioration were present.

Our basic expectation is for a steady voting pattern immediately following the realignment, followed by greater fluctuation after the midsequence adjustment when short-term forces begin to dominate election contests. One way of testing this is to use the estimates of the "expected vote" for each party for each year introduced in Chapter 3 and to measure the deviation of the actual vote from these estimates. We can plot the fluctuation of the actual vote around the expected vote at each election to indicate the impact of short-term forces on the vote over the historical sequences.

The data presented in Figure 4.1 tend to confirm our expectations, although the patterns are neither as sharp nor as consistent as one might hope. The estimates for the years after 1932 are consistent with our expectations and generally in conformity with findings derived from the individual level data provided by sample surveys. A sharp increase in the Democratic vote can be observed in 1932, and in that and the following elections, deviations from the expected vote also favored the Democrats. Decline in the Democratic expected vote can be observed in the later 1940s. In these same years, the Republican expected vote rose, and deviations from the expected vote fluctuated sharply, favoring first one party and then the other.

The patterns of the earlier decades of the century are also in conformity with expectations. The Republican expected vote

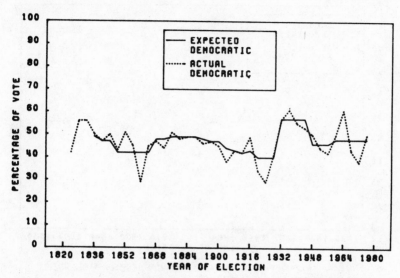

SOURCE: United States Historical Election Returns, Inter-university Consortium for Political and Social Research.

Figure 4.1a: Democratic Expected and Actual Vote in Presidential Elections, 1824-1976

rose during the early years of the periods, and deviations from those estimates also favored that party. The actual vote deviated sharply against the Republicans in 1912, reflecting the Bull Moose schism, and in that and the surrounding elections, the Democrats profited from favorable deviations from the expected vote. In the elections of the 1920s, deviations from the expected vote consistently favored the Republicans and worked against the Democrats, a pattern suggesting that through these years, short-term forces worked on balance in a single direction. This view is in accord with historical accounts of the period and can be seen as a reflection of other factors, such as the LaFollette incursion in 1924 and the difficulties experienced by the Democrats in nominating a nationally viable and attractive presidential candidate.

The behavior of the measures is much less satisfactory for the nineteenth century, reflecting in part the timing of the forma-

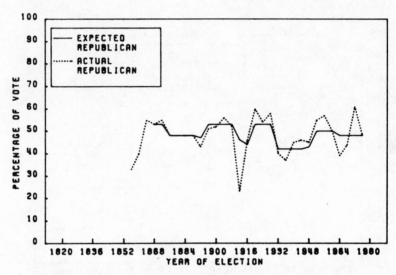

SOURCE: United States Historical Election Returns, Inter-university Consortium for Political and Social Research.

Figure 4.1b: Republican Expected and Actual Vote in Presidential Elections, 1856-1976

tion of the Republican party and the consequent absence of estimates of the Republican expected vote during the Civil War years and before. The democratic expected vote fell in the 1840s, and fluctuating deviations from the expected vote, usually in a Democratic direction, were characteristic of the 1850s. Apart from the election of 1892, however, the series provides no evidence of deterioration of the Civil War alignment, and in fact the actual vote in the 1880s virtually coincided with the expected vote. While this pattern reflects known characteristics of the period including a well-developed party system, a highly mobilized and partisan electorate, and a closely competitive system, it is hardly supportive of the view that the electorate in this period was marked by declining partisan loyalties.

A more complicated indicator of electoral volatility also depends upon the analysis technique introduced in Chapter 3. Unlike the earlier analysis, which focused on estimates of

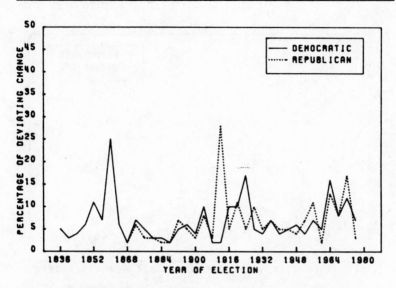

Figure 4.2: Deviating Change in Democratic and Republican Presidential Voting, 1836-1976

SOURCE: United States Historical Election Returns, Inter-university Consortium for Political and Social Research.

realigning electoral change, here we examine only the amount of deviating electoral change during each decay phase. The expectation is that increasingly large amounts of deviating change, both across-the-board and differential changes, should be observed in the decay phases. Figure 4.2 displays the total amount of deviating change, combining the estimates of surge and interaction, for Democratic and Republican presidential voting. Understandably, extremely high values appear in 1860 for the Democrats and in 1912 for the Republicans. These data show a slight tendency for deviating change to appear greater late in the decay phases, but the differences are certainly not dramatic. As in Figure 4.1, deviating change appears low between 1876 and 1888 for both parties in the presidential series.

Figure 4.3 presents similar estimates of deviating change in congressional voting, data which are singularly unsupportive of

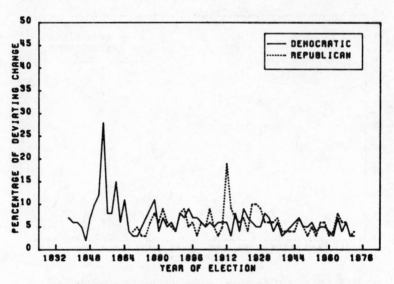

SOURCE: United States Historical Election Returns, Inter-university Consortium for Political and Social Research.

Figure 4.3: Deviating Change in Democratic and Republican Voting for the House of Representatives, 1838-1972

the idea of increasing electoral variation during the decay phase of a realignment sequence. The patterns of deviating change in both Democratic and Republican congressional voting reveal a century of relative stability, with the exception of 1912, in the Republican series. No substantial pattern of decay appears prior to either 1896 or 1932, although for the Democrats deviating change was greater in each case during the elections immediately before the realignment than after.

Clearly, the electoral volatility that seems to characterize presidential voting during periods of alignment deterioration has not affected congressional voting in the last two realignment sequences. Indeed, it is sometimes argued by contemporary political analysts that the very disassociation of presidential contests from those of the Congress is itself a symptom of partisan dealignment. Nevertheless, this disassociation means that even high levels of electoral volatility and departures from

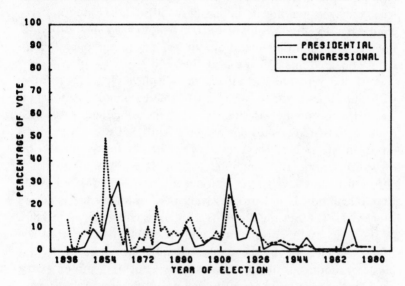

SOURCE: United States Historical Election Returns, Inter-university Consortium for Political and Social Research.

Figure 4.4: Votes for Minor Parties in Presidential and Congressional Elections, 1836-1978

strict partisan loyalty in recent presidential elections contributed very little to altering the composition of Congress. In later chapters, we will emphasize the importance of unified control of government as a prerequisite for partisan realignment; if voting for Congress has become so stable and so unresponsive to short-term forces, including those surrounding a potential realignment crisis, the possibilities for partisan realignment may be significantly altered.

A more straightforward indicator of partisan loyalties is the incidence and level of the third-party vote. The obvious expectation is higher support for minor parties during deterioration phases, reflecting growing popular disenchantment with the positions and performance of the major parties and growing dissatisfaction with the alternatives which they provided. As Figure 4.4 suggests, minor party activity and the minor party vote has sharply diminished, and virtually disappeared in the case of the Congress, since the mid-1920s, partly as a result of legal changes making it increasingly difficult for minor party candidates to obtain a place on the ballot. Even in this period, however, substantial electoral support for minor party candidates appeared in 1948 and again in 1968.

And the remainder of the series displays close conformity with our expectations. The popular vote for minor party candidates for both the presidency and the Congress rose with relative consistency during the 1840s and 1850s to reach a high point, in the case of the presidency, with the four-way election of 1860. During the remainder of the 1860s, the minor party vote fell to low levels (the Union vote in 1864 is treated as the Republican vote), and progressively rose to higher levels across the 1870s, 1880s, and the early 1890s, reaching a peak in 1892 in the case of the presidency, and in 1894 in the case of the Congress. The rise in the congressional minor party vote was most pronounced during these years, but the minor party presidential vote also rose, although only to more modest levels. The level of minor party vote for Congress and the presidency was relatively low during the 1896 realignment era and stood at substantially higher levels during the second and third decades of the century. In short, from the 1840s through 1976, the minor party vote was highest in relative terms during periods we have considered as marked by alignment deterioration and lowest during realignment eras.

Another indicator of the detachment of vote choice from partisan loyalties is a measure of aggregate split-ticket voting. Such an indicator is analogous to, but by no means the equivalent of, similar indicators based upon the individual responses provided by sample surveys. In fact, aggregate indicators of ticket splitting can be misleading under a variety of circumstances.[28] The primary weakness of these aggregate indicators like most other aggregate indicators is a conservative bias. Only net differences in the party vote for two offices, here president and Congress, are captured by subtracting the total party vote cast for one office from the total party vote cast for the other. For example, differences produced by those who vote for the Democratic candidate for president and the Republican candidate for Congress are, in effect, canceled by the differences produced by those who split their tickets in the opposite direction, and only the net difference remains. On the other hand, measures of aggregate ticket splitting have the advantage of being applicable to virtually the entire sweep of American political history, an advantage that is lacking where otherwise superior measures based upon individual level data are concerned. It should also be pointed out that this indicator is not independent of the data on third-party voting offered above. Particularly in the twentieth century, third-party presidential candidates rarely ran on a slate with congressional candidates. Thus, virtually the entire third-party presidential vote will also be counted as split-ticket voting.

Our expectations where patterns of aggregate ticket splitting are concerned are superficially straightforward. Relatively high levels of ticket splitting should be characteristic of each deterioration phase of electoral sequences. We might note, however, some of the theoretical implications of this hypothesis. We are, in effect, hypothesizing that during a realignment and the period of partisan stability that follows, voters will be likely to vote straight tickets. In other words, voters will not just vote to throw the rascal in the executive office out, but the forces which advantage the party in one race will carry over to other races as well. As will become clearer in later chapters, this is an essential element of our view of partisan realignment and one which distinguishes our treatment from those of others which at least implicitly treat partisan realignment primarily as an aspect of presidential contests. Second, during the decay phase, parties remain referents for voters, even as they desert them with increasing frequency. Thus voters split their tickets in response to short-term forces; they are more likely to abandon their party in the presidential race and return to it in voting down the ticket than to be swept into the other party's column by an appealing candidate at the top of the ticket. Clearly, other formulations are possible, but they would lead to other behavioral patterns over time than we have hypothesized.

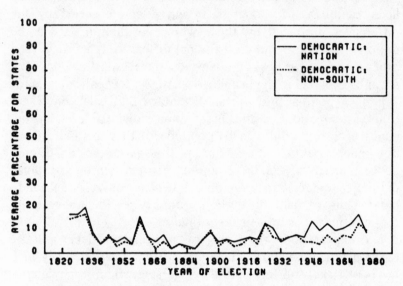

SOURCE: United States Historical Election Returns, Inter-university Consortium for Political and Social Research.

Figure 4.5a: Aggregate Ticket-Splitting for President and Congress for Democrats in the Nation and the Non-South, 1824-1976

The patterns displayed in Figure 4.5 conform to our expectations, at least for the twentieth century. As can be seen, the level of ticket splitting was relatively high during the years from 1912 through 1928 and from 1948 through 1972, although the pattern of the two parties sometimes diverged. The differences between the parties are greatest for those elections, as 1912 and 1924, in which third parties were in the field and cut disproportionately into the strength of one of the parties. Ticket splitting, at least in terms of this measure, was relatively lower in the 1930s and, most markedly in the case of the Republicans, in the elections immediately after 1896.

Once again, the measure behaves less well for the nineteenth century. Indications of high levels of ticket splitting can be observed in the case of the election of 1860, as might be expected in view of the four-cornered nature of that race. Indication of a surge of ticket splitting in both parties can also

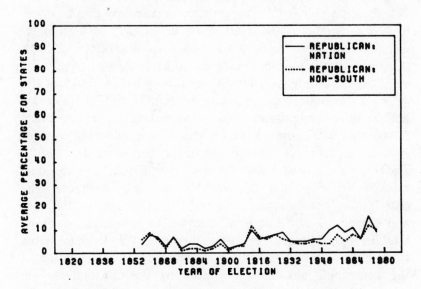

SOURCE: United States Historical Election Returns, Inter-university Consortium for Political and Social Research.

Figure 4.5b: Aggregate Ticket-Splitting for President and Congress for Republicans in the Nation and Non-South, 1856-1976

be seen in the "liberal Republican" election of 1872, but contrary to our expectations, the measure declines to very low levels for the 1880s and earlier 1890s. Once again, this pattern is explicable in terms of characteristics peculiar to the period. In the course of the 1860s and 1870s, the timing of elections was changed in a number of states. Elections to different offices were increasingly held on the same day, and the practice of holding elections at different and often temporally distant days was ended. The conditions under which elections were held in these years and the ballot form which was used severely constrained the opportunity of voters to split their tickets. The adoption of the Australian ballot in the 1890s once again increased opportunity for ticket splitting.[29] Thus the relative absence of indications of ticket splitting during the 1880s and the earlier 1890s is by no means surprising.

A somewhat different set of expectations bearing upon the deterioration phases of realignment sequences can also be investigated using the available aggregate data. As a partisan alignment decays, vote choice should be less and less associated with the normal voting patterns established early in the realignment era. This is definitely a form of electoral volatility but not the same phenomenon as the shorter term instability assessed above. Again using the method of estimating the expected vote introduced in Chapter 3, we constructed an expected vote for each state for each of the alignment eras since the 1850s. Estimates are based upon the vote in off-year congressional races; a single estimate is used for each alignment era. The correlations between these expected distributions of the vote and the actual distribution of the vote in presidential contests later in the alignment era were then assessed. Decline across time in these relations is taken as evidence of deterioration of the geographic alignment produced by the electoral realignment.

In Chapter 3, we took pains to point out that correlational techniques are not appropriate for uncovering across-the-board change, but rather can only assess change in the relative ordering of units. Obviously, that point applies to this analysis as well. However, several of the indicators presented in this section have tapped the across-the-board component of the electoral variation in the decay periods; we offer the following analysis as a supplement, not as an alternative to what has gone before.

The results of these operations for both parties are presented in Figure 4.6. As can be seen, the relation between the estimated expected distribution of the vote for both parties and the actual presidential vote declines rather consistently and progressively across the decades after the 1860s. Much the same pattern can be observed in the case of the New Deal era. In this instance, and unlike the post-Civil War era, a period of relative stability can be observed during the 1930s and much of the 1940s, followed by precipitous decline. The 1896 alignment era, however, stands out as different. Aside from the Republican presidential vote in 1912 and 1928 and the Democratic

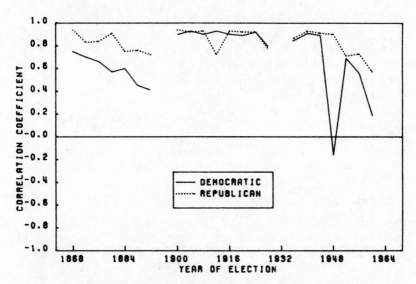

SOURCE: United States Historical Election Returns, Inter-university Consortium for Political and Social Research.

Figure 4.6: Correlation between Expected Votes Based on Congressional Voting and Actual Presidential Votes for Republicans and Democrats Following Each Realignment, 1868-1892, 1900-1928, and 1936-1960

vote in 1928, no decline can be observed in the relation between the estimated expected vote and the actual distribution of the vote across the first three decades of the century. The failure of this period to provide evidence of decay here results from the across-the-board shifts in 1912, 1920, and 1924 having little effect on correlations. But other forms of evidence presented above indicate that the period from 1912 to 1928 had relatively high levels of electoral volatility.

We have stressed that the electoral volatility and weakening of partisan loyalties during periods of electoral dealignment creates a pool of voters available for realignment, i.e., available to adopt a party preference in sufficient numbers to alter significantly the electoral strength of the existing political parties. In analyzing the historical electoral sequences with aggregate data, we have, to this point, concentrated on measures

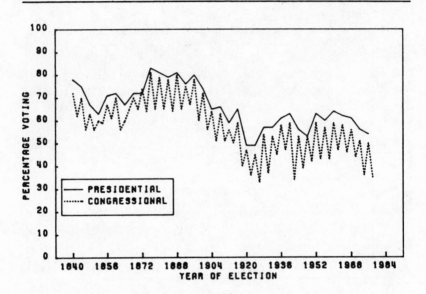

SOURCE: United States Historical Election Returns, Inter-university Consortium for Political and Social Research.

Figure 4.7: Turnout of Eligible Voters in Presidential and Congressional Elections, 1840-1978

of volatility in the partisan vote as our primary indicator of the willingness of the electorate to desert party ties in response to short-term forces in making their voting choices. Besides independents and independent-behaving voters, alternative or additional sources of "available" converts in a realignment are eligible voters who have not for whatever reasons joined the participating electorate. These would include young voters, new citizens, and the apolitical. We might hypothesize, then, that the proportion of the eligible electorate participating in elections is relatively low during the decay periods but increases during a realignment as previous nonparticipants come into the electorate on the side of the advantaged party.

Figure 4.7 plots fluctuations in voter participation from the 1840s through the 1970s. As can be seen, the years from 1896 through the mid-1920s were marked by relatively consistent decline in voter participation. A surge of participation can be observed in the election of 1928 and in the elections of the 1930s followed by declining, or at least fluctuating, participation rates from the 1940s onward. In her analysis of partisan change in the 1920s and 1930s, Kristi Andersen estimates that less than half of the newly eligible voters turned out in the presidential elections of the 1920s. Throughout that decade, there accumulated a large number of potential voters without any previous political habits, a pool of available converts which the Democrats would win two to one in the 1930s.[30]

It is more difficult to argue that other dealigning periods saw the creation of a reservoir of inactive potential voters. The mid-nineteenth century was a period of progressive relaxation of suffrage requirements and of rising participation levels. To the extent that there was a lag between these two, some such accumulation might have occurred in the 1840s and 1850s. It is even more problematic whether such a pool of inactive, eligible voters existed in the 1880s and early 1890s, since voter participation was extremely high during these years. It has been argued that these very high rates of participation were more a product of fraudulent voting, particularly in urban areas, than voter enthusiasm.[31] The population was expanding more rapidly than the census counts in these years, perhaps accounting for some of the instances of more votes than enumerated population in rapidly growing areas. There is, however, no evidence that these new voters failed to vote in large numbers during the 1880s and early 1890s, as would be required for the creation of a pool of inactive, unattached potential voters.

CONCLUSION

In this chapter, we have looked for evidence that the deterioration of partisan attachments so often noted in the contemporary era had its counterparts in other postrealignment periods, whether there is indeed a generalizable pattern of decay forming the link between the periodic realignments in American history. The evidence is neither as clear-cut nor as consistent as one might hope. Only the increase in the level of third-party activity occurs consistently in each of the hypothesized eras of dealignment. The other indicators behave as expected in some periods but not in others. Significantly, perhaps, only the contemporary era shows all the aggregate indications of the patterns we are attempting to extrapolate to other historical periods. On the other hand, if we take all the indicators collectively, every presumed decay period shows some signs of the expected instability.

Our conclusion must be similar to that which was drawn from the examination of the evidence for the occurrence of realignments: The electoral patterns alone neither uniquely identify the eras of decay nor distinguish them with certainty from other periods. To do so we must go beyond the behavior of the electorate and examine the behavior of elites and of governmental institutions that both affect and are affected by electoral patterns.

NOTES

1. See, for example, Walter Dean Burnham, *Critical Elections and the Mainsprings of American Politics* (New York: Norton, 1970), 'The Changing Shape of the American Political Universe," *American Political Science Review* 59 (March 1965), pp. 7-28, and "American Politics in the 1970's: Beyond Party?" in William Chambers and Walter Dean Burnham (eds.), *The American Party Systems* (New York: Oxford University Press, 1975).

2. Everett Carll Ladd, Jr., with Charles D. Hadley, *Transformations of the American Party System* (New York: Norton, 1975); Norman H. Nie, Sidney Verba, and John R. Petrocik, *The Changing American Voter* (Cambridge, MA: Harvard University Press, 1976); David Broder, *The Party's Over* (New York: Harper and Row, 1972).

3. Walter Dean Burnham, Jerome M. Clubb, and William H. Flanigan, "Partisan Realignment: A Systemic Perspective," in Joel Silbey, Allan Bogue, and William Flanigan (eds.), *The History of American Electoral Behavior* (Princeton, NJ: Princeton University Press, 1978), pp. 45-77; Paul Allen Beck, "The Electoral Cycle and Patterns of American Politics," *British Journal of Political Science* 9 (April 1979), pp. 129-156; Charles G. Sellers, Jr., "The Equilibrium Cycle in Two-Party Politics," *Public Opinion Quarterly* 29 (Spring 1965), pp. 16-38.

4. Paul Allen Beck, "A Socialization Theory of Partisan Realignment," in Richard G. Niemi and Associates, *The Politics of Future Citizens* (San Francisco: Jossey-Bass, 1974) pp. 200-206.

5. Kristi Andersen, *The Creation of a Democratic Majority 1928-1936* (Chicago: Chicago University Press, 1979); Philip E. Converse, "Public Opinion and Voting Behavior," in Fred Greenstein and Nelson Polsby (eds.), *Handbook of Political Science, Vol. 4* (Reading, MA: Addison-Wesley, 1975), pp. 75-169.

6. The standard party identification question is phrased as follows:

Generally speaking, do you usually think of yourself as a Republican, a Democrat, an Independent, or what? (If Republican or Democrat) Would you call yourself a strong (Republican) (Democrat) or a not very strong (Republican) (Democrat)? (If Independent) Do you think of yourself as closer to the Republican or Democratic Party?

Unless otherwise noted, the survey data are from the Survey Research Center/Center for Political Studies National Election Studies, Institute for Social Research, University of Michigan.

7. Beck, "A Socialization Theory of Partisan Realignment."

8. The discrepancy in the transmission rates of age cohorts in 1952 and 1976 is not necessarily an indication of the unreliability of the data. Other data (such as Table 4.1) suggest that some partisan change occurred in these cohorts over the two-decade period; some individuals whose partisanship was the same as their parents' in 1952 may have changed away from that party by 1976, thus lowering the rate of successful transmission.

9. See, in particular, Philip E. Converse, *The Dynamics of Party Support: Cohort-Analyzing Party Identification* (Beverly Hills, CA: Sage Publications, 1976) and Paul R. Abramson, "Developing Party Identification: A Further Examination of Life-Cycle, Generational, and Period Effects," *American Journal of Political Science* 23 (February 1979), pp. 78-96.

10. There is some evidence that responses to the party identification indicator are not monotonic. See John R. Petrocik, "An Analysis of Intransitivities in the Index of Party Identification," *Political Methodology* 1 (Summer 1974), pp. 31-47.

11. Richard J. Trilling, "Party Image and Partisan Change," in Louis Maisel and Paul M. Sachs (eds.), *The Future of Political Parties* (Beverly Hills, CA: Sage Publications, 1975).

12. Nie et al., *The Changing American Voter*, Ch. 16.

13. Less supportive of this interpretation is the fact that the combined contribution of issues and party identification also increased in 1964 and beyond.

14. Everett C. Ladd, Jr., and Charles D. Hadley, *Political Parties and Political Issues* (Beverly Hills, CA: Sage Publications, 1973).

15. Gerald M. Pomper, "From Confusion to Clarity: Issues and American Voters, 1956-1968," *American Political Science Review* 66 (June 1972), pp. 415-428.

16. See, for example, James A. Stimson and Edward G. Carmines, "The Continuing Issue in American Politics," presented at the annual meeting of the Southern Political Science Association, New Orleans, 1977.

17. Warren E. Miller and Teresa Levitin, *Leadership and Change* (Cambridge, MA: Winthrop Publishers, 1976).

18. Ladd and Hadley, *Transformations of the American Party System*, Ch. 3; Nie et al., *The Changing American Voter*, Ch. 14.

19. Ladd and Hadley, *Transformations of the American Party System*, Ch. 4.

20. Arthur H. Miller, Thad A. Brown, and Alden S. Raine, "Social Conflict and Political Estrangement, 1958-1972," presented at the annual meeting of the Midwest Political Science Association, Chicago, 1973; Arthur H. Miller, 'Political Issues and Trust in Government: 1964-1970," *American Political Science Review* 68 (September 1974), pp. 951-972.

21. *The Gallup Poll: Public Opinion, 1972-1977,* Vol. 1, Wilmington, DE: Scholarly Resources, 1978), pp. 131-133.

22. Jack Citrin, "Comment: The Political Relevance of Trust in Government," *American Political Science Review* 68 (September 1974), pp. 973-988; Warren Miller, "Misreading the Public Pulse," *Public Opinion* (October/November 1979), pp. 9-15.

23. Abramson, "Developing Party Identification."

24. See, especially, Burnham, *Critical Elections and the Mainsprings of American Politics.*

25. James L. Sundquist, *Dynamics of the Party System* (Washington, DC: Brookings Institution, 1973), Ch. 9.

26. See Melvyn Hammarberg, *The Indiana Voter: The Historical Dynamics of Party Allegiance During the 1870's* (Chicago: University of Chicago Press, 1977) and David A. Bohmer, "The Maryland Electorate and the Concept of a Party System in the Early National Period," in Silbey et al. (eds.), *The History of American Electoral Behavior.* Hammarberg's data source is county directories which contain indicators of the partisan preferences of individuals but not their actual voting behavior, while the county poll books which Bohmer uses record voting behavior but no indication of party identification or other political attitudes.

27. Converse, "Public Opinion and Voting Behavior"; Andersen, *The Creation of a Democratic Majority 1928-1936.*

28. Andrew T. Cowart, "A Cautionary Note on Aggregate Indicators of Split Ticket Voting," *Political Methodology* 1 (Winter 1974), pp. 109-130.

29. Jerrold D. Rusk, "The Effect of the Australian Ballot Reform on Split Ticket Voting: 1876-1908," *American Political Science Review* 64 (December 1970), pp. 1220-1238.

30. Andersen, *The Creation of a Democratic Majority 1928-1936,* p. 70.

31. Philip E. Converse, "Change in the American Electorate," in Angus Campbell and Philip E. Converse, *The Human Meaning of Social Change* (New York: Russell Sage, 1972), pp. 263-337.

Chapter 5

PARTISAN REALIGNMENT AND

CONTROL OF GOVERNMENT

The preceding three chapters explored patterns of change in the popular vote for president and Congress during the years from the 1840s through the mid-1970s. On the basis of the evidence presented there, we are led to the conclusion that patterns of electoral change alone are not sufficient for the demarcation of certain elections or election periods as partisan realignments. On the one hand, there is evidence of considerable stability in the relative ordering of geographical units over the years, suggesting that the major realignments of the past did not involve the large-scale electoral reshuffling often attributed to them. On the other hand, evidence appears of across-the-board realigning change in periods other than those usually identified as realigning. Nor is the evidence of the decay of electoral alignments entirely consistent.

Nonetheless, the three periods usually considered major realignments involved lasting electoral change. The realignment of the 1930s is an impressive example of lasting electoral change involving almost entirely across-the-board increases in Democratic strength. Evidence of such change can also be observed throughout the Civil War era, and we are of course prepared to accept the Civil War period as involving significant electoral change if for no other reason than the demise of one political party and the emergence of another. Electoral change appears significantly less sweeping and more temporary in the 1890s. On the basis of electoral patterns alone, it is difficult to distinguish the 1890s from several other periods which also show evidence of lasting electoral change, but which are usually not treated as involving national partisan realignment.

Analysts have implicitly considered more than just the partisan distribution of the popular vote in identifying the Civil War era, the 1890s, and the 1930s as periods of partisan realignment, even though the evidence considered and the data analyzed have usually been limited to popular voting patterns. Periods of major partisan realignment are seen as ushering in eras of stable dominance over the national political system by one or the other of the parties, and realignment periods are often treated as "policy watersheds" in the life of the nation. By the same token, the decay of partisan alignments is seen not only in terms of the detachment of voters from their previous partisan loyalties; the implied significance of this development is the increasing inability of a divided government and a weakened partisan majority to cope with national problems. In other words, partisan realignments are treated not only in terms of popular electoral change but also, at least implicitly, in terms of their governmental consequences. Indeed, in the absence of the presumption of governmental and policy consequences, it is doubtful that historical realignments would have received the scholarly attention they have.

The present chapter examines shifts in patterns of partisan control of government and in public policy that accompanied electoral change. Our effort in doing so is both to examine the governmental and policy consequences of electoral change and to enrich our conceptualization of the realignment phenomenon. While the focus here is confined to the national level, the next chapter examines change in patterns of party dominance at the state level.

PARTISAN REALIGNMENT AND NATIONAL POLICY

Impressionistic evidence clearly suggests that the partisan realignments of the Civil War years, the 1890s, and the 1930s were associated with major policy innovations, policy innovations which not only endured but also led to fundamental changes among elite groups and the populace in what was regarded as appropriate governmental concerns. Indeed, historians along with other scholars have treated these periods, both implicitly and explicitly, as critical turning points in the development of the nation. The Civil War, along with the actions of northern and southern leaders leading up to it, was a major step in the integration of the nation –one which stamped the United States, in fact as well as in theory, as a single and unified nation, rather than a loose confederation of semisovereign states, and which eliminated long-standing economic and social practices and conferred lasting legitimacy on others. However vacillating the policies of Lincoln and the Republicans may seem in retrospect, those policies involved a response to long-standing divisions and tensions and to the crisis of secession, a response that involved a massive commitment on the part of the northern population.

The meaning and nature of the policy actions, and lack of action, of the late 1890s and the first decade of the twentieth century are more difficult to identify and describe precisely. Yet these years are often identified as marking, in effect, the widespread acceptance of industrial capitalism, as involving enlargement of the legitimate sphere of action and responsibility of the central government, and as characterized by modification of the institutions of governmental politics themselves. Although the policies are often characterized in negative terms as restricting the activities of states and local governments, these

years marked a major step toward the nationalization of
politics, public policy, and political issues. The first McKinley
administration coincided with recovery from the depression of
1893, and the promise of a "full dinner pail" could be seen as
redeemed. That administration also witnessed the subsiding of
the most obvious manifestations of deep-seated discontent, best
signified by populism, which was seen at that time as threat-
ening violent civil strife.

The 1930s can be seen as a similar watershed. Rudimentary
though they were, the policies and programs of the New Deal
involved acceptance of direct action by government to promote
the welfare of society as a legitimate and major governmental
responsibility. These years marked as well the beginning of a
massive and continuing expansion of governmental intervention
into areas of national life formerly considered to be primarily, if
not exclusively, matters of private concern. The causes of
recovery from the Great Depression are debated. Yet there can
be little doubt that a measure of recovery occurred, and that
improvement of economic conditions and, perhaps more important, a vital and active concern for a suffering citizenry were
widely associated with Franklin Roosevelt, the Democrats, and
the policies of the New Deal.

It is obvious, of course, that partisan realignments did not
involve complete breaks in the continuity of public policy, nor
did they involve introduction of totally new issues into political
and governmental affairs. Social well-being had been an issue,
and the national and state governments had obviously intervened in the economic and social life of the nation before the
1930s. It is difficult, however, to escape the conclusion that
both the scope and character of intervention and the magnitude
and effectiveness of social welfare policies were different after
the 1930s than before. Big business was a fact of national life
before the 1890s, as were governmental actions designed to
benefit the business and industrial communities. But after the
1890s, it seems clear, big business was more legitimate, policies
designed to aid and encourage business and industry were more
acceptable, state regulation was less tolerable, and the role of

the agriculture sector of the nation in politics was altered. Slavery and the issues of sectionalism were major factors in American politics for decades prior to the 1860s, but the governmental actions of the 1860s and the popular response to those actions were decisive, constituting a major turning point for the nation.

In contrast, the years following these realignment eras, the impressionistic evidence suggests, were marked by governmental inertia in the formation and implementation of public policy. Historians have attached pejorative labels to these periods. The phrase "sectional conflict and compromise" has been used to describe the politics of the 1840s and 1850s, "the Politics of Dead Center" to describe the years from the latter 1870s through the early 1890s, and the "Age of Normalcy" to describe the 1920s. To our knowledge, no equivalent term has yet been applied to the 1950s, the 1960s, and the 1970s, but we can expect that when such a term is devised, it will convey a sense of ineffective government and unsolved national problems. These periods were characterized, at least in terms of modal tendencies, by ineffective government and by frequent governmental deadlock. Policy-making tended to be at best incremental rather than innovative, and deviating elections, third-party activity, and increasing divergence in the partisan outcomes of elections were common. The electoral shifts of particular population groups during such periods did not work to strengthen the existing partisan alignments, nor did they necessarily look toward the emergence of a new alignment. Rather, they reflected the appearance, or resurgence, of issues and tensions that were not subsumed under the symbols of the old realignment. They looked, in other words, toward decline of partisan loyalty and toward deterioration of the conditions of effective government.

The conceptualization of electoral sequences employed here suggests the conditions and processes through which electoral change is related to policy formation. More specifically, this conceptualization suggests interconnections between electoral change, on the one hand, and the behavior of political elites and performance of government and political parties, on the other.

In each of these historical realignments, the advantaged party came to power with unified control of the presidency and Congress and with a mandate, if not for its platform and programs, at least to take action to alleviate crisis conditions. In the face of these electoral mandates, together with the congressional tendency to accept presidential leadership in crisis situations, legislative majorities acted effectively to implement the new policy directions taken by their party and the president. To the extent that these policies were perceived as successfully managing and reducing crisis, the incumbent party's majority was sustained and even strengthened in succeeding elections; new voters and the previously apolitical and nonpartisan disproportionately developed identifications with the advantaged party, thus securing its majority status. Continued electoral success and consequent control of the Congress and the presidency allowed continuation of new policy directions long enough for them to become institutionalized and to lessen the likelihood that they would be dismantled when the majority party began to suffer occasional defeats. From this point of view, attainment of unified control of the presidency and Congress by the advantaged party, and maintenance of that control for a substantial period of time, were of central importance in each realignment for the implementation and perpetuation of new policy directions.

This conceptualization also suggests processes at work during the years following historical realignments, periods which we have termed the decay phases of electoral sequences. With the passage of time, popular and elite recollection of the crisis that had precipitated the realignment faded, and with it the salience of the issues that formed the majority party's primary appeal. New issues arose which often cut across party lines and divided party loyalists, candidates, and elected officials. Detachment of the electorate from party loyalties and defection from party ties allowed the opposing party to capture the presidency occasionally, win majorities in one or the other house of Congress, and even briefly gain unified control of government. But the

lack of clear distinction between the parties and the prevalence
of cross-cutting issues militated against partisan cohesion in
Congress and worked to prevent new or even effective policy
action. As a consequence, governmental inertia and policy deadlock tended to be the rule. Some have argued that policy inertia
during these decay phases of electoral sequences led to the
accumulation of unsolved societal problems which eventually
would assume crisis proportions and produce a new realignment.

Although rarely subjected to empirical analysis, partisan control of governmental agencies and shifts in the directions and
characteristics of public policy are integral elements in most
characterizations of partisan realignments. Indeed, and as we
have argued in earlier chapters, identification of the major
historical realignments would not be possible solely on the basis
of examination of shifts in popular voting patterns. Hence,
consideration of these conditions is necessary to the definition
of partisan realignment. These conditions of governance, moreover, lend significance to electoral changes. Unless electoral
changes had significance for partisan control of government and
for the directions of public policy, their meaning and importance in the life of the nation would not be great.

Systematic, empirical examination of public policy formation
and of the product of governmental action across a century and
a half of American history extending significantly beyond the
impressionistic evidence of the sort sketched above would be a
major undertaking indeed.[1] Such an undertaking would require
data bases and perhaps analytical and theoretical approaches
that have not yet been developed.

Our goals here are necessarily more modest. The following
sections examine the juxtaposition between electoral change, on
the one hand, and patterns of partisan control over the policy-
making agencies of the national government, on the other, in
order both to demonstrate the impact of partisan realignments
and to enrich our conceptualization of the realignment process.
In our view, unified and sustained partisan control of government was a necessary and obvious condition for the policy

innovations we usually see as the products of partisan realignments. It also appears that the margins of partisan control were
of importance in these terms, while the level of electoral
competition and the geographical distribution of shifts in voting
behavior were of critical significance for the governmental
majorities which they produced.

UNIFIED CONTROL
OF CONGRESS AND THE PRESIDENCY

Partisan control over policy-making institutions is by no
means a demonstration of the relevance of parties to policy-
making or to the development and pursuit of particular policy
directions. A party majority in the Senate or the House may
mean little for policy-making and entail little cooperation with
the president. No observer of these institutions would contend
that party labels accurately reflect policy coalitions or that the
political history of the United States can be neatly divided into
eras of majority support for a coherent set of policies versus
eras of total disarray.

Even so, it is likely that presidents with a majority of their
party in Congress have a better chance of gaining congressional
support than those facing a majority of the opposition.[2] Surely
it is the case that the performance of the parties—and particularly the degrees of agreement and unity of party members in
Congress, explored in a subsequent chapter—can be of fundamental importance to effective policy-making and innovation. If
it is granted that parties can play a role in the policy-making
process, then effective partisan control of policy-making institutions can be seen as a minimal condition for fulfillment of that
role.

Consistent unified control of some duration by a single party
is a significant condition for achieving major policy innovation.[3] Repeated successes at the polls can be taken by party
members in office as reward for policy actions taken and as
encouragement for the continuation and extension of policy
initiatives. An extended period in power allows time for pro-

gram formation and development, for new policies to be assimilated by the populace at large, to gain support, and to become embedded in the governmental and legal structures. Hence, the likelihood of reversal and dismantlement of policies and programs diminishes with the duration of control by the initiating party. Conversely, policy initiatives taken by a party only briefly in control run a greater risk of reversal when the opposing party comes to power.

The electoral realignments of the 1860s, the 1890s, and the 1930s each ushered in prolonged periods of unified control of the presidency and Congress by one or the other of the parties. As shown in Table 3.1 above, during the years since 1840 substantial realigning change, of either the "surge" or "interactive," type and for at least one party, appeared in the presidential or congressional vote in the elections of 1848, 1860-1868, 1874-1876, 1896, 1910, 1932, 1948, and 1960. Only three of these elections—1860, 1896, and 1932—also began periods of unified party control of the presidency and both houses of Congress for as long as fourteen years, as shown in Table 5.1. Democratic victories in 1932 marked the beginning of a period of united control that lasted until 1946. From 1896 to 1910, Republicans held solid, although not extraordinary, majorities in both houses of Congress, marking the end of the pattern of divided partisan control that had characterized much of the latter 1870s, the 1880s, and the early 1890s.

The pattern of the 1850s was more complicated. Republicans gained a House majority in the elections of 1854 which was reversed in 1856, and it was not until the Thirty-sixth Congress (1859-1861) that an enduring Republican majority was achieved in the House. Republicans did not gain control of the Senate and the presidency until 1861. The conditions of united Republican control achieved in 1861 and the extraordinary majorities enjoyed by the Republicans in both houses of the Thirty-seventh Congress were of course the product of southern secession. Indeed, the restructuring effects of electoral change in these years worked eventually, as is well known, to convert the southern states into a solidly Democratic stronghold and to

TABLE 5.1   Party Control of the Presidency, Senate, and House of Representatives, 1828 to 1976

	Party In Control of:						
	Presidency	*Senate*	*House*		*Presidency*	*Senate*	*House*
1828	D	D	D	1910		R	D
1830		D	D	1912	D	D	D
1832	D	[D]	D	1914		D	D
1834		D	D	1916	D	D	[D]
1836	D	D	[D]	1918		R	R
1838		D	D	1920	R	R	R
1840	W	W	W	1922		R	R
1842		W	D	1924	R	R	R
1844	D	D	D	1926		R	R
1846		D	W	1928	R	R	R
1848	W	D	[D]	1930		[R]	D
1850		D	D	1932	D	D	D
1852	D	D	D	1934		D	D
1854		D	R	1936	D	D	D
1856	D	D	[D]	1938		D	D
1858		D	[R]	1940	D	D	D
1860	R	R	R	1942		D	D
1862		R	R	1944	D	D	D
1864	R	R	R	1946		R	R
1866		R	R	1948	D	D	D
1868	R	R	R	1950		D	D
1870		R	R	1952	R	R	R
1872	R	R	R	1954		R	D
1874		R	D	1956	R	D	D
1876	R	R	D	1958		D	D
1878		D	D	1960	D	D	D
1880	R	[R]	R	1962		D	D
1882		[R]	D	1964	D	D	D
1884	D	R	D	1966		D	D
1886		R	D	1968	R	D	D
1888	R	R	R	1970		D	D
1890		R	D	1972	R	D	D
1892	D	D	D	1974		D	D
1894		[R]	R	1976	D	D	D
1896	R	R	R	1978		D	D
1898		R	R				
1900	R	R	R	D	=	Democrats	
1902		R	R	R	=	Republicans	
1904	R	R	R	W	=	Whigs	
1906		R	R	□	=	Dominant party lacks clear	
1908	R	R	R			majority	

shift some nonsouthern states marginally into the Republican column. Even so, partisan realignment was associated in these years with the termination of a period of divided partisan control over the federal government and marked the beginning of a prolonged period of united Republican control.

The election of 1920 comes close to conforming to the properties of partisan realignment. Evidence of lasting electoral change can be observed in that election marking the beginning of an extended period of Republican control of national policy-making agencies and over a disproportionate share of the state governments as well, as will be seen in Chapter 6. The Republican electoral advantage over the Democrats in the 1920s was also greater than in the early years of the twentieth century. We do not, however, ordinarily think of these years as involving the shifts in governmental policy, the emergence of a new political symbolism in response to crisis, or the new directions in political leadership that we and others have taken as elements of partisan realignment. Rather, the 1920s can better be taken as a restoration of the Republican dominance which began after 1896, and which was temporarily interrupted by the Wilson years and the progressive incursions at the state level. The decade was also a continuation, perhaps in extreme form, of the probusiness orientation in policy-making of the dominant party. The low levels of voter participation during the 1920s, moreover, do not suggest the relatively high levels of popular concern and interest that have accompanied major realignments. Nor, as is explored subsequently, do we find evidence of the increased partisan polarization among partisan elites in Congress that seems characteristic of partisan realignments. For these reasons, the 1920s do not appear as an era of national partisan realignment like the Civil War years, the 1890s, or the 1930s, despite evidence of the occurrence of lasting electoral change in the election of 1920.

Conceptualizing realignment as involving both electoral changes and shifts in patterns of partisan control of government emphasizes a central point. Historically, lasting electoral change has disrupted unified control of government and worked to frustrate policy action as well as creating unified control and the conditions of policy action. Several episodes of lasting electoral change—notably the middle and latter 1870s, the elections of 1910 and 1912, and of 1946—ended realignment eras by disrupting the unified control enjoyed by one of the parties. Each of these midsequence adjustments reduced electoral support for the recently advantaged party without yielding a clear and dependable advantage for the opposing party. Investigators who have employed only electoral data for empirical identification of realignments have been variously forced to ignore or to explain away these periods of lasting electoral change that somehow seem not to be of the same order as the 1860s, the 1890s, and the 1930s. By emphasizing unified control of government and the maintenance of that control over a substantial period of time, we emphasize also that policy initiatives and their long-term acceptance are of fundamental importance to the notion of partisan realignment. Lasting electoral changes are of interest to us as students of individual voting behavior; they are of less interest as we seek to understand change in the direction of public policy unless these electoral choices are transformed into policy outcomes.

MARGINS OF VICTORY AND CONTROL

Our interest in unified party control of the agencies of government stems from its role as a precondition for the kinds of policy initiatives associated with partisan realignments. Not only does dominance over the presidency and the two houses of Congress provide at least nominal control of the authoritative decision-making institutions involved in enacting policy,[4] it also provides the organizational control of the legislature and bureaucracy and the patronage and pork barrel opportunities which may be essential for converting "paper" majorities into governing majorities. Here again, we can surmise that the duration of the party's tenure in office is of importance. Extended control by a party affords an opportunity to shape the bureaucracy, to develop effective organization and leadership in Congress, and to utilize patronage and the pork barrel in the service of party goals.

Obviously, unified partisan control is at best only a precondition for concerted policy action, given the separation of powers in the American system and the rather notorious lack of discipline of the congressional parties during much of the history of the nation. An inept or unpopular President can fail in the leadership function to the frustration of policy action. Similarly, divided majorities in Congress or a recalcitrant congressional leadership may render a period of unified partisan control of government no more productive of concerted policy effort by the party in power than a period of divided control. At a minimum, however, concerted policy action is less likely under conditions of divided partisan control than when a single party controls both the presidency and the Congress.

It appears equally obvious that the dominant party will have a greater chance of success in its policy initiatives the larger the size of its majorities in Congress and the more impressive the president's victories at the polls. An impressive presidential victory at the polls, in the Electoral College, or both may create the impression of a mandate for campaign pronouncements and for the party platform and increase the likelihood of effective policy action. Such a victory can also create at least the illusion of coattail effects and enhance congressional cooperation. Large congressional majorities are likely to be diverse in goals and constituency bases and may be difficult to coordinate and govern. On the other hand, a party with large majorities can afford to lose some of its seats and still put the bulk of its program into effect. The party in such a position can also tolerate more in the way of lapses from party discipline and still achieve legislative success. Hence difficulties with party governance, cooperation between the president and Congress, and achieving majorities in particular policy areas may be lessened.

The importance of the margin of control in Congress for the ability of the party to take policy action is illustrated indirectly by evidence that at first glance appears contradictory— presidents advantaged with large majorities in Congress have nevertheless exercised their veto power more frequently than other presidents. While we should expect more cooperation and

less vetoes at such a time, it is quite clear from the context and
the veto messages that these Presidents were willing and able to
exercise the veto power as a weapon in controlling and leading
their own party.[5] The relationship between margin of control
of Congress and presidential vetoes may be curvilinear: Presidents facing a hostile Congress use the veto to prevent action; a
president with a large margin of control can afford to remind
the Congress of his power through the veto without jeopardizing his ability to carry out his own policy initiatives. Presidents
with narrower margins of control tread more carefully and veto
bills less frequently.

It is reasonable, then, to consider the size of majorities in
Congress and presidential margins of victory as related to the
capacities of the parties and their leadership to act effectively in
policy-making. As Figure 5.1 suggests, the three realignment
eras were unlike other periods in terms of the one-sidedness of
partisan advantages in control of Congress and presidential
margins in the popular vote and the Electoral College. The
elections of 1860, 1896, and 1932—and, for that matter, the
election of 1828—marked the beginning of extended periods of
clear and consistent unified control by one or the other of the
parties. During each of these periods, presidential margins and
party majorities in the House and Senate tended to be consistently large, although the weakening of Democratic strength in
the early 1940s is clearly evident. The Civil War and New Deal
realignments involved larger margins of partisan control than
did the realignment of the 1890s. Even so, Republican margins
of control from 1896 through 1910 were consistent and substantial. These years were marked, as can be seen, by a larger
and more consistent margin of Republican control than the
1920s, for example, when Republican electoral strength tended
to be greater. During the 1920s, the Republicans enjoyed considerable margins in presidential elections but barely won majorities in Congress in the off-years.

The differing characteristics of decay periods are also evident
in Figure 5.1. The extremely narrow, shifting, and inconsistent
margins of control of the years from 1874 through 1894 are in
striking contrast to both the immediately preceding and follow-

ing periods. Even when there was unified partisan control, as following the election of 1888 by the Republican party, the margins of control in Congress tended to be narrow and short-lived. In the years immediately preceding the Civil War, control was also narrow and often divided. While the Democrats appear to have been the dominant party after 1840, their control was often interrupted, and only during the brief period from 1853 to 1855 was their margin of control substantial.

Similar weaknesses of partisan control were also character-istic of other interrealignment periods. Wilson's extraordinary Electoral College margin in the three-candidate race of 1912 and parallel gains for the Democrats in the House of Represen-tatives and the Senate produced unified and one-sided control of the policy-making institutions, but only briefly. By 1914 Democratic control in the Congress had receded to rather nar-row margins which were reversed in 1918. Weakness of Repub-lican control in the 1920s has been noted. Although the Repub-licans dominated the politics of the decade, and their margins in presidential years were consistently large, the off-years were consistently marked by substantially narrowed majorities in Congress.

Much the same pattern marked the years after World War II. While the Democrats remained the dominant party, Republican presidential victories and, indeed, landslides were frequent. Aside from the election of 1952, however, even Republican presidential landslides were accompanied by Democratic major-ities in Congress. While the Democrats more frequently con-trolled both the presidency and the Congress than did the Republicans, their margins were often narrow. The one-sided and unified control that the Democrats exercised in the early 1960s, particularly after the election of 1964, suggests the hazards for policy innovation when control is not sustained long enough for the innovations to become assimilated. Nixon's dismantling of Great Society programs was probably consider-ably facilitated by their relative lack of institutionalization.

The margins of victory and control presented in Figure 5.1 reflect a different pattern of partisan dominance during realign-ment periods than during other periods. In general, the realign-

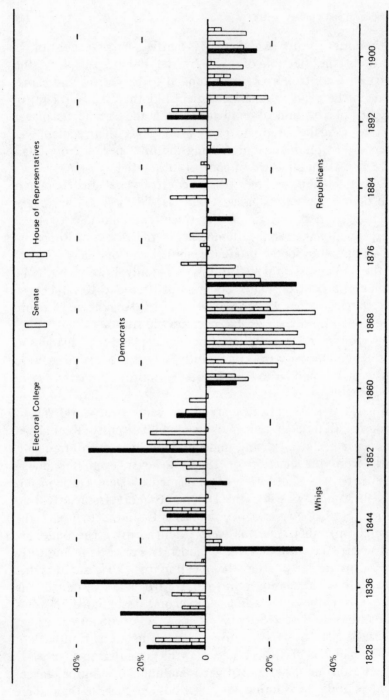

Figure 5.1: Margins of Control for Democrats and Whigs/Republicans in the Electoral College, Senate, and House of Representatives, 1828-1978

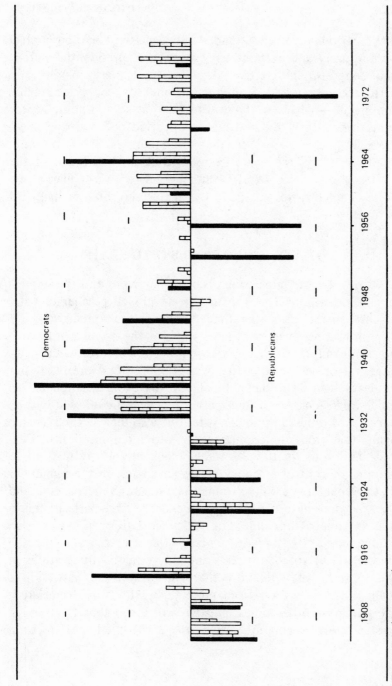

Figure 5.1: (Continued)

ment periods involved extended and consistent unified control by one party and extraordinary margins of presidential victory and congressional control. These extraordinary margins, we have argued, provided the conditions for concerted policy action, although as we have also noted at several points, these conditions clearly did not make concerted policy action inevitable. It is clear, however, that other periods—the latter nineteenth century, the years from 1910 through the end of the 1920s, and the post-World War II years—were not marked by these characteristics nearly to the degree the three realignment periods were.

TRANSLATING VOTES INTO SEATS

Obviously, the large congressional majorities and the impressive presidential victories in the Electoral College characteristic of partisan realignments reflected shifts in the popular vote. We have noted, however, that large shifts in the popular vote have not uniformly led to large margins of control in Congress or to large majorities in the Electoral College. Conversely, rather modest changes in the popular vote have on occasion led to much larger changes in the margin of control exercised by one party. Not only the popular vote, but also the electoral mechanisms that translate popular votes into representation in Congress and votes in the Electoral College are clearly relevant to margins of control in policy-making agencies. In the remainder of this chapter, we will examine these electoral mechanisms and the role they have played in producing the large partisan majorities capable of implementing policy initiatives during partisan realignments. By looking at both the average rates for the translation of votes into seats and the temporal fluctuations in these rates, we will show that the advantaged parties in a realignment benefited from more highly favorable translation rates than at other times, and we will argue that this was, at least in part, a consequence of the across-the-board electoral shifts characteristic of early elections in the realignment periods.

The electoral mechanisms for translating popular votes into Electoral College votes or seats in Congress are often referred to as capable of "manufacturing majorities." The "winner-take-all" electoral systems used in the United States—both the single member plurality system used in legislative races and the multi-member voting in the Electoral College—usually fail to translate popular votes into representation on a proportionate basis, with the Electoral College generally the more extreme and erratic in this regard. There is a substantial literature bearing upon the translation of the popular vote into seats in the House of Representatives.[6] All of the empirical evidence presented has indicated a translation rate of a two or three percentage point gain in House seats for each one percentage point gain in the popular vote. This rather high rate of gain suggests a characteristic of electoral mechanisms which would indeed inflate the legislative strength of electoral majorities.

The following pages consider the translation rates for elections to the Senate and for the popular vote for President in relation to votes in the Electoral College as well as for elections to the House of Representatives. Although not customary in the relevant literature, we use the proportions of the total vote (or total number of seats) rather than the proportions of the two-party vote.[7] Since the votes cast for the two major parties are not mirror images of each other, the proportions of the total vote are more straightforward and readily interpretable. The proportions of the total vote, because they reflect the intrusions of third parties, are also more directly related to the size of partisan majorities and are as a consequence better suited to our purposes.

The linear relationships for extended periods between the popular vote in presidential, House, and Senate elections, on the one hand, and votes in the Electoral College and seats in the House and Senate on the other, are presented in Table 5.2. The

TABLE 5.2   Translation Rates of Votes for President, Senate, and
House of Representatives

	Translation Rates of Popular Votes into Electoral College Votes	
	Democrats (1836–1972)	Republicans (1856–1972)
Swing Ratio (b)	2.9	2.6
Fit (r^2)	.56	.72
Percentage of Votes Yielding a Majority	45.2%	47.4%
	Translation Rates of Votes into Senate Seats	
	Democrats (1914–1976)	Republicans (1914–1976)
Swing Ratio (b)	2.0	2.4
Fit (r^2)	.59	.73
Percentage of Votes Yielding a Majority	45.1%	50.2%
	Translation Rates of Votes into House Seats	
	Democrats (1836–1972)	Republicans (1856–1972)
Swing Ratio (b)	1.8	1.7
Fit (r^2)	.50	.55
Percentage of Votes Yielding a Majority	45.8%	47.3%

regression coefficients ("b's") indicate the average proportion of seats or Electoral College votes won for each unit increase in the proportion of votes received. The range of values for the parties in the several races indicate a translation of popular votes into Electoral College votes of almost 3% for 1%, 2.9% for Democratic presidential candidates from 1836 to 1972. In congressional elections, the translation rates are lower in all cases for the entire period. Senate translation rates are around 2 for 1 for Democrats, with a slightly higher rate for Republicans (2.4). In voting for the House of Representatives, the rates are still lower (1.77 and 1.73 for Democrats and Republicans respectively).[8]

The second element of substantive interest to be noted in Table 5.2 is the percentage of the popular vote that yields an "expected majority" in the Senate, House, or Electoral College. By this we mean the proportion of the popular vote that would be expected to yield at least 50% representation in the House or Senate or of the votes in the Electoral College, given the translation rates characteristic of that body. Some of the literature concerned with translation rates has emphasized the Democratic bias operating in elections to the House of Representatives. The more important bias characteristic of the electoral system is of course in favor of the major parties to the disadvantage of the minor parties, which seldom gain any representation for the small number of votes they receive. This situation is reflected in the fact that the percentages of the popular vote yielding expected majorities are below 50% for both major parties (Table 5.2). Of course, these are "expected values" given the linear fit to the observed data and could not mean literally that both parties would gain majorities simultaneously.

These translation rates are the average rates over a lengthy temporal period. A better way to investigate the interaction between the translation rates and the creation of majorities in the realignment sequence is to introduce a time dimension. Figures 5.2 and 5.3 present the relationship between popular votes and strength in the Electoral College and the House for each national election from 1836 to the present. The Senate series, presented in Figure 5.4, does not begin until 1914 with the advent of popular election of senators. The lines through the figures represent the actual percentage of the popular vote. The ends of the bars represent the percentages of party strength in the Electoral College, the Senate, or the House. Thus, the length of each bar indicates the disparity between popular votes and their translation into seats or electoral votes. The dark bars in the figures indicate higher proportions of seats in the House and Senate or of votes in the Electoral College than of popular votes; light bars indicate more votes than seats or Electoral College strength. Tall, dark bars show a highly favorable rate of

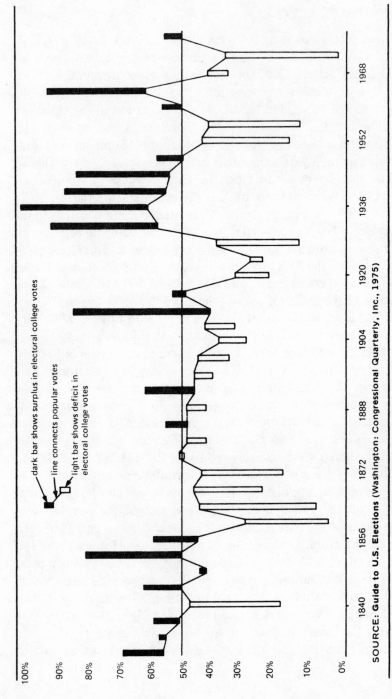

100%
90%
80%
70%
60%
50%
40%
30%
20%
10%
0%

dark bar shows surplus in electoral college votes

line connects popular votes

light bar shows deficit in electoral college votes

1840   1856   1872   1888   1904   1920   1936   1952   1968

SOURCE: Guide to U.S. Elections (Washington: Congressional Quarterly, Inc., 1975)

Figure 5.2a: Democratic Popular Votes and Electoral College Votes for President, 1828-1976

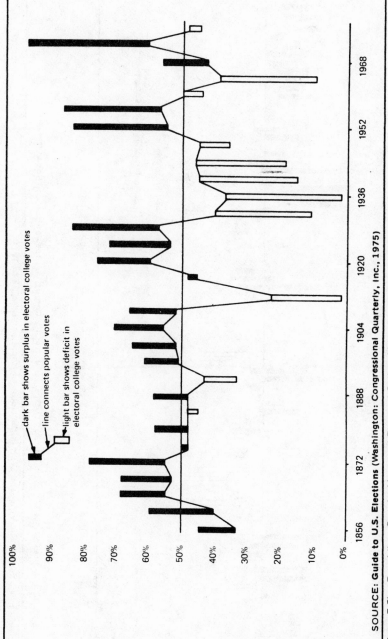

SOURCE: Guide to U.S. Elections (Washington: Congressional Quarterly, Inc., 1975)

Figure 5.2b: Republican Popular Votes and Electoral College Votes for President, 1856-1976

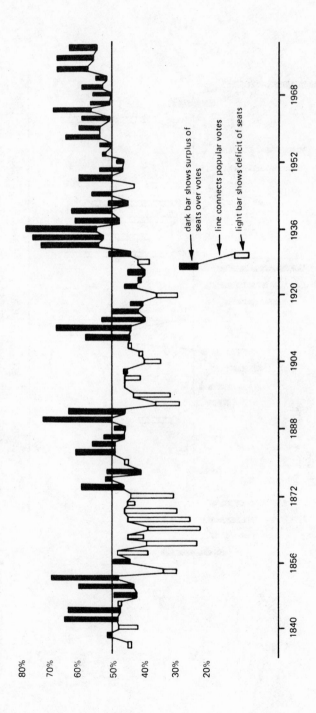

SOURCE: United States Historical Election Data, Inter-university Consortium for Political and Social Research.

Figure 5.3a: Democratic Votes and Seats in the House of Representatives, 1836-1978

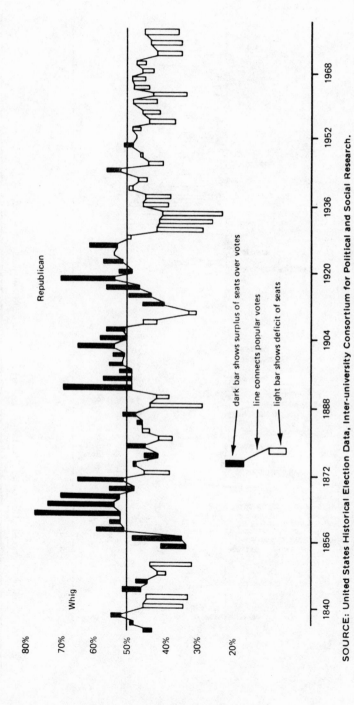

Figure 5.3b: Whig and Republican Votes and Seats in the House of Representatives, 1836-1978

179

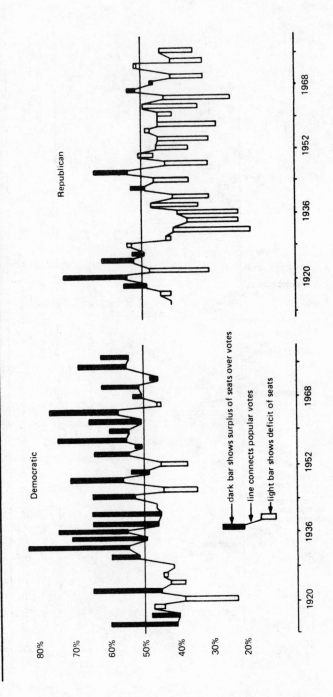

SOURCE: United States Election Data, Inter-university Consortium for Political and Social Research.

Figure 5.4: Democratic and Republican Votes and Seats in the Senate, 1914-1976

translation; long, light bars indicate a highly unfavorable rate, and short bars indicate a relatively faithful translation. These figures reveal a remarkable unevenness in the extent to which a given proportion of the popular vote was translated into strength in the Electoral College or in Congress. And this unevenness was characteristic of the Democratic, Republican, and Whig parties in all three series.

Figures 5.2, 5.3, and 5.4 suggest that the "advantaged" parties during the partisan realignments of the 1860s, the 1890s, and the 1930s benefited not only from favorable electoral responses but also from favorable operation of the mechanisms translating popular votes into margins of control. Favorable translation rates appear to have been particularly important in the initial elections of each period. In the 1860s and the 1890s, the translation rates worked to convert popular pluralities or narrow majorities into oversized majorities in the House and the Electoral College. In 1932, healthy majorities in the popular vote were converted into even larger margins in Congress and the Electoral College. The advantage of favorable translation rates did not continue consistently throughout the period of sustained control by the newly dominant party. It is likely, however, that favorable translation rates, like the margin of control itself, may have been less important for the continuation of policies than for their inauguration.

Some qualification of this general pattern is necessary. In the elections of 1856 and 1858, the Republicans enjoyed even more favorable translation rates than in the early 1860s. In another sense, however, this situation can be seen as illustrating the importance of the vagaries of electoral mechanisms. Without such favorable translation rates at the beginning of its existence, the new party might have been unable to establish itself as a viable contender for political power. Similarly, in the 1890s, the most favorable translation rate enjoyed by the Republicans was in 1894, two years before the party gained unified control of government through the capture of the presidency. We might argue that this overwhelming majority in the Fifty-fourth Congress gave the Republicans an organizational advantage that allowed them to retain firm control with a smaller margin in the next Congress.

We do not wish to imply, of course, that historical realignments were merely the products of quirks in the translation of votes into majorities. It is clear, however, that the large majorities which provided the conditions for concerted policy action were heavily dependent upon the degree of electoral competitiveness and the geographical distribution of electoral change given the operation of the electoral system. Conversion depends upon: (1) the closeness of the vote between the major parties in each district; (2) the uniformity of the shift in popular votes across districts; and (3) the size and distribution of the vote for minor parties. In general, a winner-take-all system advantages a large party whose votes are spread relatively evenly across districts, so that it wins with narrow pluralities in many districts. A large party is disadvantaged if its votes are concentrated geographically so that it "wastes" votes by winning some districts or states by large majorities rather than "using" these excess votes to convert narrow losses into pluralities or majorities in other districts or states.[9] Conversely, small parties are typically disadvantaged in a winner-take-all system if they are dispersed geographically; only if they are concentrated in a few districts, can they amass enough votes to win pluralities and gain representation.

The degree of competitiveness has a major effect upon the actual benefit a party receives from an increase in its vote. A party winning 5%—or 90%— of the vote will probably gain no additional representation from a five percentage point increase in its vote in the next election. On the other hand, a party losing in every district with 47% of the vote could (in a hypothetical example) move from 0% to 100% of the seats with a similar five percentage point increase in its vote—if its vote increases were spread uniformly across all districts.

The shifts in governmental control associated with the election of 1896 offer an illustration of the importance of the competitiveness of the electoral situation in creating majorities in policy-making institutions. As we have seen in previous chapters, the election of 1896 was marked by relatively little realigning electoral change. Yet the competitive conditions of the late nineteenth century were such that even these relatively limited electoral shifts produced a pronounced change in the partisan distribution of seats in Congress. In 1896, 19% of the total House seats changed in party control. An even larger percentage, 36%, changed party in 1894. In contrast, the much more massive electoral change of 1932 produced only a comparable shift, 21%, in partisan control of total House seats. As a consequence of the closely competitive conditions in many nonsouthern states in the late nineteenth century, the impact of even slight electoral change was greatly amplified. On the other hand, the less competitive conditions of the 1920s in nonsouthern states worked to reduce the impact of much greater electoral change in 1932.

In a competitive situation, the evenness of the geographical distribution of shifts in the electoral strength of the parties will also have an impact upon the magnitude of the translation ratio and upon the size of majorities in Congress or the Electoral College. The more evenly the vote increase is distributed geographically, the larger the resulting majorities are likely to be. In Chapter 3, we presented evidence suggesting that the major partisan realignments were characterized primarily by across-the-board shifts in electoral support rather than by differential change. And, indeed, we have argued that the perceived crises that preceded realignments have initially at least involved a rather uniform rejection of current leadership that only later resulted in permanent change in the partisan attitudes of some segments of the electorate. We also saw in Chapter 3 that during major realignments (in contrast to some other presidential elections with exceptionally popular candidates), essentially unidirectional across-the-board electoral changes were characteristic of both the presidential and the congressional vote. These across-the-board electoral surges in favor of the advantaged party, coupled with electoral mechanisms that worked to exaggerate their results, produced the oversized majorities in Congress and the impressive presidential victories in the Electoral

College which, as we have seen in this chapter, were characteristic of realignment eras.

The connection between the popular vote and seats in Congress or votes in the Electoral College worked with a consistent bias in favor of one party during realignment eras. During other periods, the bias of the translation rates was not always as large, nor did it as consistently favor one party. Other occasional elections, particularly those with large third-party votes, were marked by extreme translation rates. In most such cases, however, these extreme rates did not affect both the presidency and the Congress simultaneously. Thus the most significant characteristic of the translation ratios in American elections was the creation of large majorities of seats or electoral votes for the advantaged party during realignments. Even relatively small margins of victory in presidential and congressional voting in some realignment elections produced large majorities for the advantaged party.

The creation of large "manufactured majorities" in Congress and in the Electoral College was not in any way unique to realigning periods. It is important to appreciate the dual emphasis offered here on both electoral change and the unified control of government. Our argument maintains that electoral patterns, especially lasting electoral changes, are important primarily because of their impact on the control of government and the consequent impact on policy-making. We argue, then, that electoral change and unified partisan control of government with large majorities provided the necessary conditions for policy initiatives. These initiatives, when popularly perceived as successful, led to sustained unified control of governments, to the maintenance of policy actions, to a new balance of popular partisan attitudes, and to the retrospective view of such periods by later scholars as constituting partisan realignments.

NOTES

1. Several studies have attempted to look at policy shifts associated with particular realignments. See, for example, Barbara Deckard Sinclair, "The Policy Conse-

quences of Party Realignment—Social Welfare Legislation in the House of Representatives, 1933-1954," *American Journal of Political Science* 22 (February 1978), pp. 83-105; Barbara Deckard Sinclair, "Party Realignment and the Transformation of the Political Agenda," *American Political Science Review* 71 (September 1977), pp. 940-953; David Brady, "Critical Elections, Congressional Parties and Clusters of Policy Changes: A Comparison of the 1896 and 1932 Realignment Eras," presented at the annual meeting of the American Political Science Association, 1975; David Brady, "Congressional Policy Responses to Issues and Elections: a Time Series Analysis," undated manuscript, University of Houston; Benjamin Ginsberg, "Elections and Public Policy," *American Political Science Review* 70 (March 1976), pp. 41-49. Conversely, Susan Hansen has looked for significant changes in a single policy area, taxes, and their relationship to realignments in "Partisan Realignment and Tax Policy, 1789-1970," presented at the annual meeting of the American Political Science Association, 1977.

2. A straightforward test of this hypothesis would examine congressional support for the president's program, but no such data have been assembled systematically for a long historical period. Since 1953, *Congressional Quarterly Almanac* has calculated a presidential support score, and these scores over the years are highly related with partisan control. With the exception of 1968, in the years of unified control, presidential support scores are consistently higher than for the years of divided control; the average difference is over 15%. These findings are reassuring for the likelihood of concerted policy effort in periods of unified control of government, though similar findings are not available for earlier periods.

3. The only rival circumstance seems to be an external military threat.

4. Several expectations regarding the policy role of the Supreme Court during partisan realignments might be suggested in this context. In the early years of a realignment era, the newly advantaged party controlling the presidency and the Congress may enact rather drastic departures in law and policy. Ultimately, however, the Court must agree if these new directions are to remain viable. Since changes in the composition of the Court lag behind changes in the control of Congress and the presidency, it may be some time before the newly dominant party is able through new appointments to shift the composition of the Court to a majority likely to be favorable to the new policy directions. The striking down of New Deal legislation is an obvious example of the consequences of this time lag. On the other hand, once dominated by the political forces of the realignment, the Court may continue the policy initiatives of the realignment through judicial decision-making long after control of the elective branches of government has waned.

Recent work has linked Supreme Court nullifications of federal statutes to the occurrence of realigning elections and has concluded that (1) the Court was indeed initially hostile to the policies of the new governing coalition after a realignment, and (2) once the Court was dominated by newly appointed members, this hostility disappeared. See, for example, David Adamany, "Legitimacy, Realigning Elections, and the Supreme Court," *Wisconsin Law Review* (September 1973), pp. 790-846; Richard Funston, "The Supreme Court and Critical Elections," *American Political Science Review* (September 1975), pp. 795-811. It would well suit our analytic purposes merely to cite these conclusions and to drop the matter. Unfortunately, these findings are misleading insofar as they imply this pattern has characterized all partisan realignments. This point is made by Bradley C. Canon and S. Sidney Ulmer, "The Supreme Court and Critical Elections: A Dissent," *American Political Science Review* (December 1976), pp. 1215-1218, as well as by Richard Funston, "The

Supreme Court and Critical Elections," p. 804, n. 67. In fact, the pattern fits the New Deal era perfectly, but it fits neither the Civil War era nor the 1890s in the least. Table 5.A shows the distribution of Supreme Court nullifications by years in each of the major realignments, controlling for the date when laws were enacted. To support the expectations expressed above neatly, each set of data would reveal the pattern of the New Deal period where many federal laws were nullified initially and few laws were nullified after majority party control was achieved. Obviously, the other two periods reverse this pattern.

These differences appear to be related to the differing circumstances of the earlier realignments. In the 1890s, the Supreme Court took more initiative in implementing the policies of the new Republican administration. The Court restrained states—not the national government—by nullifying state government regulations of economic activities. Constitutionally, this placed the Republican-controlled Congress in a position to take over the regulatory policies begun by the states, and Congress played its role by doing little. Since the national Republican policy was to remove, not to further, restrictions on economic activities, there was no need for the Court to nullify federal statutes.

During the Civil War era, the Supreme Court was never dominated by the Reconstruction Republican political forces that briefly dominated the national government. The Supreme Court, as such, did not interfere successfully with civilian aspects of the conduct of the war. During Reconstruction, a traumatic era in the history of the Court, it refrained from acting in crucial matters; the failure to legitimize Reconstruction policies, however, led to congressional initiatives to limit jurisdiction and one instance of what amounted to "court packing." Ultimately, Supreme Court nullification of legislation passed by the Republican majorities came late in the period, not at the beginning as suggested by the realignment perspective.

In all partisan realignments except 1896, the newly elected president faced a hostile Supreme Court, but only during the New Deal did the Court become substantially more supportive of the policies of the realignment administration.

5. The systematic historical research on presidential vetoes is limited. Recently, there is Jong R. Lee, "Presidential Vetoes from Washington to Nixon," *Journal of Politics* 37 (November 1975), pp. 522-546. We interpret Lee's analysis as weakly supportive of the realignment perspective, with the main contrary findings associated with the administration of Andrew Johnson.

6. The most informative introduction to the several approaches to the quantitative analysis of the translation of votes into seats is in Edward R. Tufte, *Data Analysis for Politics and Policy* (Englewood Cliffs, NJ: Prentice-Hall, 1974), pp. 65-68, 91-101, 121-124. See also Edward R. Tufte, "The Relationship Between Seats and Votes in Two-Party Systems," *American Political Science Review* 68 (June 1973), pp. 540-554; James G. March, "Party Legislative Representation as a Function of Election Results," in Paul Lazarsfeld and Neil Henry (eds.), *Readings in Mathematical Social Science* (Chicago: Science Research Associates, 1966), pp. 220-241.

7. At least one other study has handled the data in this way. Thomas Casstevens and William Morris, "The Cube Law and the Decomposed System," *Canadian Journal of Political Science* 5 (December 1972), pp. 521-532.

TABLE 5.A   Supreme Court Nullifications of Federal
Statutes Following Partisan Realignments

	1861–1872 *Legislation Enacted Into Law*		
	Before 1861	*After 1861*	*Total*
1861–1864	0	0	0
1865–1868[a]	1	2	3
1869–1872	0	5	5

[a]Republican majority control achieved in 1865.

	1897–1908 *Legislation Enacted*		
	Before 1897	*After 1897*	*Total*
1897–1900[b]	2	0	2
1901–1904	1	1	2
1905–1908	1	4	5

[b]Republican majority control achieved before 1897.

	1933–1944 *Legislation Enacted*		
	Before 1933	*After 1933*	*Total*
1933–1936	0	13	13
1937–1940[c]	0	0	0
1941–1944	0	1	1

[c]Democratic majority achieved in 1939.

8. The fit of these data to the straight line is not perfect, certainly, but at least moderately strong in all cases with r^2s ranging from 0.5 to 0.7 for the data in Table 5.2. Dropping highly deviant values like 1854 in the Democratic House voting changes the b considerably from 1.77 to 1.92, but the r^2 increases only 0.01. When subperiods are considered in House voting, the relationship between votes and seats is weaker in the period from the 1880s to the 1920s and noticeably stronger before and after. The r^2s drop for relationships that include all or some of these years, and the b's, the translation rates, are lower. Cube law analysis is not reported in the text, because we believe that the simple linear regression analysis is easier to understand and because in no case is the fit of the curvilinear, cube law enough better than the straight line to warrant special attention. The correlations between actual seats and the expected values generated by the linear regression or by the cube law are approximately the same for all three races. An exception to this general finding for

Democrats and Republicans can be made by including votes for third parties. The cube law formulation fits parties with very low proportions of the vote quite well, and the linear model does not. In other words, as Tufte observed, the linear regression is appropriate to the normal range of vote percentages for major parties.

9. In the American party system since the Civil War, we might expect the Democratic Party to be disadvantaged due to the concentration of its strength in the South; however, this is somewhat offset by the low turnout in the southern states, which enables the Democratic party to win these safe seats with a small proportion of its total national vote.

Chapter 6

PARTISAN CONTROL OF STATE GOVERNMENTS

As has been seen, shifts in voting patterns in the 1860s, the 1890s, and the 1930s brought about relatively lasting change in the control of federal policy-making agencies. During each of these periods, an advantaged party gained unified control over the presidency and the two houses of Congress. In these years, shifts in mass electoral behavior led to substantially larger shifts in patterns of partisan control of the federal government. With the partial exception of the 1920s, periods following partisan realignments—those periods we have described as the decay phases of electoral sequences—were marked by increased minor party activity, by more frequent deviating elections, and by loss of unified control of the national government by the party advantaged by the earlier realignment. During such periods, electoral change did not lead to unified control of government, but worked instead to disrupt such patterns of partisan control.

It is obvious, of course, that for many of the purposes of public policy-making and implementation, control of state governments and to some degree local governments is as important as control of national policy-making institutions. Indeed, for many of these purposes, state governments historically have been more important than the national government. We expect that the behavior of state and local political systems in realignment eras will be related to the national patterns but not mirror images of them. In our view, under most circumstances, the levels of government have operated quite independently of one another. Indeed, state and local political systems responding to different constituencies and conditions regularly produce policies quite dissimilar from one another, and policies often inconsistent with federal policies as well. The realignment perspective implies, however, that during partisan realignments at the national level, state and local governments have refrained from interfering with the national policies offered in response to the realignment crisis. State and local governments have not usually implemented policies exactly like those of the federal government at each realignment, but rather have temporarily abandoned clashing and incongruent policy initiatives typical of the decay phases.

Political party organizations parallel the federal structure of government and in similar fashion encompass a wide range of state and local variation; the usual disarray of a federated political party has been overridden only partially and briefly during American history. Nevertheless, if political parties are assumed to play some role in the formation of public policy, there are several implications for partisan control of the institutions of national, state, and local governments. At a minimum during a partisan realignment, we would not expect the newly dominant party in national policy-making institutions to face unified control at the state and local level by the opposition political party. Beyond this, if unified control by one party at the national level and in a significant portion of state and local governments occurs, the likelihood of comprehensive policy action would be increased, and the blocking of policy initiatives of one level of government by another would be less likely. Furthermore, the deterioration of these conditions during a decay phase would make coherent, overall policy much less likely.

These considerations aside, it is reasonable to assume that the social and economic forces associated with realignment periods had similar effects at both the national and the state and local levels, and it is also reasonable to expect that the advantaged party benefited from these conditions in terms of election to state and local offices. While social and economic forces were systemwide and their immediate political effects could be seen at several levels of government, there is no reason to assume that the appearance of particular political consequences establishes a direction of impact from one level of government to another. Certainly, innovation in public policy is not the exclusive domain of any one level of government.

Although similar patterns of change in control of government during electoral sequences could be expected at all levels of government, investigation of patterns of control of government at the local level would obviously involve a herculean task of both data collection and analysis. Indeed, even comprehensive examination of elective state offices would be a task of major proportions. As long as attention is limited to state legislatures and governors, however, patterns of partisan control of state governments can be examined with relative ease. In the present chapter, we have limited our focus even more narrowly and have concentrated attention on: (1) the coincidence between partisan change at the state and national levels; (2) the incidence and duration of unified control of state governments by Republicans and Democrats over the years; and (3) the patterns of change in control of state governments.

STATE AND NATIONAL PARTISAN CHANGE

As we have argued in previous chapters, electoral change alone is insufficient to identify a partisan realignment. On the other hand, some shift in the partisan balance is necessary to create the unified control of government which can in turn permit the policy innovations which, in retrospect, earn an era the title of partisan realignment. By the same token, if we assume that policy innovation is facilitated by articulation between the federal government and like-minded state governments, then we must determine if there was a coincidence of partisan change in state and national elections which in turn brought unified control to the same party at both levels during partisan realignments.

Each of the national partisan realignments was associated with substantial shifts in the gubernatorial vote and with large shifts in the proportion of seats controlled by the parties in the state legislatures, resulting from shifts in the popular vote for state legislators. In the early 1930s, virtually every Democratic candidate for governor made a stronger showing than the Democratic counterpart in the 1920s. Democrats invariably gained seats in the legislature, and even though in many northern states the rural-dominated upper houses remained under Republican control, the Democrats narrowed the margin. In the 1890s, the electoral shifts were less unidirectional, but states marked by Republican gains in the vote for national office were also marked by parallel gains in the Republican vote for governor and state legislators; in the 1860s, the northern states were characterized by a similar pattern.

At least in general terms, these shifts in partisan strength at the state level coincided with change in the vote for national offices and with change in partisan control over national elective institutions. To this point, however, we have not attempted to compare systematically shifts in the popular vote for state offices with change in the vote for national offices. Comprehensive data bearing upon state legislative elections are not available, but comprehensive gubernatorial returns are at hand and provide a basis for comparison of the magnitude and pattern of partisan change in elections to offices at the two levels of government.

It is possible to construct an "expected vote" for governor for each state, just as for the presidency, although variations in the length of gubernatorial terms and in the timing of gubernatorial elections from state to state create some complications.[1]

By comparing change in gubernatorial "expected votes" with change in the presidential "expected vote" between periods before and after realignments, we can assess the degree of similarity in the realigning shifts in both presidential and gubernatorial voting. Comparisons must be limited to the realignments of the 1890s and the 1930s, because of the lack of comparability of elections and parties during the Civil War era. We would expect that the impact of national crisis would be reflected in the similarity of realigning shifts in both the presidential and gubernatorial vote. States responding strongly to national forces with realigning change in the presidential vote could be expected to show corresponding change in the vote for state offices.

The results of these comparisons are presented in Figure 6.1. As can be seen, the realignment of the 1890s was characterized by markedly similar shifts in the presidential and gubernatorial "expected votes" across the states. Although the figure reflects a number of deviant states, most of the states are tightly clustered around the diagonal line, which would represent equal "expected vote" shifts in all states in both the presidential and gubernatorial vote, and the correlation between the shifts in presidential and gubernatorial "expected vote" is relatively high ($r = .60$). In the case of the New Deal realignment, on the other hand, the relationship is much weaker ($r = .29$), and the scatter of states is skewed pronouncedly to the right. During the New Deal years, it appears, the Democratic gubernatorial vote increased, but in virtually all states, the vote for president shifted more dramatically in the Democratic direction than did the gubernatorial vote.

Although limited, the evidence suggests that in the 1890s the vote in state and national elections shifted in similar directions and in similar magnitudes. For more than a decade prior to the depression of 1893, the political system had drifted in a Democratic direction. In part, this drift was a product of the imposition of the "Southern System" in state after state of the South. But during these years, northern states also tended to move toward the Democratic Party. In the 1890s, this pattern of

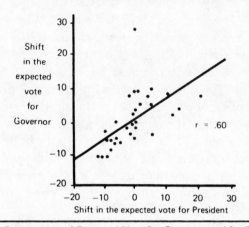

Figure 6.1a: Relationship of Expected Vote for Governor and for President before and after 1896

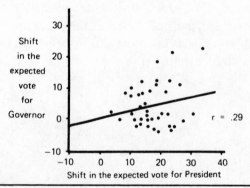

Figure 6.1b: Relationship of Expected Vote for Governor and for President before and after 1932

change was sharply and, it appears, almost uniformly reversed in the North as the vote for state and national offices in most northern states shifted toward the Republicans. In the South, the vote in national and state elections shifted even more markedly to the Democrats.

During the 1930s, electoral change at the two levels of government was less uniform. Shifts in the presidential vote toward the Democrats were not uniformly paralleled by equivalent gains in gubernatorial elections. To some degree, this dissimilarity was a product of prior electoral change. In a number of states, primarily in the Northeast, the Democratic gubernatorial vote had increased in the early 1920s, forecasting the later successes of Al Smith and Franklin Roosevelt in presidential contests. (The gubernatorial voting in the 1920s represents one aspect of the decay of the prior alignment discussed in Chapter 4.) In the South, on the other hand, several states were already voting 100% Democratic in gubernatorial elections, so no shift was possible to complement the increased Democratic percentages in presidential elections. As a region, only the Midwest shifted uniformly toward the Democrats in both the presidential and gubernatorial races of the 1930s. But whatever the patterns of individual areas, it remains the case that the national realignment of the 1930s was not uniformly translated into equivalent electoral change in elections to state offices.

PARTISAN CONTROL OF STATE GOVERNMENTS

More important than the coincidence of electoral change is the shifting of the unified control of government at the same time at both state and national levels. Shifts in patterns of partisan control over state governments are examined in Figure 6.2, which displays the incidence of united Democratic, united Whig or Republican, and divided partisan control over state legislatures and gubernatorial offices for each biennium from 1834 through 1976.[2] As can be seen, the series reflect numerous shifts, some of them major, in partisan control of state governments. Indeed, change appears as a virtually constant property of the series. But despite irregularities, the series are marked by patterns of change generally coinciding with the realignment cycle. In 1860, in 1894, and in 1932, control over state governments shifted sharply toward the parties advantaged by electoral realignment. In no other periods, with the possible

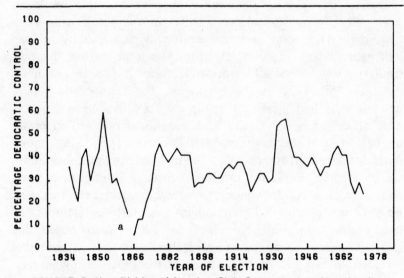

SOURCE: Partisan Division of American State Governments, Inter-university Consortium for Political and Social Research.
a. No calculations were made for the Civil War years.

Figure 6.2a: Percentage of Democratic Control in State Governments, 1836-1976

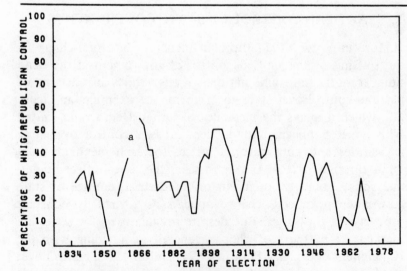

SOURCE: Partisan Division of American State Governments, Inter-university Consortium for Political and Social Research.
a. No calculations were made for Civil War years.

Figure 6.2b: Percentage of Whig and Republican Control in State Governments, 1836-1976

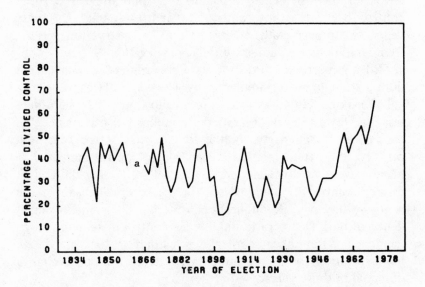

SOURCE: Partisan Division of American State Governments, Inter-university
Consortium for Political and Social Research.
a. No calculations were made for Civil War years.

Figure 6.2c: Percentage of Divided Control in State Governments, 1836-1976

exception of the 1920s, can shifts of such magnitude be
observed. Moreover, decline in the incidence of united control
can be observed following each realignment.

Shifts in partisan control were particularly marked during the
Civil War years. In state elections held in 1859 and 1860, the
new Republican Party gained united control over more than
60% of the state governments, and immediately following the
war, the incidence of Republican control rose to still higher
levels. This second increase in Republican dominance was, of
course, in part a product of the withdrawal of the Democrati-
cally controlled Confederate states and their subsequent return
under Republican control during Reconstruction. In 1864,
some 80% of the states outside the Confederacy were controlled
by the Republicans. The magnitude of Republican control
declined in the 1870s and remained at lower levels thereafter.

Moreover, the incidence of Democratic and divided partisan control over state governments tended to increase in these years, as southern states emerged from Reconstruction and the Democratic party regained legitimacy in the North.

Shifts in partisan control of state governments also occurred during subsequent realignments. By 1894, Republicans controlled approximately 46% of the states, following 1892 when there was the lowest level of unified Republican control since the formation of the party. In the first decade of the twentieth century, the extent of unified Republican control increased to higher levels, as did Democratic control, reflecting the end of divided control in many states. In the second decade of the century, however, Republican control declined, and the incidence of both Democratic and divided control increased. A high incidence of Republican control was restored in 1918 and 1920, in association with the moderate lasting electoral change observed in those years.

The shift toward the Democrats in the 1930s was also pronounced and followed a pattern similar to that of the 1890s. In the election of 1932, the Democratic party gained control of 57% of all state governments in the nation, approximately double the incidence of Democratic control of state governments in the 1920s, which had been of course based primarily in the South. In the immediately following elections, moreover, Democratic control increased to even higher levels. Beginning in the late 1930s, recession of Democratic strength can be observed paralleled by the restoration of some Republican control. By the late 1950s and 1960s, however, Democratic control declined further but was not consistently replaced by unified Republican control, reflecting a trend in recent decades toward more and more divided control of state governments.

Obviously, a marked parallel can be observed between patterns of partisan control at the state and national levels of government. These patterns in turn parallel the incidence of electoral change discussed in Chapters 3 and 4 above. In each case, a shift toward one or the other of the parties was observed during realignments; in immediately following years, the incidence of control by the advantaged party rose to still higher levels. Indications of midsequence adjustments can also be noted, followed, except in the 1920s, by increase of both divided control and united control by the opposing party.

While relatively clear patterns can be noted, the data presented and discussed above mask critical aspects of historical change in partisan control of state governments. Shifts in control are, to a degree, distorted for substantial periods by the relatively invariant nature of the "solid" South, which obscures the magnitude of the patterns of partisan control characteristic of each of the realignment periods. To eliminate these obscurities, Figure 6.3 displays the proportion of nonsouthern states characterized by united control over the state executive and both legislative houses by the parties advantaged by the three partisan realignments. In 1858 and 1859, Republicans controlled approximately 63% of the nonsouthern state governments. Republican control declined somewhat in the years immediately following, only to rise to still higher levels later in the decade. Shifts in partisan control of state governments during the subsequent realignments were even more pronounced. In 1894 and 1895, Republicans had united control over almost 66% of the nonsouthern state governments, and in 1932 and 1933, Democrats won control of almost 42% of these state governments as compared with the 11% they had controlled in 1930 and 1931. In many instances, of course, the advantaged party nationally made substantial gains in a state, winning one or two of the elective institutions, without achieving unified control of that state's government. To the extent that such increases for the nationally advantaged party at the state level indicate loss of unified control of government by the *other* party, barriers to the implementation of national policy initiatives may have been removed.

As at the national level, the magnitude of legislative majorities is an additional indicator of the ability of the advantaged party to support new policy directions. As Figure 6.4 suggests, the 1860s, the 1890s, and the 1930s were marked not only by a shift in the balance of partisan control over nonsouthern state

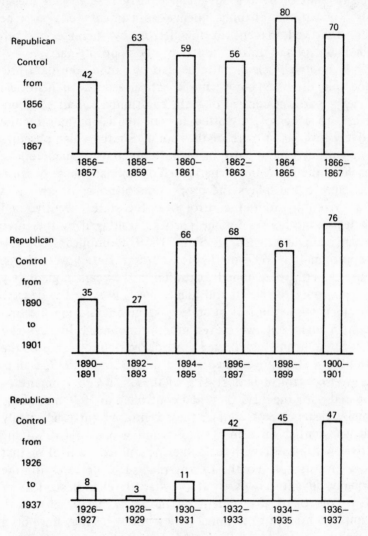

SOURCE: Partisan Division of American State Governments, Inter-university
Consortium for Political and Social Research.

Figure 6.3: Percentages of Non-Southern States with One Party Control of Executive
and Legislature in Years Surrounding Realignments

legislatures toward the advantaged parties, but also by an increase in the magnitude of control. In each of these periods, the advantaged party came to control a preponderance of the state legislatures and also attained substantial majorities in an increased percentage of legislatures. Once again, moreover, recession of control by the advantaged party can be observed. As Figure 6.4 shows, the 1870s witnessed a decline in the magnitude of control over state legislatures that paralleled declines in unified Republican control of state governments, and the same pattern can also be observed in the second decade of the twentieth century. The Democrats also experienced the same pattern of decline beginning in the 1940s.

The data displayed in Figure 6.4 suggest a further characteristic of American political history. Both houses of most American state legislatures have tended historically to be controlled by very substantial partisan majorities. When it is recalled that the data in Figure 6.4 bear upon only the nonsouthern states, and when it is also recalled that during most of the years since the mid-nineteenth century southern legislatures have been consistently controlled by large Democratic majorities, this characteristic appears all the more pronounced. This characteristic also suggests that historically, very substantial electoral change has been required to shift control of the state legislative bodies from one party to the other, which is not the case at the national level. This, presumably, is another consequence of the malapportionment of state legislatures during much of the twentieth century. Overall, the characteristics of state politics have been such as to dampen the partisan effects of even major electoral change.

DURATION OF PARTISAN CONTROL

To this point, no regard has been paid to the degree of permanence characteristic of historical shifts in control of state governments. If only the number of states marked by unified partisan control is considered without also considering the duration of control, it would be possible for relatively transitory

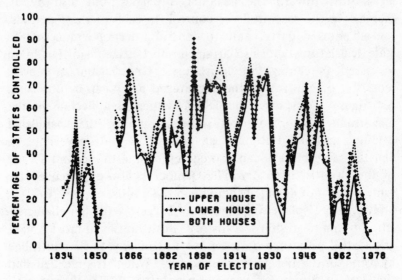

SOURCE: Partisan Division of American State Governments, Inter-university Consortium for Political and Social Research.

Figure 6.4a: Percentage of State Legislative Houses with Whig or Republican Majorities of 60 Percent or Greater for the Non-South, 1834-1977

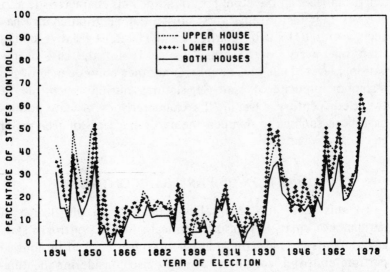

SOURCE: Partisan Division of American State Governments, Inter-university Consortium for Political and Social Research.

Figure 6.4b: Percentage of State Legislative Houses with Democratic Majorities of 60 Percent or Greater for the Non-South, 1834-1977

movements to create the impression of large and enduring shifts in control. Patterns of essentially transitory change would have only limited implications for successful government and articulation of national policy at the various levels of government as suggested by the conceptualization of partisan realignments discussed elsewhere. Moreover, since partisan realignments presumably mark points of systemic change, we need to determine first, whether there was a break in the patterns of control allowing national policy a period of dominance, and second, whether these periods indeed mark the beginning of eras of unified control rather than the mere continuation of earlier periods or gradual increase in the number of states under unified control.

Consideration of these issues is complicated by the high degree of stability that has characterized patterns of partisan control of state governments. Since the mid-nineteenth century, most of the states have been characterized by long and uninterrupted periods of solid control by one party over the legislative and gubernatorial offices. The fact is most obvious in the case of the "solid" South, but it is to be noted as well that such states as Iowa, Kansas, New Hampshire, and Vermont were marked by equally "solid" Republican control from the 1850s through the 1950s. Indeed, almost half of the states could be described as safe, one-party states for the past century, with only occasional disruptions of that dominance. Furthermore, during the past one hundred years or more, very few states have been marked both by relatively lengthy periods of unified control by Democrats *and* by relatively lengthy periods of Republican control.[3] In other words, it is clear that major and lasting shifts in control of state governments from one party to the other have not been numerous in American history either during periods of realignment or at any other time.

It is also clear, however, that historical periods of realignment were characterized by lasting change in the partisan control of many state governments. The nature of shifts in control of state governments can be assessed by considering the percentage of states characterized by unified Republican or Democratic control during each two-year period from 1856 to 1976, and the number of states during each such period in which unified control was initiated and lasted for two or more years and eight or more years (Figure 6.5).[4] It could be expected that periods of realignment would be marked by large numbers of states under the unified control of the advantaged party; more specifically, that during such periods patterns of unified control would be established and endure for substantial periods. While it makes for a complicated figure, it is necessary to distinguish between states which were already controlled by a party and those in which control shifted to the party.

As Figure 6.5 indicates, between 1856 and 1864, between 1894 and 1902, and between 1930 and 1934, partisan control of state governments shifted asymmetrically toward one or the other of the parties. For no other periods, with the exception of elections during the years surrounding 1920, is there evidence of so many shifts in control of such prolonged duration. Figure 6.5 also suggests the recession of the strength of the advantaged parties following realignments. In the elections surrounding 1876, Democrats gained control over an increased proportion of states, as a consequence primarily of the return of Democratic dominance in the South. In the years that followed, Democrats gained control over a still larger number of states, and the number of states characterized by divided partisan control also increased moderately (Figure 6.2). The early decades of the twentieth century followed a similar pattern. Republican control spread in the elections from 1894 through 1904 and was then interrupted by a briefer interlude of Democratic gains beginning at the end of the first decade of the century. In this case, however, Republican strength was regained in the elections surrounding 1920. A similar recovery of Republican strength following the New Deal realignment can also be observed in the 1940s and early 1950s. Thereafter, Republican strength again declined, and the proportion of states marked by divided partisan control also increased.

Thus, here again, it is possible to observe evidence of historical changes in patterns of control of state governments that

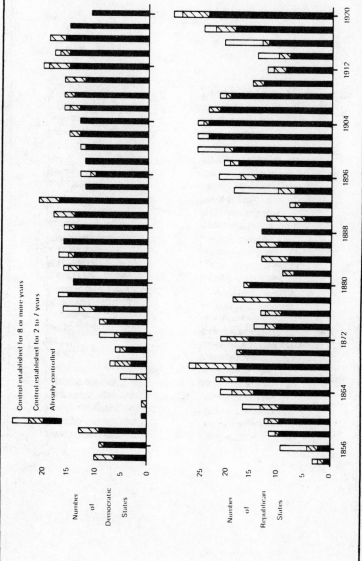

Figure 6.5: Frequency of Unified Party Control of State Governments, 1854-1974

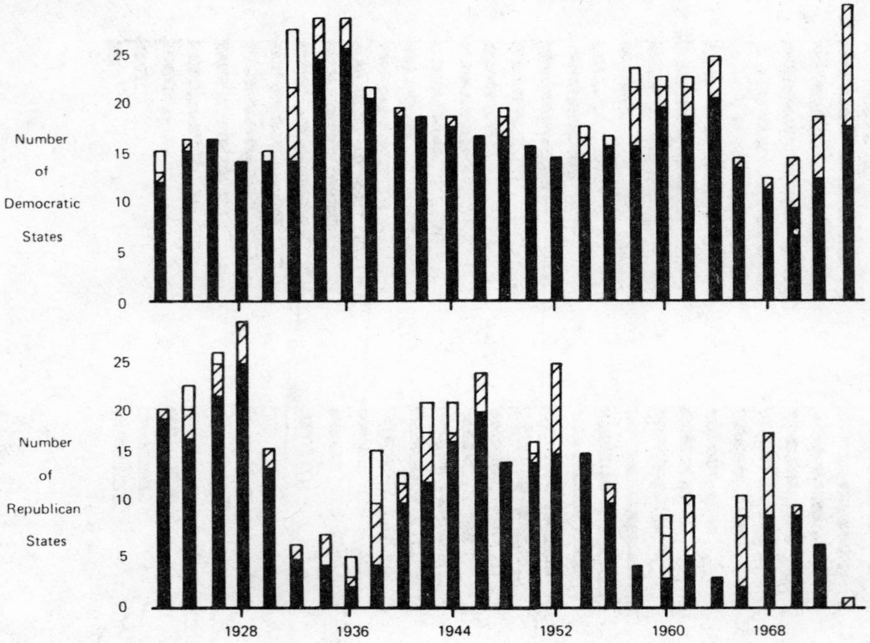

Figure 6.5: (Continued)

paralleled changes in partisan control of the national government. Yet qualifications must also be introduced. The 1920s stand out rather consistently as an exception to this summary of patterns of historical political change. That decade was not marked either by a decline in the degree of Republican control of state governments or by an increase in Democratic or divided control, as would be expected if this period were considered one of the "decay phases" of historical electoral sequences. Rather, Republican domination over state governments increased beginning in 1918 after the brief interruption of the progressive years. As was also indicated above, moreover, the same pattern of increased Republican strength can be observed where partisan control of the national government was concerned. Since indications of lasting electoral change favoring the Republicans can be observed in the elections of 1918 and 1920 (Chapter 3), it might be argued that the evidence suggests a Republican realignment at the beginning of the 1920s, a realignment restoring and strengthening the Republican dominance that had been temporarily interrupted by divisions within the party during the progressive years.

At the risk of appearing to "argue the data away," we have rejected this interpretation. As we saw, the decade of the 1920s was marked by increased minor party activity, by "minor realignments" in various states and regions, and by other indications of electoral instability.[5] Historians, moreover—relying, it is true, primarily upon impressionistic evidence—have not seen these years as marked by significant policy action on the part of government. Rather, they have seen this as a period of governmental inactivity and avoidance of pressing issues, of division within both parties, and of growing popular disenchantment with the parties, politics, and government. As we explore at greater length in the following chapter, limited indicators of elite behavior also suggest it is appropriate to see this decade as marked by the progressive deterioration of an earlier partisan alignment.

Even so, the 1920s, like other periods, introduce an element of complexity that precludes a simplistic view of the operation of the political system or an assumption of precise similarity between historical electoral sequences. It can be hypothesized, without demonstration, that the decade was marked by an increased incidence of short-term forces and by an increased susceptibility of the electorate and policy makers to those forces, but which, on balance, rather consistently worked against the Democrats and in favor of the Republicans. To push the argument further, it appears that, historically, processes contributing to the deterioration of partisan alignments disproportionately contributed to the weakening and deterioration of the minority party coalition, though without increasing the internal coherence and the capacity to govern of the majority party and without enhancing the loyalties of the electorate to that party. Such a view is at least superficially compatible with the evidence not only of the 1920s, but also of the 1840s and 1850s and of the years from the 1950s through the 1970s.

A second, in some respects more important qualification need only be noted in passing here. While relatively systematic patterns of change in partisan control of state governments can be noted across the years from the 1840s through the mid-1970s, it is also apparent that in many states, including northern as well as southern states, shifts in partisan control did not occur during any phase of these historical sequences. Realignments did work historically to shift the balance of partisan strength in various states. In terms of control of state governments, however, it is also clear that a large proportion of states were not affected significantly by historical realignments. Indeed, the data presented in Figure 6.5 could be more accurately described as suggesting massive stability rather than disruptive or frequent change.

PARTISAN CHANGE AND REALIGNMENT

An improved view of the nature and magnitude of historical partisan change can be gained by examining in greater detail periods that were marked by the largest incidence of change in partisan control of state governments, the major partisan realignments. A more complex assessment of change during these periods can be made by combining a measure of duration of partisan control with variations in patterns of change. This examination compares the form of control before and after each realignment and allows assessment of shifts toward the advantaged party that did not establish unified control. These comparisons must be limited to the 1890s and the 1930s. The emergence of the Republican party and the disappearance of the Whigs in the 1850s, combined with the suppression of the Democratic party in the South during Reconstruction, render the elections preceding and following the Civil War noncomparable for present purposes.

Table 6.1 provides a detailed examination of the nature of partisan change during the realignments of the 1890s and the 1930s by taking into account the partisan complexion of the state both before and after the realignment. For purposes of the examination, the elections of 1896 and 1932 are treated as the realigning elections of the periods, and arbitrary periods of four and eight years following these elections are used to classify states as characterized by "mixed" or "unified" partisan control.[6] Obviously, the results displayed in the table would be different if another election—or, perhaps, a bloc of elections—was selected as the point of realignment for each realignment era, or if periods other than four and eight years were employed. The differences, however, would not be great, and the impression of limited change conveyed by the table would remain.

Regardless of the minor differences between the four- and eight-year coding in Table 6.1, it is obvious that in neither realignment did many states shift from unified control by one party to unified control by the other. Using the less demanding criterion of four years, only three states shifted from united Democratic control to united Republican control around the election of 1896, and only seven shifted from Republican to Democratic control around 1932.[7] Lasting gains in terms of united partisan control during these realignments came about primarily as states already under divided partisan control shifted

TABLE 6.1   Patterns of Change in Unified Control of States Before and
After 1896 and 1932[a]

Patterns of Change in Unified Control of States	1896		1932	
	8-year	4-year	8-year	4-year
Became Democratic				
Republican to Democratic	--	--	4%	19%
"Mixed" to Democratic	--	--	10	13
Became "Mixed"				
Democratic to "Mixed"	2%	2%	--	--
Republican to "Mixed"	--	5	31	27
Became Republican				
"Mixed" to Republican	39	34	--	--
Democratic to Republican	--	7	--	--
"Stable"				
Democratic to Democratic	30	30	27	29
"Mixed" to "Mixed"	20	7	21	4
Republican to Republican	9	16	6	8
Number of States	44	44	48	48

[a]The rules for coding unified control before and after 1896 and 1932 are in footnote 7.

to united partisan control by the advantaged party. Taken in total, moreover, the table suggests that these realignments brought about lasting change in partisan control in only a minority of the states, and even in some of these, change was relatively transitory.

There were also differences in the patterns of change during these two realignments. Prior to 1896, about one-half of the states (44% by the four-year standard, 54% by the eight-year) were characterized by divided partisan control; two-thirds of these states shifted to united Republican control. Prior to the 1930s, about one-third of the states (27% by the four-year standard and 36% by the eight-year) were under divided control, and a smaller proportion became Democratic. To look at Table 6.1 in another way, very few states emerged from the 1896 realignment with divided control, not more than 20% by either criterion. After 1932, on the other hand, a much larger proportion were marked by divided control, one-third by the four-year standard and one-half by the eight-year.

Almost certainly, the degree of partisan competition affected the impact of electoral change upon patterns of partisan control of state governments. Intensive partisan competition prior to 1896 was reflected in the large number of states marked by divided partisan control of the elective agencies of government and in the relatively smaller partisan majorities in state legislative houses (see Figure 6.4). These competitive conditions worked to amplify the effects of electoral change and resulted in the shift of a substantial number of states to united Republican control. The less competitive conditions of the 1920s were reflected in both the lower incidence of divided partisan control of state governments and in the greater incidence of large partisan majorities in state legislatures. Apparently, the one-sided Republican dominance of the 1920s, as well as the increasing malapportionment of state legislatures, worked to dampen the effects of major electoral change in 1932 upon patterns of control of state governments. In consequence, rather than shifting fully into the Democratic camp, a substantial number of states shifted from united Republican to divided control.

Taken in total, the data suggest the limited impact of the two national realignments upon patterns of partisan control of state governments. In a substantial number of states, partisan control of state governments did not change. We can surmise that in these states, partisan delegations in legislatures grew or declined and gubernatorial majorities of the popular vote shrank or increased but without change in partisan dominance. Two other, more disruptive, patterns of change also emerged. In the first, the state governments controlled by the nationally disadvantaged party were disrupted by the loss of one or another elective institution, though without establishment of united and durable control by the opposite party. In the second, the national realignment was associated with electoral forces that produced lasting and united control by the advantaged party. Either effect, it may be surmised, was of potential significance for policy-making and the conduct of government. The first pattern, which probably best describes the Civil War and New Deal, obviously constituted a more limited opportunity for the advantaged party to undertake new policy initiatives at the state level. Since it is these realignments that are generally considered the most successful in policy innovation, we might suppose that divided control of state governments allowed the imposition of federal policy on the states. The second pattern, which was more characteristic of the realignment of the 1890s, constituted a greater opportunity for the advantaged party to undertake new directions in policy-making and government. However, the Republican gains doubtless led to declining interference by states in business matters and contributed to the national policy of laissez faire. Finally, it is clear that the partisan effects of historical partisan realignments varied from state to state and indeed from one realignment to another.

INTERSYSTEMIC ASSOCIATIONS

We have argued that the major partisan realignments of the Civil War years, the latter 1890s, and the 1930s worked to "articulate" the nation in partisan terms. These periods were marked by relatively pervasive unidirectional shifts toward one or the other of the parties at the electoral level and in terms of the executive and legislative agencies of state and national governments. It is true that these shifts were neither entirely pervasive nor completely unidirectional. In each of these periods, some regions, states, or smaller areas either did not realign or shifted in a partisan direction opposite to the national tide. Even so, these major realignments gave to one party in each case control over the presidency and the Congress and over executive and legislative bodies in an increased proportion of the states.

In contrast, the 1840s and 1850s, the period from the 1870s through the early 1890s, the second and third decades of the twentieth century, and the years from the 1950s through the first half of the 1970s were characterized by increased partisan "disarticulation." These periods, the evidence suggests, were marked by increased instability. Here again, the evidence is by no means entirely consistent. The latter decades of the nineteenth century stand out as a period of immense electoral stability, at least in terms of the measurement techniques we have used, and the decade of the 1920s was not marked by an increased incidence of divided control of government or by increased control by the minority Democratic party. On the other hand, both periods witnessed increased minor party activity; evidence of electoral instability can be observed in the 1920s, and the latter decades of the nineteenth century were characterized by the erosion of the strength of the Republican party and by divided and shifting control of government.

We have argued that the increased partisan articulation characteristic of major realignment periods can be seen as related to the greater decisiveness in public policy-making and implementation that historians have attributed to these periods. On the other hand, the increased "disarticulation" of other periods has been seen as working, along with other factors, to frustrate policy initiative and innovation and concerted policy action.

It is obvious that neither the existence of stable and reliable partisan majorities within the electorate nor unified partisan control of the elective agencies of government guarantees decisive, dynamic, or concerted policy-making or implementation. Parties are often divided; historically, American parties have never been completely national organizations or monolithic entities, and policy initiative can be blocked and frustrated by the courts and state and national bureaucracies. On the other hand, if we assume that political parties are—or can be, and in some historical cases have been—policy coordinating agencies, then we can also argue that conditions of partisan articulation make effective and concerted national policy action possible and more likely. Indeed, in view of the multilayered nature of American government, the sharing of power at all levels and the possibility at all levels of both policy initiation and policy veto, it can be argued that political parties are necessary mechanisms for the formation, enactment, and implementation of concerted and coherent public policy. Yet the evidence can be taken as suggesting that only at times of national crises are the parties able to perform that function.

The evidence marshalled in this and the preceding chapters leads almost inescapably to the conclusion that the American political system has been characterized by major inertia. Even under the conditions of tension and crisis during realignment eras, electoral change was not great. Certainly, electoral change during these periods did not involve the massive reshuffling of the electorate that the literature sometimes suggests. Decreases in electoral stability can be observed in other periods, but these changes must also be seen in relative terms. In fact, the primary generalization that emerges would comment upon the durability of partisan alignments.

Patterns of control of state government particularly suggest a similar generalization. The relatively limited change in these patterns during realignment periods and the advantage enjoyed by the parties in many states in terms of the massive size of legislative majorities suggest a further inertial factor. Clearly, truly large-scale change has been required to shift the balance of partisan strength in most of the states. Historically, it appears, conditions approaching national crisis have been required to bring about even those modest shifts.

NOTES

1. Procedures followed in calculating the "expected vote" are described in Chapter 3 above. Because of variations in gubernatorial terms, lasting change has been operationalized for these purposes in terms of twelve-year spans rather than as a fixed number of elections, as in the case of Congress and the presidency.

2. The data on the partisan composition of state legislatures in historical depth from before the Civil War to the present were compiled by Walter Dean Burnham and are available from the Inter-university Consortium for Political and Social Research. Information bearing upon the incidence of unified partisan control of the legislatures and governors' offices in all states can be presented in relatively straightforward fashion. Even here, however, difficulties are encountered because of variations in the timing of elections and in the length of terms of office. Never have a majority of the states held elections at the same time for terms of equal length. During the last century, states have been characterized by one-, two-, three-, and four-year terms, and some gubernatorial and legislative elections have been held each year. In Figure

6.2 and elsewhere in this chapter, scores for each state are calculated for two-year periods even though the timing of elections and the terms of office have varied widely.

3. Since the 1850s, over two-thirds of the states have been marked by at least one period of fourteen or more years of unified control of legislative and gubernatorial offices by one of the parties. Very few states—only eight—have been marked by periods of unified partisan control by both the Democratic and Republican parties for as long as eight years.

4. The selection of periods of two or more years and eight or more years is, of course, arbitrary.

5. One additional piece of evidence is the reduced correlation between presidential and gubernatorial voting during the 1920s reported by Paul Allen Beck, "The Electoral Cycle and Patterns of American Politics," *British Journal of Political Science* 9 (April 1979), p. 133.

6. In order to determine the pattern of change or stability for each state, it is necessary to code the years immediately before and after each realignment as unified or mixed control. In order to allow for state differences in the timing of elections and the duration of realigning changes, a year on either side of the realignment was selected as an anchoring point for the coding of unified control before and after each realignment. These years were 1890, 1896, 1926, and 1934. A state was coded as having unified control before or after a realignment if it was under unified control for a continuous period of four years (or eight years) including the appropriate anchor year. All other patterns were coded as mixed control. For example, in coding control of states before and after the realignment of 1896, the four-year codes for these hypothetical states would be:

	1888	1890	1892	1894	1896	1898	1900	Scored
State A	Dem	Dem	Dem	Mix	Rep	Rep	Rep	Dem to Rep
State B	Mix	Dem	Dem	Mix	Mix	Rep	Rep	Dem to Mix
State C	Mix	Dem	Mix	Rep	Rep	Mix	Mix	Mix to Rep

7. It is extremely rare to find a state that has switched abruptly from eight or more years of unified control by one party to eight or more by a second. Between the 1850s and the present, it has happened only once. In 1932, the state of Washington established eight years of Democratic control after eight years of Republican control. Three other states shifted control with only a brief gap, South Carolina around 1876, West Virginia around 1930, and California around 1956. From all the remaining states, only two others, Delaware and Louisiana, have at any time in their history had as much as eight consecutive years of unified control by more than one party.

Chapter 7

CONGRESS AND PARTISAN CHANGE

In certain elections—those identified as components of partisan realignments—lasting electoral change worked to accord to one or the other of the parties a marked degree of dominance over the national political system. The perspective developed in Chapter 1 suggests a variety of expectations concerning the impact of the electoral forces and political circumstances of these periods upon partisan elites. The most obvious impact was among officeholders. The shifts in partisan dominance examined in Chapters 5 and 6 above clearly indicate that substantial change in the occupancy of elective offices occurred during historical realignments. We would also surmise, moreover, that change in the occupancy of public office extended to the local level, to the bureaucracy and other appointive offices, and included leadership roles outside the structure of formal governmental officeholding.

The realignment perspective leads, as well, to expectations of change in the behavior and attitudes of partisan elites, whether as a consequence of the entry of newcomers into office and other leadership roles, of shifts in the orientation of incumbents who survived electoral realignment, or both. Change in the issue content of politics and narrowing of the range of politically salient issues could be expected along with greater agreement, consensus, and singleness of purpose among partisan leaders. We would also expect political leaders inside and outside of government to align themselves more clearly and dramatically around the issues that developed during realignments, to express their views with increased intensity and reduced ambiguity, and to perceive more clearly political divisions within the mass public, if only because of the sharpened popular concerns and divisions provoked by crisis. Presumably, the primary agents for conveying this increased clarity of political cleavages were the political parties. The parties naturally would also become victims and beneficiaries of the heightened affect surrounding cleavages during realignments.

At other periods, when alignments were beginning to decay, electoral shifts can be taken as indications of the presence of new or resurgent political issues and forces which cut across prevailing partisan alignments and which worked to weaken partisan control, hence to reduce the effectiveness of the parties as governing and policy-making mechanisms. Presumably during these decay periods, political issues and forces would work to lessen the unity and singleness of purpose of partisan elites. Political leaders would be free of a single, dominant set of symbols; leaders and followers would respond to more varied and cross-cutting issues; and many leaders and followers would experience periods of political calm or apathy.

Other views of the political process would lead to different, even contrary, expectations. If we viewed constituency pressures, demands of interest groups, and considerations of party organization as relatively constant and irresistible forces at work on all political leaders, then we would expect no uniform shifts in behavior and attitudes, changes in issue orientations, or in unity and agreement regardless of realignment sequences. Indeed, the "overlarge" majorities characteristic of dominant parties during realignments, and the probable greater diversity of those majorities, might lead to expectations of greater disunity and lack of agreement rather than increased unity.

It is obviously impossible to measure on a comprehensive scale the behavior and attitudes of political leaders during historical eras. It is possible, however, to examine in relatively satisfactory fashion one segment of that elite, the members of the United States Congress. The voting behavior of members of Congress ought to provide a good testing ground for propositions about partisan elites in general. Congressional voting is not only a highly visible political act, but it is accompanied by strong expectations on the part of the public and of elites that on salient issues, voting will reflect policy goals based on constituency preferences and reflected in campaign commitments.

The basic expectations about congressional behavior are straightforward enough. *First,* accompanying the electoral shifts marking realignments, there would be a high degree of turnover among members of Congress as incumbent members of one party were replaced by newcomers of another party. High turnover rates, therefore, would work disproportionately to the advantage of one of the parties. High turnover rates would be followed by relatively greater stability in the composition of the legislature for some years. Increase followed by decrease in congressional turnover would occur independently of any long-term trends toward higher or lower turnover rates. Furthermore, an increase in turnover during realignments would be in addition to turnover caused by institutional changes such as reapportionment. During decay phases, turnover would be more erratic and occasionally to the benefit of one party and then the other.

Second, we would expect the party blocs in Congress to behave in more distinctively dissimilar ways immediately following realignment. The realignment issues would work to polarize the parties and lead to dissimilar voting behavior for at least a few years. In other periods, more varied issues and diffuse attention to problems would lead the parties to become more similar in voting behavior and incidentally would contribute to decline in agreement on major concerns among members of the same party.

At first glance, a *third* expectation also seems to follow straightforwardly from the realignment perspective. During the years of unified control of government following realignments, in comparison with decay phases, we might expect party cohesion to be high, especially within the ranks of the advantaged party. The forces outside Congress that produced electoral change and brought about unified control of government could be seen as likely to influence both old and new members of the advantaged party to unite around a legislative program related to the issues of the realignment. In this view, unity and agreement in Congress on goals and programs would be reflected by high levels of partisan cohesion in voting behavior.

As will be seen, this expectation is not supported by the data of roll call voting. It is not, however, an expectation that follows necessarily from the realignment perspective. We can surmise that the large majorities enjoyed by the dominant parties during realignments tended to be diverse in constituency orientation and bases. Because of the size of these majorities, we can also surmise, lapses from strict party discipline could be more readily tolerated than in the case of smaller majorities without jeopardizing party goals and programs. Put differently, the capacity of a larger partisan majority to act effectively in policy terms is less dependent upon rigorous party discipline.

This general pattern of expectation concerns both the immediate results of electoral forces—that is, the determination of winners and losers—and the more indirect effects of political forces, such as perceived constituency pressures and demands. Obviously, electoral change is directly associated with control of the House of Representatives and the Senate, especially after 1912, as well as with turnover in membership. The two forms of electoral change discussed in preceding chapters, across-the-board change and differential change, do not have the same implications for the partisan composition of Congress. Since across-the-board change disproportionately benefits one party and hurts the other, it involves more potential for enhancing party control and producing large majorities than does differential electoral change. Moreover, in the short run, it does not matter whether these shifts are lasting or not. A high rate of turnover that provides an advantage to one party creates an opportunity for that party to take effective policy action; how lasting the advantage is depends to a considerable degree on what is done with the opportunity.

In this chapter, membership turnover and voting behavior in both the Senate and the House of Representatives are examined. For some aspects of the investigation, we are dependent on available scholarship which provides more information on the House than the Senate. Of course, the late introduction of popular election of senators limits the direct influence of electoral forces on the composition of that chamber to the period since 1912. Staggered terms further complicate analysis of the Senate, although the result should usually be no more than temporal diffusion of the impact of realignment forces. In a comprehensive survey of Congress, it is obviously necessary to include analysis of the Senate, regardless of the relative neglect of that body in earlier research. Consideration of the Senate has the further utility of providing rudimentary indications of the effect of institutional differences between the two chambers.

Many scholars have called attention to a connection between congressional behavior and significant policy departures during realignment periods, although often these observations, as in our case, have been based on impressionistic evidence.[1] At a minimum, many scholars would probably agree that realignment years were marked by increased coherence of policy purpose and action. It would be a major undertaking, however, to assess rigorously the variations in policy patterns in Congress over a century and a half or more, and no attempt has been made here to measure the content of public policy or systematically to assess shifts in policy direction associated with partisan realignments.

MEMBERSHIP CHANGE

Obviously, when a party establishes a large margin of control in either the House or Senate, a substantial change in member-

ship is required. The data displayed in Chapter 5 clearly show
that realignment eras were characterized by series of fairly
one-sided congressional elections which resulted in one-sided
partisan domination of both the Senate and the House. During
decay phases, there were sometimes congressional landslides in
favor of one or the other of the parties. Only the period from
the late 1950s through the late 1970s stands out as an equivalent period of sustained, one-sided control of Congress by one
party. During that period, of course, sustained Democratic
control of Congress was not paralleled by consistent control of
the presidency.

The primary question for the present analysis concerns the
manner in which electoral change was reflected in membership
turnover rates. To what extent did realigning elections bring
large numbers of new members to Congress, and were realigning
elections followed by relative stability in Senate and House
membership? Such realignment variations should be independent of the long-run trend toward lower membership turnover
in Congress that has marked well over a century of American
history.[2] The literature on career patterns and political motiva-
tion of congressmen offers explanations for lower voluntary
turnover in recent decades, and studies of redistricting and
incumbency factors suggest reasons for greater safety in congressional seats over the years.[3] These factors do not, however,
preclude the periodic appearance of realignment effects.

Membership turnover has been calculated in two ways in the
recent literature.[4] For our purposes, it is desirable to give the
uncorrected proportion of first termers, which reflects the number of nonincumbent representatives who were elected to each
Congress without regard for whether they occupied an existing
seat or a new seat created through reapportionment and regardless of prior service in Congress. The simple index of all first
termers, which we will use subsequently, is shown in Figure 7.1.
The "percentage replacement" index, which corrects for newcomers resulting from reapportionment, was also calculated.
The differences between the two indexes are minor for our
purposes, since they indicate that no significant cases of high

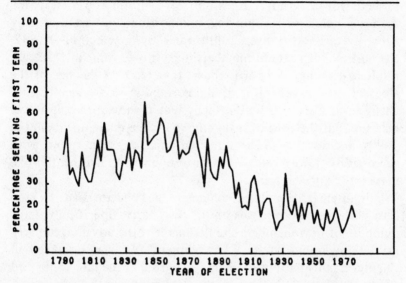

SOURCE: Guide to U.S. Elections (Washington, Congressional Quarterly, Inc., 1975).

Figure 7.1: Percentage of First-Term Representatives, 1790-1976

turnover were merely a result of adding seats to the House through reapportionment. Hence, we have displayed only the index of first termers.

The data in Figure 7.1, show that each of the three historical partisan realignments was characterized by a high rate of turn-over in comparison with immediately preceding and following elections. Other elections also produced high rates of member-ship turnover. As noted above, the congressional elections of 1894 involved a more massive shift in House membership than did those of 1896. There were also, as the figure indicates, high levels of membership change in the House in various elections of the nineteenth century not usually considered as realigning, most notably in 1816, 1842, 1874, and 1882. These elections, however, were not followed by prolonged periods of dominance by the advantaged party. Apparently, short-term forces, such as the supposed voter reaction to a congressional pay increase prior to 1816 or the impact of the financial panic of 1873, pushed House turnover rates above the norm for these years. Although elections following reapportionment were usually above average in turnover, as illustrated by the election of 1882, the all-time high rate of membership turnover came in 1842 as a result of the one reapportionment that reduced the size of the House.[5] But in general, a declining trend in House membership change was disrupted by unusually high turnover rates, however measured, at the time of realignments. While realignments in the 1890s and in the 1930s reflected this long-term trend with successively lower rates of turnover, each realignment broke markedly from the trend.

Our interest in partisan congressional behavior leads to concern with the turnover patterns of each party. Specifically, large numbers of new members should augment the advantaged party at the beginning of each realignment. As was discussed in Chapter 5, this pattern of change occurred in the late 1850s and 1860s, in the 1890s, and in the 1930s, when the advantaged parties added large numbers of new members to their congressional contingents. The simple evidence presented in Chapter 5 shows changes in control of Congress and in the size of majorities. Of necessity, the advantaged parties gained more than they lost as majorities were attained. In subsequent elections, the newly dominant parties tended to lose strength, though without losing their majorities. Even in the elections of 1896, the Republicans lost ground in the House to the Democrats, because, it might be said, they had won so overwhelmingly in 1894. There were in 1896 more Democratic freshmen than Republican, and over three times as many Republican incumbents as Democrats lost in an election marking the beginning of fourteen years of Republican control of both Houses of Congress and the presidency.

Data bearing on the party affiliation of first termers, as percentages of the entire House, are given in Figure 7.2. These data show clearly that in major realignments, there were extremely one-sided gains for the advantaged parties, but the partisan imbalance in newly elected members was not lasting. Newly elected members in 1932 were almost entirely Demo-

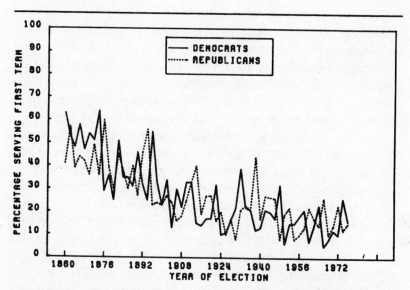

SOURCE: Guide to U.S. Elections (Washington, Congressional Quarterly, Inc., 1975).

Figure 7.2: Percentage of First-Term Democratic and Republican Representatives, 1860-1976

crats, and the large membership turnover in 1894 was even more overwhelmingly Republican. In 1860 and the two following elections, the Republicans also enjoyed a considerable advantage. In each case, however, after these initial elections, the new majority party lost the advantage in change in House membership, and turnover rates became more evenly balanced between the parties, or even tipped to the advantage of the opposition. The extreme partisan advantages in House membership change during realignments were not characteristic of other periods. During nonrealignment eras, turnover rates tended to be lower, more evenly balanced between the parties, and frequent shifts in partisan advantage worked to the benefit of first one party and then the other. This pattern can be taken as a further aspect of the decay of partisan alignments. In these years, there were no occasions when one party sustained the favorable turnover rates required to establish firm control of the House.

It is more difficult to determine the number of incumbents who were forced to withdraw as a result of the political forces associated with realignments or to assess the extent to which realigning elections led to unusually large numbers of electoral defeats. Considering only outright electoral defeat in every twelfth year from 1872 to 1956, King and Seligman demonstrate a considerably higher rate of defeats in 1896 and 1932 than in other elections considered.[6] Electoral defeat as a source of turnover became all the more important in the twentieth century when legislative career patterns changed, when the apparent electoral advantages of incumbency became more pronounced, and as the incidence of House first termers declined.[7]

Electoral vulnerability did not extend to the three or four representatives in top leadership positions of the House. During the past century, these individuals were rarely defeated in general elections (only one Democrat and one Republican in the entire period) or even opposed for renomination.[8] It is likely that chairmen of major committees were also relatively invulnerable to defeat due to realigning electoral change or other constituency-based disruptions, but the overall composition of committees is another matter. Committee composition, even major committee composition, was disrupted during realignments as Brady has shown.[9] The level of turnover in committees was not necessarily higher during the realignments, but shifts in partisan control of the House altered committee composition with likely policy consequences.

It appears, then, that the electoral disruptions that marked partisan realignments were translated quite directly into change in the membership of the House of Representatives. But what of the Senate? It was obviously protected from the immediate impact of electoral change by staggered terms and, until 1914, by indirect election. We know, of course, that control of the Senate was established by the advantaged party during each historical realignment, and we would expect the same basic pattern of turnover as in the case of the House, only spread over a longer period.

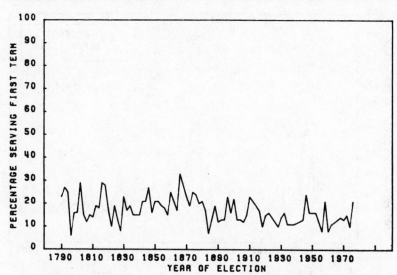

SOURCE: **Guide to U.S. Elections** (Washington, Congressional Quarterly, Inc., 1975).

Figure 7.3: Percentage of First-Term Senators, 1790-1976

The incidence of membership turnover in the Senate and the party affiliation of first-term senators are shown in Figures 7.3. and 7.4. Aggregate turnover rates were quite similar for the entire period and were so constrained by the combination of staggered terms and the accidents of retirement that little in the way of realignment effect can be observed. On the other hand, the party advantage in membership turnover appears, as expected. The historical realignment eras were marked by a series of elections with repeated, relatively one-sided partisan distributions of new members favoring the advantaged party. During and following the Civil War, the Republicans enjoyed the advantage in terms of new members. Between 1894 and 1904, Republicans, again, were the major gainers in all elections except 1896, and from 1930 to 1936, new senators were largely Democratic.

Obviously, during realignments there was less immediate impact on the composition of the Senate. This pattern appears,

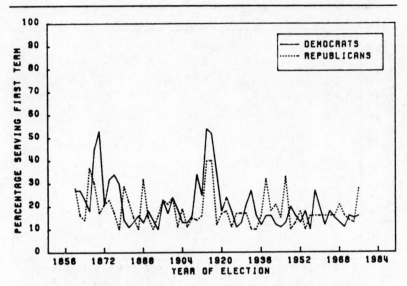

SOURCE: Guide to U.S. Elections (Washington, Congressional Quarterly, Inc., 1975).

Figure 7.4: Percentage of First-Term Democratic and Republican Senators, 1860-1976

however, to have involved only a systematic delay and temporal spreading of the impact of new electoral forces. The institutional differences between the House and Senate are best described as the relative invulnerability of the Senate to temporary electoral change, as the stable nature of the data series presented in Figure 7.3 suggests. It is also noteworthy that in each partisan realignment, the advantaged party had already gained a substantial edge in the Senate by winning new seats before gaining the presidency.

PARTY VOTING IN CONGRESS

The changing composition of the Senate and the House of Representatives is comparatively easy to chart. It is much more difficult to describe significant patterns of partisan behavior in these legislative bodies or to assess the policy implications of that behavior. The roll call votes cast by members of legislative bodies are frequently employed by analysts for these purposes. Roll call voting behavior, of course, is by no means an infallible guide to all aspects of the attitudes and activities of members of Congress—much less to those of political elites more generally—and, obviously, roll call votes provide little indication of decisions reached in the committees, the caucuses, the cloakrooms, and the other arenas of congressional decision-making. On the other hand, the data of congressional voting behavior constitute the most simple, consistent, and substantial resource available for systematic examination of the role of political parties in historical policy-making.

In considering the voting behavior of the congressional parties during realignment periods in comparison with decay phases, our expectations as to patterns of voting behavior in the House and Senate are twofold. In the first place, we expect that the two parties were more distinctly dissimilar in voting behavior in Congress early in realignment eras and tended to become more similar during the later years of each such era. In other words, we anticipate that Congress was more sharply polarized in partisan terms early in realignment eras as the parties took opposing positions on the issues of the day. Our second set of expectations concerns fluctuations in the unity and cohesion of the congressional parties in relation to the realignment cycle. As suggested above, however, and as discussed more fully below, these latter expectations are not borne out.

In examining congressional voting behavior, it is obviously important to distinguish between patterns of change associated with realignment sequences as opposed to those associated with other forces at work in the political system. Congressional voting behavior has been marked by gradual, long-term change during the past century or more.[10] Hence, it is particularly necessary to separate shorter-term changes in partisan unity and polarization from longer-term trends. The expected patterns of voting behavior should appear in both the House and the Senate, although differences in timing can be anticipated where the latter body is concerned.

Previous studies of Congress—such as those of Lowell, Turner, and MacRae—have employed techniques essentially similar to those used here. These studies, however, have focused upon relatively limited sets of Congresses and upon the House of Representatives only. A recent study by Clubb and Traugott examines the House during all Congresses from 1861 through 1974.[11] Their analysis, extended here to include the Senate, permits more comprehensive examination of partisan dissimilarity and cohesion during three historical realignment periods.

PARTISAN POLARIZATION

It is essential initially to assess the pattern of coincidence between the occurrence of realigning electoral change, on the one hand, and variations in dissimilarity (or cleavage) between the blocs of party members in Congress, on the other. For this purpose, the familiar index of unlikeness will be used as an indicator of dissimilarity. This index affords a partial means to assess the degree to which the two parties voted in opposition to each other. The index ranges from 100 (indicating perfect polarization, with all voting members of one party voting together on one side of an issue and in opposition to all members of the other party) to 0 (indicating no difference in the voting by members of each party on an issue). The index was computed for each record vote in the Senate and the House of Representatives in each Congress from the Thirty-seventh (elected in 1860) through the Ninety-fifth (elected in 1976) and averaged to create a single score for each chamber and Congress.[12] On the basis of the formulation and findings discussed above, the index can be expected to fluctuate in association with the realignment cycle. High levels can be expected at the time of partisan realignment and declining levels during the years that follow until the next realignment when higher levels should again appear.

Party voting in the House of Representatives can be examined by drawing upon and extending the earlier work of Clubb and Traugott. A similar examination of Senate voting, presented here for the first time, follows. Party unlikeness scores for the

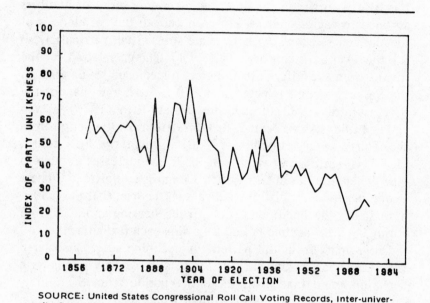

SOURCE: United States Congressional Roll Call Voting Records, Inter-university Consortium for Political and Social Research.

Figure 7.5: Index of Party Unlikeness for the House of Representatives, 1860-1976

House for the period from 1861 through 1978 are displayed in Figure 7.5. Impressionistically, the scores suggest a pattern of decline associated with each realignment sequence. The scores were relatively high at the beginning of each sequence and declined irregularly during the years that followed. In other words, at the beginning of each period, the House parties tended to vote in opposition to each other more frequently; during the following years, the degree of opposition between the parties tended to decline. The pattern appears most strongly for the two twentieth-century periods and weakest for the years following the Civil War realignment. The uneven pattern in the latter period appears, however, to be at least in part a reflection of the extreme score for the Fifty-first Congress (1889-1891).

These impressions can be systematically confirmed by correlating the unlikeness scores for each Congress with time—or in this case, a surrogate for time, the ascending series of numbers assigned to each Congress. For each period, the correlations of the unlikeness scores with time are substantial, particularly so for the twentieth century (Table 7.1). The correlation for the period from the Fifty-fifth Congress (elected in 1896) through the Seventy-second (elected in 1930) is -.82, and that for the Seventy-third (1932 through the Ninety-fifth (1976) is even higher (-.88). As suspected, the correlation for the period from the Thirty-seventh Congress (1860) through the Fifty-fourth (1894) is significantly weaker at -.37, but increases notably to -.63 when the deviant Fifty-first Congress is omitted.[13] These strong negative correlations indicate, of course, that the unlikeness scores declined, and the parties became more alike in voting behavior as time passed following each realignment.

Quite apart from the pattern of declining scores associated with each realignment era, the series is marked by a long-term declining trend that spans the entire period from the Thirty-seventh through the Seventy-fourth Congress. The correlation with time for the entire period is -.69, with a fairly gentle regression slope (b = -.53). Since the calculations are based upon Congresses rather than individual years or sessions, the regression coefficient indicates that the party unlikeness scores for the House dropped by an average of about five points during each twenty years of the entire period. Within this long-term trend, however, fluctuations associated with the realignment eras are apparent. As they should be, given expectations outlined above, the regression slopes within each period are steeper than the long-term trend, particularly so from 1897 through 1933 (b = -2.02) and from 1933 through 1978 (b = -1.31). In other words, during the two most recent realignment eras, the decline in unlikeness scores was about twenty points every twenty years after 1897 and fifteen points every twenty years after 1933. Obviously, these within era changes were much greater than the longer trend. The gentle slope for the period from 1861 to 1897 (b = -.56) increases significantly (-.83) with the omission of the Fifty-first Congress. Even during this from 1897 through 1978, the partial regression coefficients for

TABLE 7.1a   Regression of Index of Party Unlikeness on Congress
             Number for the House of Representatives, 1861–1978

	Intercept (a)	Regression Coefficient (b)	Correlation Coefficient (r)	Coefficient of Determination (r^2)
1861–1896	59	–.56	–.37	.14
1897–1932	71	–2.02	–.82	.67
1933–1978	52	–1.31	–.88	.77

TABLE 7.1b   Regression of Index of Party Unlikeness on Congress
             Number and Temporal Distance from Realignments for
             the House of Representatives, 1861–1974

	Regression Coefficient (b)	Correlation Coefficient (r)	Coefficient of Determination (r^2)
Congress Number, 1861–1978	–.57	–.74	.54
Distance from Realignment, 1861–1978	–1.50	–.69	.48

period, the decline in party unlikeness was about eight points
every twenty years once the Fifty-first Congress is omitted.

The independence of the two patterns, their relative strength,
and their combined statistical relationship to the unlikeness
series can be assessed more precisely by regressing the unlikeness scores jointly on time and on a variable contrived to
measure the temporal distance of each Congress from the most
recent realignment.[14] Because of the differences observed
above, the analysis is carried out both for the entire period and
for the period from 1897 through 1978. The results of the two
multiple regressions are reported in Table 7.2. As can be seen,
both the long-term trend and the contrived realignment variable
contribute to statistical explanation of the series of partisan
unlikeness scores. For both the entire period and the subperiod

TABLE 7.2   Multiple Regression of Index of Party Unlikeness on
            Congress Number and Temporal Distance from
            Realignments for the House of Representatives,
            1861–1978

	Standardized Regression Coefficient (Congress Number)	Standardized Regression Coefficient (Distance from Realignment)	Coefficient of Multiple Correlation	Coefficient of Multiple Determination
1861–1978	−.40	−.43	.82	.68
1897–1978	−.63	−.41	.88	.78

from 1897 through 1978, the partial regression coefficients for the long-term trend are generally similar (b = −.40 and −.63 for the two periods respectively) with those associated with realignment (b = −.43 and −.41). Both, however, are strong and the realignment effect is independent of the longer-term trend.

Once again, the analysis suggests differences between the latter nineteenth century and twentieth century. Time and the realignment variable in combination provide a slightly better explanation for change in the unlikeness series after 1897 (R = .88) than for the entire period (R = .82). Taken in combination, moreover, and as signified by the coefficients of multiple correlation, the two variables provide a more powerful explanation of the series than either variable taken separately.[15]

The data suggest, then, that partisan voting in the House since 1861, at least as measured by the index of party unlikeness, has been characterized by long-term decline and by cyclical fluctuations associated with partisan realignments. In general, the level of partisan voting was highest during Congresses early in realignment periods and tended to decline during the years that followed until there was a resurgence of party voting associated with the next realignment. Both long-term decline in party voting and cyclical fluctuations in association with partisan realignments were most pronounced after 1897, and the period from 1861 to the mid-1890s stand out as dissimilar.

During this earlier period, decline in partisan voting was substantially more moderate and irregular.

These dissimilarities are, of course, in keeping with the view of the latter nineteenth century as characterized by a strong and maturing party system and the twentieth century as marked by progressive partisan deterioration. Following the realignment of the 1860s, the decline in partisan polarization in the House, it appears, was inhibited by the stronger partisan institutions and structures of the latter decades of the nineteenth century and by the emotion-laden issues and cleavages resulting from the traumas of Civil War and Reconstruction. On the other hand, the progressively weakening partisan institutions and structures of the twentieth century might be seen as contributing to the more precipitous decline in polarization following the realignments of the 1890s and the 1930s.

It appears obvious, at least on first consideration, that Senate voting during these years should have followed patterns similar to those observed in the House of Representatives. If major electoral realignments worked to produce partisan polarization in the House, then similar effects could be expected in the Senate. The institutional differences between the two chambers suggest, of course, the need for some modification of these expectations. The length and staggered nature of the senatorial term could be expected to dampen the effects of partisan realignment and, to an even greater extent, the effects of temporary electoral change. Since all senators do not stand for election at the same time, the effects of the political forces of realignments or of other major, but short-term electoral forces would be somewhat diffused and their impact upon senatorial voting lessened. Of greater importance, perhaps, the mode of indirect election of the Senate by state legislators prior to 1914 may have worked to tie senators more closely to partisan organizations than was true of members of the House. In the Senate, in other words, party connections and dependence in the nineteenth century might be seen as stronger than in the case of the House. Viewed in these terms, comparison of partisan voting patterns in the Senate with those of the House

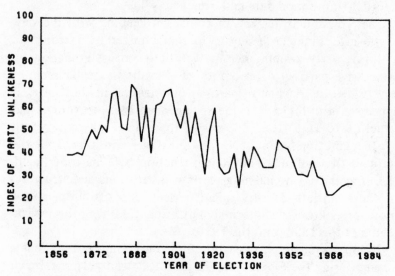

SOURCE: United States Congressional Roll Call Voting Records, Inter-university Consortium for Political and Social Research.

Figure 7.6: Index of Party Unlikeness for the Senate, 1860-1976

provides a means to gain some indications of the consequences both of institutional differences and of processes at work in the partisan system since the 1860s.

The series of unlikeness scores for the Senate, calculated for the same period and in the same fashion as for the House of Representatives, is marked by numerous irregularities (Figure 7.6). As in the case of the House, cursory examination of the series gives an impression of long-term decline in partisan unlikeness across the entire period. Closer inspection suggests a curvilinear pattern. The scores for the 1860s are low and rise irregularly across the latter decades of the century to reach a high point during the years surrounding the turn of the century. Thereafter, the scores decline and decline with considerable consistency through 1978. The years after the 1890s, of course, conform most closely to the expectations outlined elsewhere. Contrary to these expectations, however, the scores for the 1930s suggest only a moderate increase in partisan voting at

TABLE 7.3   Linear Regressions of Index of Party Unlikeness on Time
(Congress Number) for the Senate, 1861–1978

	Regression Coefficient	Correlation Coefficient	Coefficient of Determination
1861–1978	−.50	−.65	.42
1861–1897	1.06	.53	.28
1897–1933	−2.12	−.82	.67
1933–1978	−.77	−.76	.57

best, and these years viewed impressionistically hardly seem to interrupt the twentieth-century decline in the partisan polarization of the Senate.

Here again, simple statistical manipulations provide a more precise view of the characteristics of the series. As Table 7.3 indicates, the series of unlikeness scores can be described as marked by long-term decline over the entire period. Thus the linear regression of scores for each Congress on time—or Congress number—yields a middling correlation ($r = -.65$) and a moderate regression coefficient ($b = -.50$).[16]

Further elucidation of the characteristics of the series can be gained by regressing the scores for each realignment era taken separately on time. It appears that during the third-party system (1861 to 1897), the Senate was characterized generally by increasing partisan polarization as the rise in the unlikeness index scores shows. The upward slope for the period was relatively steep ($b = 1.06$), and the scores increased by approximately ten points in twenty years, with a moderately strong correlation of .53 (Table 7.4). The two realignment periods after 1897, on the other hand, were both marked by decline in unlikeness scores as shown in Table 7.3, with regression coefficients of −2.12 for the years from 1897 through 1933 and −0.77 for the years from 1933 through 1978. In both cases, moreover, the correlation coefficients are high ($r = -.82$ and −.76 respectively). In short, Senate partisan voting, at least as measured by the unlikeness index, was marked during the period from 1861 through 1978 first by a rising trend in the

TABLE 7.4   Multiple Regression of Index of Party Unlikeness on Time
(Congress Number) and Temporal Distance from
Realignments for the Senate, 1897–1978

	Regression Coefficient (Congress Number)	Regression Coefficient (Distance from Realignment)	Coefficient of Multiple Correlation	Coefficient of Multiple Determination
1897–1978	–.70	–.50	.83	.69

nineteenth century and then by a declining trend in the twentieth.

It remains to be asked whether in the Senate, as in the House, shifts in partisan behavior were associated primarily or at all with the cycle of partisan realignments, only with a longer trend, or some combination or both. Can we observe in the Senate around the longer-term trend the same pattern of surge and decline in partisan voting in association with realignments that was observed in the House? Did partisan realignments bring with them in the Senate increases in partisan polarization as they did in the House, and did partisan polarization in the Senate progressively decline during the years that followed realignments as it did in the House?

The multiple regression of the unlikeness index jointly on time and the same temporal distance from realignment variable that was used for the House of Representatives provides information bearing upon these and related questions. In the case of the Senate, however, it is only useful to examine the two realignment periods following the 1890s and the 1930s. The rising trend in the Senate unlikeness series for the latter nineteenth century—or, in other words, the increase in Senate partisan polarization during these years—suggests the absence, or retardation, of deterioration of Civil War polarization in that body. As the partial regression coefficients indicate (Table 7.4), both variables contributed substantially to the decline in partisan voting in the Senate during the twentieth century, although the longer-term trend apparently influenced change in Senate partisan voting (b = -.70) somewhat more strongly than did realignment processes (b = -.50).

It is also clear that a break in congressional partisan voting occurred during the years surrounding the turn of the twentieth century. The patterns of party unlikeness during the latter decades of the nineteenth century in both the Senate and the House were different from those of the twentieth century. For the House, decline in partisan voting was less marked in the latter nineteenth century than in the twentieth; in the Senate, partisanship increased during the latter decades of the nineteenth century. In contrast to the latter nineteenth century, partisanship in both Houses of Congress, as measured by the index of unlikeness, declined precipitously in the twentieth century.

PARTISAN UNITY AND COHESION

Indications of shifts in partisan polarization in the two Houses of Congress can be observed over the years from 1861 to the mid-1970s. It remains to be asked whether the same patterns of change were characteristics of the internal cohesion of the congressional parties. The perspective developed in Chapter 1 might be taken as suggesting that change in partisan cohesion in Congress should, in general, parallel shifts in partisan polarization. In terms of this perspective, the political tensions, the heightened emphasis upon a narrowed range of issues, and the conditions of crisis that characterized historical periods of electoral realignment should have led to increased cohesion among party members in Congress. On the other hand, during decay phases, declining party unity could be expected as a consequence of shifts in electoral alignments, of growing electoral instability, and of the appearance of new and varied issues that cut across the issues of the earlier realignment.

To assess patterns of partisan unity in the House of Representatives and Senate, we can again draw upon and extend work reported elsewhere.[17] For these purposes, the familiar Rice index of party cohesion is used to measure the extent to which members of the same party voted together on roll calls. The index ranges from 0 to 100, with 100 indicating that all voting members of a party voted on the same side of the issue and zero indicating that the voting members of the party were divided, with half voting on one side of the issue and half voting on the other.[18] The index was computed for both parties and both chambers on all record votes in all Congresses of the period from 1861 through 1978 and averaged to create a cohesion score for each party in each Congress. This operation yields for analysis average Republican and Democratic cohesion scores for the House of Representatives and the Senate for each Congress from 1861 through 1978. Despite its simplicity and defects, the index allows comparison of cohesion both from Congress to Congress and from one party to the other.

Examination of the cohesion scores and statistical analysis of the series indicate that change in House and Senate cohesion does not consistently parallel the trends in partisan polarization observed in the preceding section. The pattern of fluctuation appears different for the two parties, but in neither case do the parties consistently conform to the expectations sketched above. More specifically, the scores do not suggest that electoral realignments introduced periods of high cohesion for either advantaged or disadvantaged parties, and the long-term trends characteristic of the unlikeness series appear much less clearly in the case of the cohesion series.

Taking the time period as a whole, there is little indication of long-term decline or of consistent fluctuation in relation to the realignment cycle. The regression of the cohesion scores on time for the entire period and for both parties in the House (Table 7.5) reveals only a negligible trend in either case, and the correlation coefficients for both parties are low. In general, the Senate scores follow contours similar to those observed for the House. The Senate scores, however, tend to be consistently lower and give an impression of greater regularity than those of the House. However, like the House cohesion scores, the Senate scores do not suggest the clear and consistent trends that marked the index of partisan unlikeness.

TABLE 7.5   Regression of House and Senate Cohesion Scores on Time,
             for Realignment Eras, 1861-1978

	Intercept	Regression Coefficient	Correlation Coefficient	Coefficient of Determination
House				
1861-1978:				
Democrat	69.7	-.09	-.24	.06
Republican	72.1	-.06	-.13	.02
1861-1897:				
Democrat	70.5	-.46	-.37	.14
Republican	58.6	1.01	.54	.29
1897-1933:				
Democrat	82.1	-1.19	-.77	.60
Republican	87.6	-1.30	-.81	.65
1933-1978:				
Democrat	62.9	.12	.21	.04
Republican	72.6	-.41	-.56	.32
Senate				
1861-1978:				
Democrat	70.5	-.26	-.51	.26
Republican	59.9	.01	.02	.00
1861-1897:				
Democrat	66.1	.02	.02	.00
Republican	-39.9	1.94	.73	.53
1897-1933:				
Democrat	77.4	-1.15	-.75	.56
Republican	75.7	-1.26	-.77	.60
1933-1978:				
Democrat	49.5	.51	.65	.42
Republican	61.0	-.17	-.19	.03

The same operation applied to the cohesion scores for the
House and Senate for each realignment era taken separately
(Table 7.5) indicates dissimilar patterns both from one party to
the other and from one period to the next. Only the years from
1897 through 1933 were marked in both chambers by clear and
consistent decline in the cohesion scores of both parties. Democratic cohesion in the House and Senate declined during the years
from 1861 through 1897, although the trend was relatively weak

and irregular. Republican cohesion in these years rose, but with considerable irregularity. Cohesion scores for the years from 1933 through 1978 are also dissimilar. In the Senate, Democratic cohesion rose modestly and irregularly; the Republican scores are without trend. Republican cohesion in the House was marked by a relatively modest declining trend, that of the Democrats by faint increase. Taken in total, there is little indication of systematic shifts in congressional cohesion in relation to the cycle of partisan realignments.[19]

Consideration of the intercept terms in Table 7.5 and examination of the average cohesion scores (not presented here) suggest relatively small differences between the parties during realignments. In both the House and Senate, the cohesion of the advantaged Republicans during the Civil War realignment tended to be low in comparison to that of the Democrats. The same pattern was characteristic of the New Deal years. In this case, the cohesion of the advantaged party, the Democrats, was again low in both chambers in comparison to that of the disadvantaged Republicans. In both instances, it appears, the large majorities enjoyed by the advantaged parties allowed them to function effectively despite relatively lower voting cohesion. The disadvantaged parties, reduced to small and presumably more homogeneous minorities, were more highly cohesive. The data suggest, in other words, that in these instances, electoral realignments and the changes in membership associated with them may have worked to promote greater cohesion among the members of the opposition party than among members of the majority party.[20] The pattern of the 1890s realignment was different. There was little difference between the two parties, and the cohesion of both tended to be high.

In several respects, examination of congressional voting behavior suggests a confusing picture. The voting patterns of the two chambers were not consistently the same, and the three realignment eras were marked by several dissimilarities. Moreover, our examination of partisan polarization—the degree to which, on the average, the two parties voted in opposition to each other—appears at odds with our examination of partisan cohesion—the degree to which, on the average, members of each party voted together. The evidence suggests partisan polarization in Congress was marked both by relatively clear long-term trends and by shorter-term fluctuations associated with the cycle of partisan realignments. Measures of partisan cohesion, on the other hand, are marked by much less in the way of consistent trend or clear pattern.

A much more consistent picture emerges when the characteristics of the two measures of congressional voting are taken into account. The cohesion index, of course, treats both parties separately. Hence, it reflects the degree of internal cohesion both in votes on which the parties tended to vote on the same side of an issue, as well as in votes on which the parties took opposing positions. In other words, unanimous votes on which all members of both parties vote on the same side of an issue yield cohesion scores of 100 (perfect unity) just as do votes on which all members of one party vote in opposition to all members of the other party. As a consequence, it is possible for a rising trend in cohesion scores to coincide with a declining trend in unlikeness scores.

Viewed in these terms, the evidence suggests that the parties were more sharply polarized during periods of partisan realignment. Apparently, clear policy differences led the parties to take opposing positions on an increased proportion of the issues voted on in Congress. The internal cohesion of the parties, on the other hand, was not consistently higher during realignments than at other times. While the differences were not great or completely consistent, the disadvantaged party, reduced to a small minority, managed to maintain relatively greater internal unity in opposition to the policy initiatives of the advantaged party. On the other hand, during two of the three partisan realignments considered, the large majorities enjoyed by the advantaged parties were either less tractable and less easily disciplined, or because of the size of these majorities, unity was less necessary for legislative success. As a consequence, the advantaged party tended to be less unified. During the years following realignments, the internal cohesion of the parties did not change in consistent fashion. Policy differences between the parties, however, tended to recede, and the majorities of the two parties more frequently voted on the same side of issues, with the consequence of diminished polarization.[21]

PARTISANSHIP IN THE HOUSE AND SENATE

This examination of partisan voting in the House and Senate began as an effort to discover changes in the role of the political parties within these policy-making bodies. Partisan realignments have been seen not only as involving lasting shifts in the partisan behavior and attitudes of the electorate, but also as policy watersheds in the life of the nation, characterized by policy initiative, innovation, and coordination. Such diagnosis of the policy correlates of partisan realignments relies primarily on impressionistic evidence, since systematic analyses of change in policy-making have not been carried out across the long sweep of American history.

It is reasonable to argue, however, that if political parties are to function as policy-making agencies and to function with relative effectiveness in that role, and if they are to serve as mechanisms which reflect and aggregate the interests and demands of the national population and translate those interests and demands into policy, several minimal conditions must be met. These conditions include among others: (1) effective control of the policy-making agencies of the nation, (2) policy differences between the parties, (3) a degree of unity among party elites, and (4) structures, linkages, and organizations which facilitate coordinated action.

Historically, the evidence suggests, partisan realignments have worked to produce the first two of these conditions. The realignments of 1860, 1896, and 1932 brought with them a high degree of unified and lasting control of the policy-making agencies of the federal and the various state governments. Analysis of House and Senate partisan voting behavior suggests that these partisan realignments also involved a relatively high degree of distinctiveness between the parties.[22] In general, at the time of each major realignment, the parties tended to be more highly and more sharply polarized. There is no consistent evidence of increase in the internal unity and cohesion of the parties in Congress at the time of realignments. On the other hand, the large majorities gained by the advantaged parties during realignments were such as to allow effective policy action even under conditions falling well short of perfect discipline.

Our evidence does not bear directly upon questions of partisan structure, organization, and linkages. However, partisan realignments tended, with considerable uniformity, to shift control of government at the national, state, and, it is likely, local levels toward one of the parties. Hence, realignments produced a measure of partisan articulation to the multilayered governmental system. Sustained control of government produced opportunities for the advantaged parties to develop programs and policies, to gain control of the bureaucracy and appointive offices, to develop organization in Congress, and to employ patronage and the pork barrel in the service of party goals. Following realignments, these conditions tended to disappear. Control of government became less consistent, shifts in control of government became more frequent, and the incidence of divided control increased. In Congress, the magnitude of partisan majorities declined, and partisan polarization diminished. Hence, opportunities for innovative and sustained policy initiatives diminished as well.

The evidence considered in this chapter clearly suggests an association between partisan polarization in Congress, on the one hand, and the cycle of partisan realignments, on the other. That association is most consistent in the case of the House of Representatives, and strongest for both chambers in the twentieth century. From some perspectives, however, fluctuations in voting behavior in relation to partisan realignments are substantially less interesting than are the indications of long-term decline in congressional partisanship which our evidence provides. Declining partisanship has been characteristic of the

House for over a century; in the Senate, a similar trend has continued virtually uninterrupted since the turn of the century. The patterns of change associated with realignments do not dominate the data considered here, and clearly all of the many political forces involved in realignments only produced deviations from longer trends. However significant, the transition from decay phases to realignments interrupted, but did not reverse, these longer-term trends.

NOTES

1. See, however, Barbara Deckard Sinclair, "Party Realignment and the Transformation of the Political Agenda: The House of Representatives, 1925-1938," *American Political Science Review* 71 (September 1977), pp. 940-953; Benjamin Ginsberg, "Elections and Public Policy," *American Political Science Review* 70 (March 1976), pp. 41-49; David W. Brady, "Critical Elections, Congressional Parties and Clusters of Policy Changes: A Comparison of 1896 and 1932 Realignment Eras," presented at the American Political Science Association meeting, 1975.

2. Michael R. King and Lester G. Seligman, "Critical Elections, Congressional Realignment and Public Policy," in Heinz Eulau and Moshe M. Czudnowski (eds.), *Elite Recruitment in Democratic Politics: Comparative Studies Across Nations* (Beverly Hills, CA: Sage Publications, 1976), pp. 263-299; Allan G. Bogue, Jerome M. Clubb, Carrol R. McKibben, and Santa A. Traugott, "Members of the House of Representatives and the Processes of Modernization, 1789-1960," *Journal of American History* (September 1976), pp. 275-302; Garrison Nelson, "Partisan Patterns of House Leadership Change, 1789-1977," *American Political Science Review* 71 (September 1977), pp. 918-939; Nelson W. Polsby, "The Institutionalization of the U.S. House of Representatives," *American Political Science Review* 62 (March 1968), pp. 144-168; Morris P. Fiorina, David W. Rhode, and Peter Wissel, "Historical Change in House Turnover," in Norman J. Ornstein (ed.), *Congress in Change* (New York: Prager, 1975).

3. H. Douglas Price, "The Congressional Career–Then and Now," in Nelson Polsby (ed.), *Congressional Behavior* (New York: Random House, 1971), pp. 14-27.

4. Polsby, "The Institutionalization of the U.S. House of Representatives." The correction for the return of former congressmen is appropriate for assessing institutionalization but not for the assessment of change brought about by an election. Fiorina et al. corrected the total of newcomers for the number of new seats added to Congress in each election and calculated a "percentage replacement" more accurately reflecting the extent to which incumbents lost seats in each Congress.

5. Fiorina, et al., "Historical Change in House Turnover," pp. 31-34.

6. King and Seligman, "Critical Elections, Congressional Realignment and Public Policy," page 268, Table 10.1. This characteristic is not at odds with the steadily

increasing tendency (not associated with realignments) for turnover to result from defeat. The rate of defeat for 1896 is also well above the average for the surrounding decades.

7. Price, "The Congressional Career—Then and Now," p. 17, Figure I. This effect is not solely a function of new districts, although that, too, contributes. H. Douglas Price, "Congress and the Evolution of Legislative Professionalism," in Ornstein, *Congress in Change*, p. 12.

8. Randall Ripley, *Party Leaders in the House of Representatives* (Washington, DC: Brookings Institution, 1967), Ch. 2, especially Tables I, III, and IV on Speakers, Majority Leaders, and Minority Leaders; Nelson, "Partisan Patterns of House Leadership Change, 1789-1977."

9. Brady, "Critical Elections, Congressional Parties and Clusters of Policy Changes;" Nelson, "Partisan Patterns of House Leadership Change, 1789-1977."

10. Jerome M. Clubb and Santa A. Traugott, "Partisan Cleavage and Cohesion in the House of Representatives, 1861-1974," *Journal of Interdisciplinary History* 7 (Winter 1977), pp. 375-401. Similar trends are suggested in David W. Brady, Joseph Cooper and Patricia A. Hurley, "The Decline of Party in the U.S. House of Representatives, 1887-1968," *Legislative Studies Quarterly* 4 (August 1979), pp. 381-407, on the basis of a shorter time series and employing somewhat different measures.

11. Clubb and Traugott, "Partisan Cleavage and Cohesion in the House of Representatives, 1861-1974."

12. The index is simply the difference between the percentage of each party that voted in favor of a measure, subtracting the smaller number from the larger. The index is marked by a variety of serious, although obvious, limitations. It is a highly aggregated measure and consequently is insensitive to differences across policy areas or to variation in behavior among individual legislators. The scoring between 0 and 100 guarantees that the averages of the index calculated for each roll call are bounded, which facilitates comparisons over the years. However, the averages may conceal quite dissimilar distributions of scores for individual roll calls. Even so, the average index provides a crude means to assess the extent to which there were partisan differences in voting and to compare the partisan performance of members of Congress across the period in question.

13. A substantial proportion of the roll call votes in the House during the Fifty-first Congress, as in the following two Congresses, were on procedural matters. The ruling in the Fifty-first Congress by Speaker of the House Thomas B. Reed (Republican) that members present but not voting should be counted for quorum purposes provoked a heated struggle between Democrats and Republicans. (See Howard W. Allen and Robert Slagter, "Congress in Crisis: A Study of Personnel and Policy Change in the U.S. Congress During the Depression and Electoral Realignment of the 1890s," presented at the annual meeting of the Social Science History Association, 1979. The struggle over "Reed's Rules" in this Congress involved frequent and systematic abstention on roll call votes by many Democrats. For some purposes, this rule fight can be seen as spuriously inflating the average unlikeness score for the Fifty-first Congress.

14. For this purpose, a "temporal distance from realignment" variable was contrived by coding the Thirty-seventh, Fifty-fifth, and Seventy-third Congresses—elected in 1860, 1896, and 1932—"1" on the variable, the Thirty-eight, Fifty-sixth, and Seventy-fourth Congresses—elected in 1862, 1898, and 1934—"2," and so on.

15. Application of a second and in some respects more rigorous procedure reflects the same pattern. In this case, the unlikeness scores were regressed on time (Congress number), and residual values were computed. The residual values can be seen as the variations in the unlikeness scores that remain after the effects of the long-term trend are removed, or controlled, to use a different terminology. Obviously, the residual values for each realignment era should also be negatively correlated with the time during each era if realignment effects are statistically independent of the long-term decline in partisan unlikeness. The results of this procedure also suggest the independence of the two patterns. The correlations of the residual values with time are strong for the period from 1897 through 1933 ($r = -.71$) and for the period from 1933 through 1972 ($r = -.74$). For the period from 1861 through 1897, however, the correlation between time and the residual values is nonexistent ($r = -.01$). Here again, this result is to some degree due to the one deviant case, the Fifty-first Congress. Once that Congress is removed, the controlled relationship is stronger, although still modest ($r = -.26$). The differences between these results suggest, as in the case of the analysis reported in the text, that trends in House voting patterns in the latter nineteenth century were different from those of the twentieth.

16. The series can better be described as curvilinear. A second degree polynomial provides a substantially better fit ($R = -.71$) than the linear model. For the use of polynomials in regression, see Hubert Blalock, *Social Statistics* (New York, 1972), pp. 459-464.

17. Clubb and Traugott, "Partisan Cleavage and Cohesion in the House of Representatives, 1861-1974."

18. The Rice index is simply the absolute difference between the percentage of the members of a party voting "yea" on a roll call and the percentage voting "nay." The reasons for possible differences between the pattern of unlikeness scores and the pattern of cohesion scores will be obvious. The index of unlikeness reaches its maximum (100) only on roll calls on which all voting members of one party oppose all voting members of the other and falls to 0 on all those roll calls in which the parties divide in exactly the same proportion. The Rice index of cohesion treats each party separately. Thus on unanimous votes, the cohesion scores for both parties is 100. On any given roll call, the cohesion scores for one party may be 100, indicating perfect unity, and those of the other party may be 0, indicating that one half of the members of that party supported the issue while the other half opposed.

19. The results of the multiple regression of the cohesion series on time and the contrived realignment variable, described above, for the entire period from 1861 through 1974 and for the subperiod from 1897 through 1974 reinforce this conclusion. Considering the period as a whole, the time and realignment variables are only faintly related to the cohesion series for both parties and chambers. The relationships are somewhat stronger, particularly in the case of the House Republican scores, for the subperiod beginning in 1897, but they are neither as strong nor as consistent as was characteristic of the unlikeness series. It is possible to show that on party votes in the House of Representatives, defined as those roll calls on which a simple majority of one party was opposed by a simple majority of the other, Democratic and Republican cohesion was marked by patterns similar to those observed in the case of the partisan unlikeness series (Clubb and Traugott, "Partisan Cleavage and Cohesion in the House of Representatives, 1861-1974"). The finding is, of course, as would be expected; the frequency of party votes in Congress is of necessity closely related to

the index of party unlikeness. Both Democratic and Republican cohesion in the House was marked, however, by a long-term decline after 1897, ending in an increase at the time of the New Deal realignment. Here again, the latter nineteenth century stands out as different. Democratic cohesion on party votes did decline after the Civil War realignment, but more modestly and less regularly than that of either party after the realignment of the 1890s and the 1930s. Republican cohesion, on the other hand, increased. Both patterns provide yet another indication of the increasing partisanship of elite political behavior during the decades following the Civil War.

20. This impression is not entirely congruent with other findings. The relationship between change in the membership of the House and partisan voting in that body has not been systematically investigated over time. Brady, however, has examined this relationship for the Fifty-fifth Congress (1897-1899) and the Seventy-third (1933-1935). He shows that in both Congresses, newcomers who were members of the advantaged party and who had taken a seat formerly held by the opposing party voted more consistently with their party than did other members. The contrasts in party voting were 8% higher for "switched seat" Republicans in 1897 as compared to other Republicans and 7% higher among "switched seat" Democrats in 1933 as compared to other Democrats. Brady's analysis was concerned, however, only with the first session of each Congress, and it is unclear whether these differences would also be characteristic of subsequent sessions, or whether more frequent party voting was an attribute of newcomers to the House during realignments or of newcomers more generally. Brady, "Critical Elections, Congressional Parties and Clusters of Policy Changes."

21. The point is confirmed by examination of change in the proportion of "party votes" (defined as votes on which a simple majority of the voting members of one party opposed a simple majority of the other party) across these years. Although not reported here, the incidence of party votes followed a pattern in both chambers essentially similar to that of the unlikeness scores reported above.

22. Data presented by Paul Allen Beck suggests that the decades of the 1830s, 1840s, and 1850s were marked by a similar pattern of partisan polarization in the House. See Beck, "The Electoral Cycle and Patterns of American Politics," *British Journal of Political Science* 9 (April 1979), pp. 129-156.

Chapter 8

THE DYNAMICS OF PARTISAN CHANGE

In undertaking the present study, we set out to elucidate and assess what we take to be widely accepted views of the political history of the United States. Drawing upon the work of others, we developed an extended and modified formulation of the realignment perspective in our initial chapter as a point of departure for empirical investigation. Extensive and diverse arrays of historical evidence were then examined in subsequent chapters. That examination suggests patterns of change and stability in general conformity with our reformulated version of the realignment perspective. Evidence of lasting change in the partisan distribution of the popular vote appears at temporal points usually seen as major, national partisan realignments coinciding with widespread stress and tension that approached national crisis. Shifts in partisan control of the federal government and of state governments can be observed during each of these periods, and we can surmise that similar patterns of partisan change occurred at the level of localities as well. Coinciding evidence of change in the degree of partisan polarization and partisanship in Congress also appears and lends added credence to this broad interpretation of the contours of American political history.

Most of us would agree, without demanding presentation of much in the way of detailed evidence, that these periods were also times of major policy change. The case is clearest for the New Deal years, if only because these years are more nearly within the reach of personal experience. But the weight of scholarship also treats the New Deal years as a time of sharp change from the policy orientations and governmental directions of the past, although the passage of time has involved diminishing assessment of the degree and magnitude of policy reorientation during these years. Few would contest the view that the Civil War years marked major change in the life of the nation; old, lingering, and seemingly insoluble issues were finally frontally addressed, at the cost of bloodshed and disruption of the nation. The case for the 1890s is less persuasive, but here again the weight of scholarship has assigned to these years major significance as a turning point in the policy life of the nation. And if we look into the more distant past, the Age of Jackson and of "Common Man Democracy" seemingly also stands out as a point both of lasting electoral change and of policy departure. Thus, we have seen these periods as times of relative partisan articulation, when the parties assumed well-defined and clearly opposing positions, when their positions constituted responses to recognized national issues and cleavages, and when they managed to a greater degree than in other periods to link together and give a measure of coherence to the diverse and potentially conflicting jurisdictions and agencies of government in the nation.

The political patterns of the years following partisan realignments also convey a sense of similarity. The characteristics of these periods include (although by no means with complete uniformity) frequent oscillations of the partisan distribution of the vote; frequent deviating elections; third-party movements; shifts in partisan control of government; and decline of partisanship and partisan polarization in Congress. Contemporary observers and historians alike have tended to describe these periods as marked by ineffective and divided government, by unsolved—indeed, unaddressed—national problems, by dissatisfaction with the mechanism of government, and by incremental rather than innovative policy-making.

We have taken these characteristics as indications of the deterioration of prevailing alignments. With the passage of time after historical realignments, new issues arose which were not subsumed by the issue dimensions produced by the realignment and which, as a consequence, cut across the areas of issue agreement providing the basis for the prevailing alignment. Demographic change resulted in the diminution of some groups and increase in the size of others, thus altering the mass basis of partisan alignments. The composition of the electorate changed as older voters were supplemented and replaced by new voters who had not experienced the circumstances of the earlier realignment and whose partisan ties were as a consequence weaker. Partisan cleavages were blurred, the needs and demands of the electorate became less clear and grew increasingly conflicting. Hence, politicians were faced with conflicting demands and unstable support, popular response to policy positions and actions became less predictable, and the conduct of government was rendered more difficult.

Once again, the evidence is most clear, although by no means unqualified, for the contemporary period. The evidence comes in the form of erosion of the strength with which individual attachments to the parties are held, increasing incidence, particularly among the young, of individuals who identify with neither party, and appearance of new issues which sometimes cut across and sometimes coincide with the positions of the parties. Since our more crude and indirect indicators behave in generally similar ways for both early and contemporary periods, we have inferred that similar underlying processes were at work during equivalent earlier periods. Thus, we have taken periods following historical realignments as times of increasing partisan disarticulation when party positions were less well defined and less clearly opposing, when the parties were less attuned to the needs and demands of the electorate, and when they functioned less well to link together and give coherence to the political and governmental life of the nation.

While our evidence conforms in general ways to this broad description and interpretation of American political history, we also confront a number of serious limitations. The similarities between the several realignment and deterioration periods are by no means precise, and the parallels between the contours of the various data series are far from perfect. Thus a variety of qualifications must be introduced and numerous exceptions noted. Moreover, we have contented ourselves for the most part with examination of the parallels between data series; we have not attempted to explore the relationships between the underlying processes which those data series reflect. Rather, we have, in effect, postulated a nexus of elite and popular attitudes and a set of mediating factors which link those processes together. While these postulates are in conformity with our evidence and are, we believe, in accord with established scholarship, they are supported only in limited ways by our empirical evidence.

Our reformulation of the realignment perspective also involves a conceptualization of the process of partisan realignment which differs from that to be found in the relevant literature, although we believe elements of our conceptualization are implicit in the work of others. The task in the present chapter is to develop and assess this alternative conceptualization of the realignment process. To do so, we can draw upon related scholarship, but we must also venture in more speculative directions. To look ahead, this alternative conceptualization of the realignment process reconciles several apparent contradictions, is in accord with the findings of other investigations, and also allows us to accommodate more of the diversity of American political history.

THE MECHANICS OF PARTISAN REALIGNMENTS

The question of timing has always been an important aspect of discussions of partisan realignment. Debate arises over when the New Deal realignment "really" occurred—1928 or 1932 or possibly 1924 or 1936?[1] Did the realignment of 1896 occur in 1896, or was that election the culmination of a set of electoral changes occurring throughout the 1890s, as MacRae and Meldrum suggested for Illinois?[2] Should the Civil War realignment be dated at 1860 or 1864 or in the 1850s?[3] In essence, the question becomes: When did the change in the underlying partisan division of the electorate occur? When did voters switch to the advantaged party? The relatively better data which are available for the New Deal realignment than for earlier realignments allow consideration of the substantive and analytical issues these questions imply.

Scholars have become wary of assuming that the electoral changes in a realignment come primarily or even substantially from conversions from one party to another. Using recall data from surveys conducted in the 1950s by the Survey Research Center of the University of Michigan, both Philip Converse and Kristi Andersen have argued persuasively that the New Deal realignment came not primarily through conversion of partisan loyalties but rather through the processes of mobilization.[4] Andersen's analysis, in particular, shows that a pool of new and inactive voters with weak or no partisan loyalties developed in the 1920s. Under the impact of the Great Depression and the earlier stimulus provided by the circumstances of the election of 1928, these "delayed" voters entered the electorate in large numbers in 1932 and 1936; most, Andersen estimates the proportion at 90%, voted Democratic. These Democratic gains in the 1930s were further augmented by young and newly eligible voters. In the 1930s, newly eligible members of the electorate voted in elections more frequently and more immediately than in the 1920s, and these new voters also disproportionately voted Democratic.[5]

This formulation relieves a theoretical tension between interpretations of the New Deal realignment as the product of large-scale conversion of individual partisan identifications, on the one hand, and, on the other, an extensive literature which argues persuasively on empirical and theoretical grounds that individual partisan identifications are highly durable and rarely change once formed.[6] But in terms of the question of the timing of realignments, it simply forces the phrasing to be modified from "when did voters switch to the advantaged party" to "when did their partisan loyalties develop or change?"

Different techniques of analysis have yielded different answers to this question, as we saw in Chapters 2 and 3. Regardless of the techniques used, however, analyses of historical realignments, because of reliance upon the data of election returns, have tended to take behavioral change as evidence of attitudinal change. Thus the first election which departs from preceding elections in terms of the distribution of the popular vote and which resembles following elections is taken as the realigning election and as marking the appearance of a new distribution of individual identifications with the parties. The analysis of variance technique employed in Chapter 3 above is also subject to this tendency, although we have attempted to differentiate conceptually change in voting behavior from attitudinal change and have emphasized additional elements of the realignment process. This same tendency is no less present when one uses breaks in correlation matrices, as Pomper and others have done,[7] or Burnham's discontinuity variable.[8] This view of attitudinal realignment as occurring simultaneously with changes in voting behavior is equally true of discussions of secular realignment.[9] In short, in the absence of individual measures of partisan attitudes, the tendency is to take voting behavior as a direct indication of attitudinal identifications. Furthermore, the dating of realignments is made in terms of the first indication of behavioral change, and concomitant attitudinal change is assumed.

Nor is this tendency to date realignments in terms of behavioral change and to treat attitudinal change as the instantaneous concomitant of change in voting behavior limited to analysts who have relied exclusively on the data of election returns. In Andersen's analysis of the New Deal realignment, Democratic identifiers who reported in the 1950s that they had never switched parties and who also reported that they had cast their first vote in 1928 or in the 1930s for the Democratic presidential candidate are assumed to have been Democratic identifiers at the time of their first vote. To put the matter more strongly, the assumption seems to be that first-time voters are promptly affiliated with the party of the first presidential candidate for whom they voted, even though they may have been apolitical nonvoters in previous years.[10] Even when the analytic techniques and data do not demand it, the view seems to be that attitudinal change occurs simultaneously with behavioral change and that, therefore, behavioral change offers evidence that a realignment has occurred.

Unfortunately, this assumption of instantaneous development of partisanship does not appear to be in accord with accepted knowledge of the formation and development of partisan attitudes. Substantial research suggests that the partisan identifications of first-time voters, whether youthful, newly eligible members of the electorate or "delayed" voters, tend to be weak and subject to change. Partisan identifications grow in strength and become more deeply seated with repetitive exercise of the franchise.[11] A better assumption, and one equally congruent with the data, would view the new, first-time Democratic voters of 1928 and the 1930s as at most weak Democratic identifiers, as independents, or even as apolitical at the time of their first vote. Had there not been vigorous policy action on the part of the Democratic administration which could be taken as successful in producing a measure of economic relief and recovery, or the promise thereof, it is likely that at least some of these new voters would have lapsed back into earlier habits of nonparticipation, become independents, or even switched to the Republicans.

Other evidence from the New Deal realignment offers further indication that the notion of realignment occurring simultaneously with the initial behavioral changes may require modification. On the basis of the *Literary Digest* polls conducted in the 1930s, Shively has inferred that in 1932 middle-class and working-class voters voted Democratic in similar proportions. With a measure of economic relief and recovery, and more importantly, as the directions of New Deal policies were established, middle-class voters returned to the Republican fold, while working-class voters did not.[12] In a similar vein, our analysis in Chapter 3 above suggests that a substantial portion of the electoral change favoring the Democrats in the elections of 1932 and 1936 was deviating, indicating that some voters temporarily defected from their Republican loyalties under the impact of the Depression, returning to their more traditional loyalties by the end of the 1930s.

Here again, Andersen's analysis is instructive. According to her estimates, in 1932, Republican identifiers still narrowly outnumbered Democratic identifiers (by a margin of 27% to 26%). A substantial portion of the Roosevelt margin in that year, she surmises, must have come from Republican identifiers who defected from their party to vote Democratic and from independents.[13] In terms of these estimates, the presidential election of 1932 might well be classified, although Andersen does not do so, as a deviating rather than a realigning election, even though it was the first in a long series of Democratic presidential and congressional electoral victories. By 1936, again in terms of Andersen's estimates and classifications, Democratic identifiers had come to outnumber Republicans by 33% to 25%. Clearly, however, even in that election, the Democratic presidential landslide was dependent upon the vote of independents and defecting Republicans. That dependence is further confirmed by a 1937 Gallup poll, also reported by Andersen, which indicated that some 20% of the Roosevelt vote came from individuals who considered themselves Republicans or independents.[14] While this support by Republicans and independents for the Democrats was transitory and seems not to have represented long-term attitudinal change, it helped produce the large Roosevelt electoral majorities in 1932 and 1936 and the extraordinary Democratic majorities in Congress during the earlier 1930s. These congressional majorities were large enough to overcome divisions within the congressional party and to allow enactment of New Deal legislation. As we have noted, Democratic partisan cohesion in Congress did not increase during the New Deal, but extraordinary majorities allowed concerted policy action nonetheless.

We can take the argument one step further. The deviating Republican vote and the independent vote, as well as the vote of former nonparticipants and of the newly eligible, for Democratic candidates in 1932 can readily be seen as a response to the Great Depression and a rejection of the policies of the Hoover administration rather than an endorsement of the Democracts. It can be imagined that without vigorous policy action on the part of the new Democratic administration and without at least modest signs of economic recovery, this support would not have continued in subsequent elections. In this eventuality, Democratic electoral strength in 1936 would have receded, or, indeed, Roosevelt might have been a one-term president. In either case, the partisan distribution of the vote in 1936 would probably have assumed a pattern different from that of 1932; from the standpoint of analysis of voting returns, the latter election would appear as only another example of a deviating election. In our view, in other words, importance must be assigned to events after 1932—and particularly to vigorous New Deal policy action and to modest economic relief—in sustaining, reinforcing, and augmenting Democratic electoral strength.

This argument, of course, assigns a substantially greater role than other interpretations to vigorous policy action and to alleviation of the effects of the Great Depression—whether policy action and economic relief and recovery were actually causally related is irrelevant—in the formation and development of a new distribution of partisan loyalties during and following the New Deal. This construction is not directly supported by empirical evidence. It is, however, congruent with the available evidence, in better accord with accepted knowledge of the formation and development of partisan attitudes; as we will suggest, it also allows us to accommodate a broader array of historical events.

Given these items of evidence, theoretical considerations, and assumptions, we can recast the elements of the New Deal realignment in somewhat more abstract terms. The first element was the availability of a pool of unattached and probably apolitical potential voters, reflected by the high rates of nonpar-

ticipation in the 1920s, who were susceptible to mobilization
into the active electorate and into Democratic identification.
The second element was a set of precipitating events in the form
of the Great Depression and national economic collapse. The
third was electoral rejection of the Hoover administration and
the Republicans, though without any necessary implication of
endorsement of the Democrats. Vigorous policy action by the
Democrats which was facilitated by extraordinary majorities in
Congress and which coincided with a measure of, or the promise
of, economic relief and recovery constituted a fourth element.
These developments can be seen as reinforcing and, indeed,
rewarding voting behavior and as necessary for the final element
of the realignment, the formation of a new and lasting distribution of partisan loyalties (a new "normal" vote, in other words)
which favored the Democrats.

It is obviously difficult to apply this construction to earlier
realignments. Even the rather meager individual attitudinal data
available for the New Deal realignment are lacking for earlier
realignments. Moreover, the high level of mass electoral participation and the intense mass partisanship which are usually seen
as attributes of the latter nineteenth century and which our
evidence also suggests, make it difficult to conceive of a pool of
unattached voters, similar to that of the 1920s, who were
available for realignment. As a consequence, it is difficult at
first glance to imagine the realignment of the 1890s without
also postulating large-scale conversions of partisan attitudes
from Democratic to Republican identification. It is possible to
assume, of course, that the mechanics of partisan identification
worked in different ways in earlier years than they have since
the 1940s, and that partisan conversions could occur more
readily and more frequently in those early years. Such an
assumption, however, would be at odds with the intense partisanship that numerous scholars have attributed to the mass
electorate of the latter nineteenth century.

Examination of the evidence suggests, however, that neither
an assumption of this sort nor postulation of massive conversions of individual partisan identifications is necessary to

account for the realignment of the 1890s. Although at odds with other interpretations which treat the 1890s as marked by large-scale realigning change, our analysis in Chapter 3 suggested that these years were characterized by extensive deviating electoral change, but only relatively modest realigning change. Viewed in these terms, and without imagining large-scale conversions of individual loyalties, the pool of unattached or weakly identifying voters need not have been large to account for the realignment. Our analysis also provides limited evidence of the loosening of partisan attachments in the 1880s and earlier 1890s in the form of the third-party movements that dot these years, high turnover rates in Congress, and frequent shifts in partisan control of the agencies of state and national government. This rather limited evidence finds additional support in the plight and complaints of experienced politicians who, Marcus suggests, found the electorate of the latter 1880s and early 1890s increasingly unpredictable.[15]

An additional item of evidence is to be found in voter participation rates, although reliable estimates of participation rates are notoriously difficult to construct, particularly for the nineteenth century. The best estimates indicate that national voter participation in the presidential election of 1896 was less than 5 percentage points higher than in the election of 1892.[16] But this is a net national figure, and it conceals turnout declines of over 15 percentage points in Alabama, Delaware, and Georgia and of more than 5 percentage points in Arkansas, Illinois, Louisiana, and New Hampshire. In 11 other states, voter turnout also declined, although more modestly. On the other hand, turnout increased by an estimated 22 percentage points in Michigan, by 15 in Kentucky, and 13 in Idaho. All told, 7 states registered turnout increases in excess of 10 percentage points, in 14 additional states increases exceeded 5 percentage points, and 6 more states were marked by still less sharp increases. These turnout changes suggest a pattern of entry into and withdrawal from participation that could account for the Republican majority in 1896 without postulation of large-scale attitudinal conversions.

If we add to these changes in turnout the progressive decline in voter participation beginning after 1896, it is clearly possible to account for realigning change in the 1890s solely in terms of shifts in the composition of the participating electorate. Taken in total, then, there is little need to treat the 1890s realignment as primarily the product of conversions of partisan loyalties, a view in accord with our evidence and with very extensive evidence of the durability of partisan identifications.

Given these considerations, the realignment of the 1890s can be seen as involving essentially the same elements as the realignment of the 1930s. The data suggest the equivalent of a pool of unattached, or weakly attached, voters susceptible to realignment which may have been augmented after 1896 by withdrawal from the electorate, or failure to enter the electorate, of significant numbers of potential voters. The precipitating event was provided by the depression of 1893; the elections of 1894 and of 1896 were marked by a regional surge toward the Republican party and rejection of the Democrats. Recovery from depression could be seen as redemption of Republican campaign promises, and the Republicans could appear as the party of stability, progress, and prosperity. Thus voting behavior was rewarded and reinforced, and a new division of partisan loyalties was formed. The consummation and consolidation of the realignment can be seen in the further additions to the Republican coalition in 1904 and continuing declining turnout which, outside the South, tended most pronouncedly to weaken the Democrats.

At first blush, application of this construction to the realignment of the 1860s confronts different difficulties. The availability of a pool of voters susceptible to mobilization into new partisan identifications is readily suggested by the voting patterns of the 1840s and 1850s in terms of departures of the congressional vote from the presidential vote, frequent shifts in the distribution of the vote, oscillations in partisan control of government, and frequent third-party movements of considerable strength. Economic depressions—or recessions—in 1853 and 1857 no doubt gave additional aggravation to continuing national crises centering upon sectionalism, colonization of the West, and slavery. In these circumstances, the new Republican party appears as only one more of the minor party movements of the era formed in this case out of the wreckage of the Whigs and dissident Democrats. The Republicans did not, of course, gain majorities in either 1856 or 1858, and national divisions and crises remained unmet. There is every indication, moreover, that the elections of 1860 left the Republicans still unequipped to function effectively as a majority party; Lincoln was obviously a minority president faced with substantial opposition within his own party and, had the South remained in the union, Republican majorities in Congress would have been marginal. As we have also seen, the Republicans in Congress after 1860 were not highly cohesive, and it seems unlikely that in the face of southern Democratic opposition the party would have proven to be an effective instrumentality to confront a national crisis.

It was obviously southern secession that brought national crisis to a head, provided a focal point for policy action, and gave to the Republicans the extraordinary majorities in Congress necessary to compensate for divisions within the party. Southern secession could then be frontally addressed, the ensuing war vigorously prosecuted, northern dissidence suppressed, sectional divisions and conflict directly confronted, and a new and deeply seated distribution of national partisan identifications formed. Without southern secession, the fate of the Republican and Democratic parties might well have been substantially different. The pattern of the realignment of the 1860s suggests for us a further conclusion: In historical realignments, the circumstances through which partisan control of the agencies of government was achieved were less important than the course of events after the achievement of control. To put it more bluntly, electoral change need not always be an ingredient in establishing the unified control of government that results in partisan realignment.

We have engaged here in an admittedly rather speculative reconstruction of three historical realignments. This reconstruction is in our view equally in conformity with the evidence as alternative interpretations, it helps account for the high degree of continuity in voting alignments across historical realignments that we have observed, and it accords well with the richer data available for the New Deal realignment. Our reconstruction also appears in better accord with theoretical and empirical knowledge of the nature, basis, formation, and development of partisan attitudes in the contemporary era. In this reconstruction, we have stressed the appearance of vigorous policy action by an advantaged party and the coinciding reduction of tension and crisis as central elements of realignment, although we have not argued that it was necessarily the policy actions of the advantaged parties that led to reductions of crises and tensions. It is this element of our reconstruction that will allow the circumstances of additional historical elections to be cast in a different perspective. In so doing, of course, we also add additional plausibility to the reconstruction.

PARTISAN REALIGNMENTS
WHICH MIGHT HAVE BEEN

When we examine the historical record, a number of elections can be singled out which appear to be marked by many of the circumstances of partisan realignment, but which are usually not identified as realigning elections. One of the clearest examples is the election of 1892. That election came at a time of apparent widespread dissatisfaction with the alternatives provided by the two major parties, dissatisfaction focused primarily upon the Republicans. The 1890 elections to the House of Representatives can only be described as a Republican disaster. While control of the Senate was retained, the party delegation in the House was reduced by 78 seats, from a narrow majority (166 Republican seats to 159 Democratic seats) in the Fifty-first Congress, elected in 1888, to a one-sided Democratic majority (235 to 88 seats) in the Fifty-second Congress. In the elections of 1892, the Republicans recovered House strength but remained a limited minority (127 Republicans and 218 Democrats). The Democrats, however, captured control of the Senate and the presidency.

Thus the Democrats emerged from the elections of 1892 with unified control of the elective agencies of the federal government, with an extraordinary majority in the House, with a vigorous president in the White House, and the tides of political fortune clearly running in their favor. Indeed, historians have surmised that the election of 1892 was the beginning of what might have been a long Democratic supremacy.[17] But the depression of 1893 intervened almost before the new administration was inaugurated; Cleveland was confronted by a divided party in Congress, and party policies were seen as aggravating rather than improving depressed economic conditions. The image of the Democrats as successful managers of government was destroyed before it was established. The Democrats were rejected in the House elections of 1894, control of both the Senate and the presidency was lost in 1896, and a Democratic realignment-in-the-making came to an end.

Similarly, the elections of the early 1850s can be seen as a missed opportunity for Democratic realignment. There is ample evidence of loosening partisan attachments and of dissatisfaction with both parties during the latter 1840s and 1850s, and popular disenchantment seemingly focused primarily upon the faltering Whigs. In the House elections of 1850, the Democrats increased their majority from 112 seats in the Thirty-first Congress to 140 seats in the Thirty-second, while the Whig minority fell to 88 seats and the Democrats retained control of the Senate. In 1852, Democratic majorities in both chambers increased to approximately 68% in the House and 61% in the Senate, and the Democratic presidential candidate was elected. Had the party solved or successfully compromised sectional divisions, a Democratic realignment could have been envisioned. Their failure, however, led to defeat in the House elections of 1854. Thus in both cases, the incapacities of political leadership and the course of events over which the leadership had no control turned what now appear as incipient realignments into no more than two additional examples of deviating elections.

A further example of potential but unrealized partisan realignment is provided by the elections of the early 1960s. Following the 1964 election, Burnham, Pomper, and other

political observers saw the possibility of a Democratic realignment in the traditional style.[18] Voting patterns had shifted
dramatically and on balance in favor of the Democrats,
although national surveys also showed that the distribution of
partisan identification within the electorate had not shifted in
commensurately dramatic fashion. In terms of voting behavior,
the South shifted toward the Republicans, and much of the
North moved toward the Democrats. In fact, the disruption of
national electoral patterns in presidential voting was more dramatic in 1964 than that accompanying any of the realignments
of the past. In 1964, the distribution of the Democratic presidential vote at the state level was negatively correlated with the
previous century and a quarter of presidential voting. Clearly
then, as Burnham and Pomper correctly perceived, the early
1960s appeared to be the beginning of a Democratic realignment. In 1960, the Republicans were defeated, and unified
Democratic control of the federal government was established.
Aided by the unpopularity of Goldwater and perhaps by the
traumatic memories of presidential assassination, the Democrats
won the elections of 1964 by landslide proportions. Thus the
Democrats gained extraordinary majorities in both chambers of
Congress, and the presidency was occupied by a Democrat of
recognized and heralded ability to deal with the legislative
branch. President Johnson offered a policy agenda of broad
scope designed to cope with long-standing national problems,
revitalize the New Deal coalition, and win new Democratic
adherents in an age of affluence. The Democratic majority in
Congress overcame internal divisions and enacted an unpre-
cedented proportion of that agenda into law.

By 1968, it was evident that a Democratic realignment had
not occurred, and political analysts and observers were already
discussing a potential Republican realignment. Nevertheless,
from the present perspective, discussions in the mid-1960s of a
potential Democratic realignment were thoroughly appropriate.
Basic elements of partisan realignment seemed to be present,
including massive change in voting behavior, unified partisan
control of government with large majorities in Congress, and

concerted policy initiatives addressed to major national problems.

Yet partisan realignment did not occur. The Johnson administration became ever more deeply mired in Vietnam, the ghettos began to burn, national tensions were not relieved but were exacerbated, and short-term voting support for the Democrats was not converted into new and stronger Democratic partisan identifications. There is evidence that blacks did realign. Black electoral participation increased in 1964 and remained thereafter at higher levels than in earlier years. A lasting increase in the proportion of blacks expressing Democratic partisan identifications can also be observed, reflecting, it appears, a response to the vigorous civil rights and antipoverty actions of the Johnson administration. But other groups did not undergo equivalent change; voting behavior did change temporarily, but partisan attitudes did not, and realignment did not occur. Thus the failure of leadership and the intrusion of unforeseen and perhaps uncontrollable events prevented consummation of partisan realignment.

Taken in total, it appears that a revised view of the process of partisan realignment is necessary in order to accommodate both empirical evidence and theoretical knowledge. In our revised perspective, major stress is placed upon the need to differentiate sharply between voting behavior, on the one hand, and political attitudes, on the other. A massive literature effectively demonstrates on numerous fronts that the evidence of voting behavior does not provide a direct and reliable basis for inferences about the structure and distribution of individual partisan attitudes. The revised perspective developed here also places major stress upon the strength and continuity of partisan attitudes and argues that, once formed, individual partisan attitudes change only rarely. As a consequence, a high degree of stability must be seen as a dominant characteristic of American electoral history. Historical realignments are seen not as the products of large-scale conversions of individual partisan identifications, but to a much larger degree the results of movements into and out of the active electorate by potential voters and of adoption of partisan identifications by the apolitical, by independents, and by weakly identifying voters.

And finally, the role of political leadership, governmental action, and the course of historical events are seen as central to the formation of new distributions of partisan attitudes and to consequent lasting shifts in dominance over government from one party to the other. Thus this view argues that the electorate, in past times and today, has been capable of perceiving and rewarding with new and strengthened partisan loyalties political leadership and governmental action perceived as successful and responsive. Conversely, the electorate has also been capable of punishing, by withholding loyalties, political leadership and governmental action perceived as unsuccessful and unresponsive.

Obviously, none of these points is original with us. Other scholars have noted or elaborated these ideas in the context of the realignment perspective. We argue, however, that the theoretical implications of these ideas, taken together, have been ignored. Scholars have, in the main, continued to regard the electorate as the primary producer of a partisan realignment; indeed, they continue to look to the electorate for signs that a realignment is or is not in the making. In contrast, our perspective emphasizes that the electorate, in reaction to events and to leadership it sees as inadequate, may create the conditions for a partisan realignment by rejecting the party in power and giving unified control of government to the opposition. Whether or not the potential realignment comes to fruition lies in the hands of the partisan leadership and its ability to make the kinds of policy decisions that win the long-term support of newly eligible, weakly identified or unidentified, and formerly apolitical members of the electorate. Only then is the temporary rejection of the party in power converted into a lasting change in the partisan division of the electorate.

Furthermore, the initial role of the electorate in creating unified control of government may vary considerably. There may be massive electoral change as in 1932 or minimal change as in 1896, depending upon competitive conditions, or electoral change may be virtually nonexistent as in the 1860s, when secession and Civil War produced the same effect. We can even imagine an electorally dominant party—hypothetically, the Republicans during the Hoover years—reacting effectively to crisis and thereby enhancing and solidifying electoral dominance. These possibilities explain, in part, why analysts of electoral change have found it so difficult to agree in identifying particular elections as realigning. They have employed an inadequate conceptualization of the realignment process, and they (and we) have erroneously interpreted voting behavior as a direct indicator of partisan attitudes.

We are not arguing here that the American electorate is uninformed or irresponsible. Quite the opposite, we see the electorate as quite capable of making judgments about the quality of the political leadership itself and of the policies the leadership offers. This is clear in the electorate's willingness to reject unsuccessful leaders and to return to office successful ones. It is also clear in the willingness of individuals to deviate from their partisan identifications and vote against candidates of the party with which they identify. The development and maintenance of strong electoral attachments to the parties has been in response to effective political leadership and government, or at least the appearance thereof. Failure to develop such attachments is equally a response to inadequate leadership. We do argue, however, that the role of the electorate is essentially reactive. The electorate cannot, unfortunately, create effective leaders; it can only provide the conditions, in the form of unified control of government, under which leaders may effectively function.

Yet the nature of the American political system is such as to impose major obstacles to coherent and effective leadership and government. The complex arrangement of geographical jurisdictions and constituencies works to nullify group demands, while the multilayered governmental system creates what amounts to a multiplicity of "veto groups."[19] Tension and crisis during historical realignment eras worked to narrow and focus issue concerns and provided the conditions for effective government. In these circumstances, partisan attachments were formed and reinforced. The erosion of partisan attachments and the diminution of issue coherence following realignments historically entailed erosion of the conditions of effective government and leadership. Increasingly, national problems were left unresolved and needs remained unmet. These conditions historically led in turn both to further decline in partisan attachments and eventually to the circumstances of crisis and tension that produced the conditions for a new realignment.

Two questions remain to be considered in the following chapter. The first of these concerns an assumption underlying much of the present study. Without in any way denying the relevance of specific historical circumstance or the effects of factors peculiar to particular historical eras, we have assumed that during the period considered here, the mechanisms through which partisan attitudes are formed and maintained have remained essentially the same. We have assumed, in other words, that formulations based primarily upon investigations of the middle decades of the twentieth century can be meaningfully applied to earlier periods, if modifying conditions are specified. But clearly, the latter nineteenth century. appears different. Various historians and other scholars have contended that these years effectively constituted a radically different political universe and hence that entirely different attitudinal and political mechanisms must be envisioned to understand those earlier years. The question is whether acknowledged differences are sufficient to vitiate our conclusions.

A second question concerns the contemporary period. Various scholars have argued that by the 1970s, the American political system had passed "beyond realignment"; they have foreseen the imminent demise of political parties. This view has been taken by some as undermining the validity of "realignment theory" as an interpretation of the past. Obviously, if the American system has passed beyond realignment, if parties are on their way to inevitable disappearance, then the sequences we and others have seen as characteristic of the historical past will not be repeated. It is equally obvious, however, that the realization of this possibility would not in itself invalidate our formulation as a description and explanation of past politics. On the other hand, such a realization would suggest that our formulation has little utility as a means to comprehend the contemporary era and even less as a means to assess the likely directions of the future.

NOTES

1. See, for example, Samuel Lubell, *The Future of American Politics* (New York: Harper and Row, 1951); Jerome M. Clubb and Howard W. Allen, "The Cities and the Election of 1928: Partisan Realignment?" *American Historical Review* 74 (April 1969), pp. 1205-1220; and W. Phillips Shively, "A Reinterpretation of the New Deal Realignment–Based, of All Things, on the *Literary Digest* Poll," *Public Opinion Quarterly* 75 (1971-1972), pp. 621-624.

2. See Duncan MacRae, Jr., and James A. Meldrum, "Critical Elections in Illinois: 1888-1958," *American Political Science Review* 54 (September 1960), pp. 669-683.

3. See, for example, James L. Sundquist, *Dynamics of the Party System* (Washington, DC: Brookings Institution, 1973) and Gerald Pomper, "Classification of Presidential Elections," *Journal of Politics* 29 (August 1967), pp. 535-566.

4. Philip E. Converse, "Public Opinion and Voting Behavior," in Fred I. Greenstein and Nelson W. Polsby (eds.), *Handbook of Political Science*, Vol. 4 (Reading, MA: Addison-Wesley Publishing, 1975), pp. 137-148; and Kristi Andersen, "Generation, Partisan Shift, and Realignment: A Glance Back at the New Deal," in Norman H. Nie, Sidney Verba, and John R. Petrocik, *The Changing American Voter* (Cambridge, MA: Harvard University Press, 1976).

5. Andersen, "Generation, Partisan Shift, and Realignment," p. 88.

6. See especially Angus Campbell, Philip E. Converse, Warren E. Miller, and Donald E. Stokes, *The American Voter* (New York: John Wiley, 1960), Ch. 7.

7. Pomper, "Classification of Presidential Elections."

8. Walter Dean Burnham, *Critical Elections and the Mainsprings of American Politics* (New York: Norton, 1970), Ch. 2.

9. V. O. Key, "Secular Realignment and the Party System," *Journal of Politics* 21 (1959), pp. 198-210.

10. Andersen, "Generation, Partisan Shift, and Realignment," pp. 88-90. In fact, Andersen makes a more extreme–and we think, unreasonable–assumption that individuals adopt a partisanship when they first enter the *eligible* electorate even if they do not cast their first vote until several elections later. Thus those who eventually become Democrats in the 1930s are referred to as "potential Democrats" in the 1920s.

11. Campbell et al., *The American Voter*, Ch. 7.

12. Shively, "A Reinterpretation of the New Deal Realignment."

13. Andersen, "Generation, Partisan Shift, and Realignment," pp. 92-93.

14. Andersen, "Generation, Partisan Shift, and Realignment," p. 93.

15. Robert D. Marcus, *Grand Old Party: Political Structure in the Gilded Age, 1880-1896* (New York: Oxford University Press, 1971), p. 17.

16. The estimates are from Bureau of the Census, *Historical Statistics of the United States: Colonial Times to 1970*, Part 2 (Washington, DC: Government Printing Office, 1975), pp. 1071-1072.

17. See, for example, Samuel T. McSeveney, *The Politics of Depression: Political Behavior in the Northeast, 1893-1896* (New York: Oxford University Press, 1972).

18. Walter Dean Burnham, "American Voting Behavior and the 1964 Election," *Midwest Journal of Political Science* 12 (February 1968), pp. 1-40; Gerald Pomper, *Elections in America* (New York: Dodd, Mead, 1968), pp. 118-121.

19. This view is developed in W. Dean Burnham, Jerome M. Clubb, and William H. Flanigan, "Partisan Realignment: A Systemic Perspective," in Joel H. Silbey, Allan G. Bogue, and William H. Flanigan (eds.), *The History of American Electoral Behavior* (Princeton, NJ: Princeton University Press, 1978) and originally presented at the Mathematical Social Science Board Conference on Historical Voting Behavior, Cornell University, 1973.

Chapter 9

PROSPECTS FOR PARTISAN POLITICS

Our examination of American political history, as we suggest at the conclusion of the preceding chapter, places us in the midst of two clusters of uncertainties. One of these concerns the differences and similarities between the political conditions and characteristics of the latter decades of the nineteenth century and those of the middle decades of the twentieth. From the perspective of the present examination, the uncertainty lies in whether it is sensible to apply to the latter decades of the nineteenth century a view of partisan and political processes that rests heavily upon research into the political phenomena of the years from the 1950s through the 1970s.[1] Is it sensible to assume that the mechanisms through which partisan attitudes are formed and maintained have remained essentially the same across more than a century, or is it necessary to assume fundamentally different mechanisms to explain and make sense of the political life of the last half of the nineteenth century?

A second cluster of uncertainties concerns the likely fate of political parties and partisanship in the latter twentieth century.

A number of political analysts and commentators have argued
on the basis of both contemporary and historical data that the
political parties are losing the support of the public and with it
the capacity to function and govern.[2] The discussion has taken
various forms, but the main thrust is that the American people
have lost confidence in political parties, are cynical about political leaders, and are either too sophisticated or too apathetic to
identify with parties. And there is more to the argument than
its implications for mass political behavior, since the conclusions drawn concern the potential demise of the parties and the
party system, indeed, the capacity of the political system to
survive. A reasonable question is whether or not the present
examination helps in any way to elucidate the prospects of the
party system.

The two sets of uncertainties are obviously interrelated.
Researchers and commentators have observed long-term patterns of political change and have taken them as indicative of
fundamental differences between the latter nineteenth century,
on the one hand, and the middle decades of the twentieth, on
the other. These same patterns of change, combined with factors seen as peculiar to the 1960s and 1970s, are also taken as
forecasting the end of political parties. In this chapter, we will
consider whether long-term change invalidates comparison of
the contemporary period with earlier periods and whether these
patterns of change are such as to preclude revitalization of the
party system.

These questions cannot be answered on the basis of empirical
data alone. Brief consideration of change in the social and
institutional environment of politics during the past century or
more does provide a basis for assessing the nature, sources, and
significance of patterns of political change during that same
period. That consideration also explains some of the inconsis-
tencies we have observed in comparing the several realignment
and decay periods. Predicting the future of the political parties
is a different and more difficult matter. To accept or convincingly to refute the view that the parties have fallen to such a
low state in the contemporary period that recovery is impos-

sible would require substantially stronger theory than is now available. Here again, however, consideration of long-term processes of change suggests the sources of the difficulties confronting the party system. We believe, moreover, that the perspective on American politics developed in our initial chapter and extended in the preceding chapter aids in identifying factors that will influence the fate of the party system in the latter twentieth century. Before turning to these issues, it is necessary to review the patterns of political change we have observed.

A few examples can serve to illustrate the types and variety of evidence that are sometimes taken as both indicative of fundamental change in American politics and as forecasting the end of the party system. Shifts in popular participation in elections since the nineteenth century have been frequently discussed. Turnout in elections rose across the nineteenth century to high points in the 1870s, 1880s, and 1890s.[3] Thereafter, participation declined to its historical nadir in the elections of 1920 and 1924. A measure of recovery came with the elections of 1928 and the 1930s and continued through 1960, although the high levels of the late nineteenth century were not achieved. In the elections of the 1960s and 1970s, turnout was irregular but tended to decline, though without reaching the low points of the 1920s. It is possible—indeed likely—that the estimates of participation during the latter nineteenth century are inflated to some unknown degree.[4] Even so, there is indication of substantial change in the level of popular participation in politics, and these patterns of change have been taken to mean that the political parties have increasingly lost the capacity to mobilize the mass electorate.

In Chapter 4, several series of data documented the variation in partisan loyalties as reflected in mass voting behavior, and evidence of long-term trends as well as cycles associated with the realignment sequences were observed. For example, our measure of aggregate split-ticket voting indicates that the presidential vote and the congressional vote were closely related during the latter nineteenth and early twentieth centuries, but the relationship declined thereafter. Here again, the New Deal years brought a measure of restoration, and the distribution of the vote for president and Congress was more closely related in the 1930s and early 1940s than during the earlier decades of the century. But decline was again resumed. This progressive disassociation of the presidential and congressional vote suggests differing perceptions of the presidency and the Congress on the part of the electorate, declining capacity of the parties to integrate the appeals of various candidates for office, and hence a decline in the relevance of the parties to governmental processes.

To note a further illustration, voting patterns within Congress also seem to suggest a decline in the relevance of the parties as policy-making agencies. A sharp decline in partisanship and polarization in both the House of Representatives and the Senate can be observed since the beginning of the twentieth century. In the House and Senate, these trends were interrupted, and, at least in the House, a measure of restoration was achieved with the New Deal realignment. In neither chamber, however, were the levels of the early years of the twentieth century or the latter years of the nineteenth regained, and the declining trend was soon resumed. By the 1960s and 1970s, these indicators had reached their lowest point in well over a century. These trends might be taken as reflecting the failure of political parties to serve as programmatic coordinators of governmental policy, and as further indication of the decline of the party system.

In part because of the nature of the available data, our indications of partisan deterioration are most consistent for the second and third decades of the twentieth century, and still less consistent for the latter nineteenth century. These differences might be seen as suggesting that during each successive decay phase, partisan deterioration has been more pervasive and more profound. Hence the implication might be that contemporary partisan deterioration differs in kind, rather than just in degree, and that recovery of the parties is unlikely if not impossible.

Taken together, these historical trends and differences seem to suggest that the capacity of the parties to mobilize the mass electorate, to pose and implement clear policy alternatives, and to integrate government has progressively declined. Thus they seem to lend credence to the view that the party system is well on the way to disappearance. They also seem to suggest that the basic attitudinal mechanisms of the mid-twentieth century were dissimilar in essential ways from those of the nineteenth. Yet neither of these conclusions seems to us appropriate. In the remainder of this chapter, we will consider the implications for the decline of political parties of both the long-term trends and the presumed change in attitudinal mechanisms over the last century. The contention that popular political attitudes toward parties were generated differently a century ago and hence cannot be compared with public opinion since World War II is a specific example of a more general argument. Without denying that historical conditions are always changing, always dissimilar in endless ways, and that relationships or patterns from one set of conditions to another are inevitably not exactly the same, we are not so pessimistic about the appropriateness of comparison in general. Each comparison must be evaluated on its merits, and that applies to the assessment of attitudinal mechanisms in different historical eras. We now turn to that assessment. To do so, however, it is necessary to recall briefly the nature of the nineteenth century as well as the social, economic, and institutional changes that have occurred in the United States over the last hundred years.

THE CHANGING CONTEXT OF POLITICS

In many respects, the political world of the latter nineteenth century appears strikingly different from that of the middle of the twentieth. The remarkably high levels of participation in elections and the evidence of extremely strong partisan consistency of voting behavior and of intense individual attachments to the parties seem strikingly at odds with the experiences of the mid-twentieth century. On the basis of these manifest differences, various scholars have argued that the models and theories of individual political attitudes and behavior developed through survey research conducted from the 1950s through the 1970s cannot be applicable to the nineteenth century.[5] Thus the tendency among these scholars has been to postulate a fundamentally different political universe for these years and to argue the need for fundamentally different models and theories of individual political attitudes and behavior. In fact, quite the reverse seems to be the case. If we remember the nature of the models and theories developed since the 1950s, then the patterns of political behavior and the evidence of political attitudes for the latter nineteenth century appear almost exactly as we would predict on the basis of those models and theories, given the social, economic, and institutional characteristics of the times.[6]

In a variety of ways, the characteristics of the nineteenth century were well calculated to produce high rates of participation on the part of the eligible electorate, intense partisanship, strong attachment to the parties, and strong party organizations. The world of the nineteenth century, however complicated it may have seemed to its inhabitants, was simpler than the world of more recent times. This was a world, as Wiebe has put it, of "island communities" in which the bulk of the inhabitants lived in relative isolation from each other.[7] The predominantly rural nineteenth-century population was less economically interdependent, and its economic well-being was less sharply differentiated than was the case later. Thus economic groups and divisions apparently played a lesser role in the political life of the nation than in later years. Put differently, this was a world of small and relatively homogeneous groupings in which social psychological factors exerted more consistent political pressures and contributed to high levels of partisanship. In these terms, relatively consistent and interrelated social pressures constitute an explanation for strong individual partisanship which is an alternative to the pervasive, well-developed, and coherent political ideologies sometimes assumed as characteristic of these years.

Substantial research suggests that in the nineteenth-century setting, religious and ethnic groups and cleavages played a larger role in shaping mass political behavior than in the middle decades of the twentieth century.[8] It is likely that this research has exaggerated the role of religious and ethnic factors in nineteenth-century politics and has tended to substitute a monocausal ethnocultural explanation of nineteenth-century political behavior for an equally implausible monocausal economic explanation.[9] Nor is it necessary to accept the inference that many members of the nineteenth-century electorate had a tightly constrained "belief system" which closely linked theological positions and beliefs with political attitudes and partisan preferences. Rather, in this simpler society, highly cohesive religious and ethnic groups with well-developed political orientations and loyalties worked in both positive and negative ways to shape and reinforce political attitudes and behavior. The simpler group structure of those years meant, moreover, that the individual was less frequently subject to conflicting group pressures in political life.

It is also likely that processes of political socialization were more effective than they would become in later years. In this less complex world, families were more closely knit and more central to the lives of their members, while alternative and potentially conflicting sources of political socialization were less prevalent and less powerful. Hence, it is plausible to assume that the family functioned more effectively to transmit and shape partisan identifications and political attitudes with the consequence of stronger individual partisanship and more strongly held political values.

If the social environment of the nineteenth century differed from that of the twentieth, the political environment differed as well. The nineteenth century was, in general, a period of party building. The signposts of this process in the earlier nineteenth century include acceptance of uniform party labels, the development of local, state, and national party organizations, progressive democratization of the franchise, and the appearance of national party programs. The latter decades of the century were, above all, a period of growth of parties and of development of partisan linkages within the political system. A pre-

dominantly local and overtly partisan press gave to the parties a
near-monopoly over political information. A patronage system
reached into thousands of post offices and customs houses
across the nation. The nominating process was dominated by
local and state party organizations which served as gatekeepers
to political office. Through such organizational mechanisms,
historians have argued, politicians of the time were able to
sound their electorates almost as effectively and certainly more
cheaply than do modern politicians with their public opinion
polls.[10] This fact aside, these mechanisms constituted potent
tools for campaigning and for mobilizing the electorate.

The political institutions of the time were also conducive to
strengthening partisanship and party organizations. In the 1860s
and the 1870s, the practice of holding elections at different
times in the various states was gradually abandoned as was the
practice within states of holding elections to different offices at
different times. Instead, elections to national and to a lesser
degree state offices were increasingly concentrated at a single
time. Under the conditions of the party ballot system, this
modification reduced the opportunities for voters to divide
their votes between the candidates of different parties, and
straight ticket voting of the "party strip" appears to have
become the rule.[11] Polsby and his collaborators have also traced
for these years the development of strong partisan structures
and the increasing role and power of the speaker as party leader
in the House of Representatives.[12] At the same time, indirect
election provided a link between United States senators and
state party organizations and an opportunity to impose sanc-
tions for breaches of party loyalty.

Latter nineteenth-century politics were marked by other
characteristics calculated to facilitate intense partisanship on
the part of the electorate and strong party organization. In
these years, it appears, intense symbols from the past loomed
large, and the partisan loyalties of the time were strongly
anchored in the recollections of the traumatic events of Civil
War and Reconstruction. Regional loyalties derived from these
experiences undoubtedly reinforced partisan attachments.

Surely the partisan realignment symbols of the Civil War and Reconstruction were extremely potent, and their heritage accounts in considerable degree for the durability of the two parties emerging from that era.

It appears as well that something of a disjunction existed between national politics, on the one hand, and state and local politics, on the other. Paradoxically, that disjunction facilitated party integration and organization across the three levels of government, although perhaps at the expense of specific political content and relevance. The distinction between national politics and issues, on the one hand, and those of the state and local levels, on the other, was sharper in these years, and the impact of national policy upon the individual was undoubtedly less direct and apparent than it became in the years following. National politics tended to focus upon essentially symbolic issues derived from the Civil War and Reconstruction and upon national issues, such as tariff and monetary policy and the like, which were relatively remote in practical terms from the daily lives of the electorate. Immediate, practical, bread-and-butter political issues were largely in the purview of state and local governmental agencies. These conditions worked to shield the national parties and the national government from potentially disruptive local issues and cleavages. Since for much of the electorate, the issues of national politics and the actions of the national government could take on an essentially symbolic hue, they could be seen as coinciding with local issues and with the positions of state and local parties. Partisan integration could thus be preserved.

Other conditions and institutions of the time were also conducive to high levels of electoral participation. The population of the latter nineteenth century was, of course, poorly educated in comparison with that of the middle decades of the twentieth. On the other hand, particularly outside the South, levels of literacy were already high during the nineteenth century. Women, blacks, and recently arrived immigrants—groups which under nineteenth-century conditions were least well educated— were either totally or disproportionately excluded from the eligible electorate. The eligible electorate was, then, to a large degree composed of the portion of the population most likely to concern itself with politics and to participate in political affairs. The close competitive conditions of the latter nineteenth century and the intensely partisan character of the electorate placed a premium on turning out the vote. Under these conditions, electoral mobilization was a primary function of the parties. We can surmise that they were aided in that function by other politically relevant secondary groups and the norms of the period which placed a value on electoral participation.

This view of the political arrangements and characteristics of the latter nineteenth century is of course heavily inferential. In developing this view, we surely are not bemoaning a lost golden age of American democracy. A high level of voter turnout is not in itself evidence of a politically involved and informed electorate. Accounts and reports of latter nineteenth-century politicians and other observers of the political scene do tell us of the very large attendance at political functions of the period, the rapt attention given to the lengthy speeches to which political figures were addicted, and the continuation of political gatherings and rallies over periods of several days. Such reports must be discounted in some degree, just as the reports of attendance at more modern political gatherings must also be discounted. Even so, these reports suggest that mass participation in politics in these years was not confined to the mere casting of votes, and they might be taken as reflecting substantial popular interest in political affairs. But here again, interest is not the same as information, and it could be surmised that in the more isolated world of the nineteenth century, political gatherings and elections were primarily important as sources of entertainment and as opportunities to meet distant neighbors and acquaintances and to gain some contact with a larger world. By the same token, intense partisanship is not in itself evidence of either high levels of political interest or information, nor are strong political parties necessarily responsive. Indeed, there is some basis for arguing that the political parties of the late nineteenth century functioned primarily as mechanisms to frustrate political responsiveness and accountability rather than as means to those ends.

The point is, however, that we need not postulate any particular level of real political interest, information, or involvement on the part of the latter nineteenth-century electorate to account for the political characteristics of the period. We need not, in other words, assume either a highly interested, informed, and involved electorate or, at the opposite extreme, an unthinking, militarily drilled electorate.[13] We can imagine a simpler society in which the number of individual group affiliations were more limited and in which conflicting group pressures on the individual voter were less frequent. In this simple society, the political parties could function as genuinely strong psychological reference groups which were reinforced by a relatively limited number of other highly cohesive and politically salient secondary groups with clear political standards. We can add to this vision relatively limited access to political information by the mass electorate and the high degree of control over available political information enjoyed by the parties, which helped to shield voters from cross pressures and from unfavorable news about candidates and policies.

And other elements can be added to the vision as well. They include the institutional arrangements of the time, such as the public casting of ballots, the form of the party ballot, and the absence of registration requirements. They also include the essentially symbolic character of national issues, at least from the perspective of the grass roots, and the apparent disjunction in issue salience between national politics and government, on the one hand, and state and local government and politics, on the other. With this vision of the latter nineteenth century, the evidence of lack of electoral response to short-term political forces, of relatively invariant partisan voting behavior, of intense mass partisanship and strong partisan identifications, of high levels of political participation, and of a highly integrated partisan system seems fully explicable. With that explication, the need to postulate a fundamentally different political universe and a fundamentally different model of political attitudes and behavior for the nineteenth century largely disappears.

Beginning in the 1890s and continuing thereafter, changes that had been underway for decades culminated in change in the parameters of political life. The nature of these changes are obvious and require little elaboration. An increasingly complex national economy gradually replaced the simpler economic structure of earlier years. Beginning in the 1890s and the early years of the twentieth century, the local partisan press was increasingly replaced by a less overtly partisan national press, eventually by national wire services, and still later by even more powerful and pervasive media of mass communication. News and information became more richly available and less influenced by partisan perspective; the heavily political fare of the past was replaced by more varied content, with the probable consequence that the concern of readers and listeners was distracted from the purely political.

These changes, coupled with increasing urbanization and improvements in transportation, completed the destruction of the system of isolated "island communities" of earlier years, and a more integrated nation developed. Issues of national scope multiplied and decision-making increasingly shifted from local and state governments to the national level. Change in the group structure of society also occurred. Trade unions, professional and trade associations, and other secondary groups of potential relevance to politics multiplied. Thus group pressures upon political behavior and attitudes also multiplied and became more complex and conflicting.

This pattern of social, economic, and demographic change, it can be surmised, was calculated to weaken partisan identification and to reduce the strength and role of political parties. The turn of the century and the decades following also witnessed a series of institutional changes and reforms which can be seen as working to disrupt partisan linkages within the national political system and as contributing to the weakening of the political parties. These changes included the introduction of secret voting and of the Australian ballot, which increased the opportunity for ticket splitting and contributed to reduction in the partisan consistency of the vote; the introduction of the direct primary, which reduced the control of party organizations over the nominating process; the spread of nonpartisan approaches to government at the local level; and the introduction of direct election of senators, which worked to disrupt the link between the state and national parties.

And other institutional changes were implemented as well. Personal registration requirements increased the "opportunity costs" of voting, with the consequence, there is good reason to believe, that those segments of the population which were politically least involved, interested, and informed—those segments, in other words, which were most likely to vote their partisan identifications—were disproportionately discouraged from voting.[14] At the same time, women and naturalized immigrants and their offspring entered the potential electorate in increasing numbers, but these hurdles slowed their movement into the active electorate. A concentrated attack upon political corruption and machine politics looked toward disruption of the system of favors that served to link some of these same segments of the electorate to the political system. At another level of government, the "unhorsing" of "Uncle Joe" Cannon in 1910 as Speaker of the House of Representatives and the roughly simultaneous assault on Senate Majority Leader Nelson W. Aldrich symbolized the assault upon party government in Congress, the institutionalization of the seniority system in that body, and the rise of a system of autonomous standing committees.

Doubtlessly, other factors contributed to decline in the indicators of popular political participation, partisan electoral behavior, and partisanship and polarization in Congress. The realignment of the 1890s brought a drop in electoral competition and with it a decline in the incentive for electoral participation. It is likely, however, that institutional modifications also contributed to the decline in electoral competition that has continued with only limited interruptions into the 1970s. The early decades of the twentieth century were also marked by an attack on the system of party organization that had developed in the nineteenth century. Political reformers described that system as corrupt and undemocratic. Whatever the merits of the case, the evidence suggests that the institutional changes resulting from this attack weakened political parties, or, at the least, reduced their capacity to function as agencies of political mobilization and integration.[15]

Broad processes of social and economic change go far, then, toward explaining political trends observable in the earlier twentieth century in terms of the models and theories of individual political attitudes and behavior alluded to above. As the nation became socially and economically more complex, the psychological group structure of society also became more complex and more varied, and the number of politically salient reference groups multiplied. The centrality of the parties as psychological political groups diminished as the number of politically salient and conflicting alternative groups increased, and the electorate was more frequently confronted by conflicting group pressures. At the same time, political issues multiplied and became more diffuse; some of the symbolic hue that had colored politics in earlier years faded; and the disjunction between national as opposed to state and local politics and government was to some degree bridged. The national information flow increased, became more varied and pervasive, and its partisan coloration declined. These processes of change strained the parties as mechanisms of political mobilization, organization, integration, and policy formation, while simultaneously a broad pattern of institutional change imposed still further strain.

ON THE FUTURE OF POLITICAL PARTIES

What we have described is the development of a social and institutional environment that is substantially less conducive to strong partisanship on the part of the electorate, to high levels of mass political participation, and to strong partisan organization than that of the latter nineteenth century. This development helps to explain the differences in the characteristics of the several decay phases observed in Chapter 4. That the deterioration of the Civil War alignment appears less pronounced than the deterioration of the 1896 alignment, which in turn appears less pronounced than that of the New Deal alignment, is explicable when these broad patterns of change are taken into account. Our summary of these patterns of change also leads, however, to the conclusion that evidence of deterioration of the parties and of partisanship, both within the electorate and among political leaders, cannot be casually dismissed.

Even if we argue convincingly that the contemporary patterns of political behavior are much like those in earlier decay phases, there is still the possibility that long-term forces are introducing drastic and irreversible changes. These longer-term trends, it can be argued, have been accentuated in the middle decades of the twentieth century, with the consequence that the contemporary era has become even less congenial to political parties and partisanship. Increasing social and economic complexity has continued apace, bringing with it proliferation of cross-cutting and conflicting group pressures and a further decline in the centrality of political parties. National issues and problems have become ever more diffuse and have assumed global dimensions and ramifications. Thus the formation of clear and consistent policies and programs has become immensely more difficult, and the repercussions of policy failure in terms of popular confidence and the further weakening of the parties have increased. News and information media have proliferated, become more powerful, less restrained, less supportive of any political party, and have taken on a more prominent role in the political life of the nation. Educational levels have risen phenomenally. As a consequence, or so it can be argued, better informed voters stand less in need of the cues provided by the parties; they are increasingly more capable of determining their own responses to the issues, problems, and political pronouncements and personalities of the day. A demographic bulge in the number of young people being socialized politically came, moreover, at a time when large numbers of adults were engaging in ticket splitting and vacillating voting behavior. Thus the signals transmitted to them through the socialization process may well have been those of partisan independence and weak attachments rather than those of strong identification.[16]

While these trends and patterns of change appear impressive, they do not constitute evidence that the party system is necessarily on its way to inevitable disappearance. Predictions of the demise of the party system seem to rest primarily upon three interrelated sets of arguments. One of these is the view that the deterioration of parties and partisanship has passed a "point of no return" and has reached such a low state that recovery is no longer possible. This view is based in part upon the prolonged deterioration of the New Deal alignment. Conditions have been right, so the argument goes, for partisan realignment since the 1960s. None has occurred; hence the mechanisms that produce realignments have gone awry. A second set of arguments concerns factors which are seen as peculiar to the 1960s and 1970s, or at least heightened during these years, and which are also taken as detrimental to the party system. The third concerns the grievous and perhaps insoluble problems seen as confronting the nation.

Evidence of progressive electoral detachment from the parties during the 1960s and 1970s was summarized in Chapter 4. But the obverse must also be noted. A substantial portion of the electorate still identifies with the parties, and partisan identification remains a primary determinant of voting behavior. The relevant data, in short, provide no evidence that the electorate is no longer capable of identifying with parties or that a "point of no return" has been passed, beyond which heightened identification with the parties is no longer possible.

. It is worth noting, moreover, that the party system, to the distress of its critics, has survived extraordinary social and political change in the past, which suggests that historically the system has proven highly adaptable to changing circumstances. The system has survived other periods of apparent weakness and severe popular disenchantment. The latter 1840s and the 1850s constituted one such period, when both the Democrats and the Whigs moved toward the compromising center and effectively avoided the pressing and divisive issues of the day. The result was the disappearance of one of the major parties and, it appears, increased disaffection from the other. It is true that a new party emerged as the Whigs faltered and collapsed. But the new Republican Party was an essentially regional party with little strength outside the North, and it is plausible to contend that national crisis in the form of secession and civil war was required to convert the new party into a viable political organization.

It can be argued, of course, that in the 1840s and 1850s, the party system was still in its formative stages. Hence the difficulties of the parties in these years might better be interpreted as "growing pains" than as signs of weakness of the system and threats to its continuation. In these terms, the second and third decades of the twentieth century constitute a better case. The series of Democratic victories in the elections from 1910 through 1916 reflected severe and disruptive divisions within the Republican Party, and these divisions continued, albeit in somewhat less virulent form, across the 1920s. It is reasonable to believe that both parties lost adherents across the 1920s, and, as declining voter participation rates clearly suggest, neither party effectively attracted the new, potential electorate.

These difficulties were probably most severe for the Democrats, and an observer at the time would not have been totally unreasonable in predicting that the party was in decline and on its way to fragmentation and collapse. In part, Democratic difficulties were simply those of the minority party. Because of its smaller size, normal processes of political socialization brought fewer new adherents to the Democrats than to the Republicans. The Democratic Party was also divided between an urban northern wing and a rural southern wing. In the context of the times, the two wings shared few commonalities of interest, aside from acquisition and retention of office. Moreover, the southern wing was heavily and narrowly based upon the repressive institutions and practices of the South. Hence, Democratic capacity to develop and present meaningful policy alternatives to those of the Republicans was severely limited. An impartial observer, cognizant of these divisions, and with the dramatic illustrations of the national convention of 1924 and the presidential election of 1928 in mind, might have sensibly predicted that the Democratic party was in the last stages of collapse. It is plausible, then, to view the health of the party system as no better in the 1920s than in the 1970s. Yet political parties survived and, indeed, seemingly underwent a measure of revitalization in the 1930s. On these grounds, a further revitalization would appear possible today.

Predictions of the disappearance of parties, however, are also based upon characteristics of the 1960s and 1970s that are seen as unique to these years. Burnham and Ladd and Hadley particularly have argued that the deterioration of parties and partisan processes are irreversible because of several developments, including the pervasiveness of mass media, the emergence of a postindustrial society with its differing social characteristics and class structure, and increasing distrust and cynicism toward social and political institutions.[17] Here again, these views are debatable.

That the news and information media, television primarily, have come to be more important channels of communication appears undeniable, but it is less obvious that this development must necessarily be at the expense of political parties. The political parties as organizations and party leaders use the media, again especially television, to communicate partisan messages both as news and as advertising. The impact is particularly strong during campaigns, perhaps, mainly for conveying information. Patterson and McClure have demonstrated the capacity of campaigns to inform voters about issue positions without changing their partisan attitudes.[18] The availability of television to many candidates who would otherwise have lacked effective means of reaching voters may partially account for ticket splitting among the most salient races. Such factors as incumbency are easily conveyed by the mass media and may diminish somewhat the impact of party and issues on vote choices. On the other hand, should support for party positions become a salient characteristic, as it would in a realignment of the traditional sort, the media would provide an opportunity for conveying to voters the candidates' records of support of party programs and endorsement by party leaders. Thus, in different circumstances, the availability of more information about candidates may encourage straight ticket voting rather than the reverse. But basically, the media are channels that can be used either to enhance or undermine the impact of parties, depending mainly on the decisions of the political leadership. The mass media have not caused the decline of parties, although they have carried information that has hurt the parties. The media and the media-based commentators are not independent political institutions; the media are not in a position to replace parties. Despite their capacities to make and distort news, the media provide opportunities that can serve equally well to undermine or revitalize parties.

It is possible to accept the argument that the class structure of a postindustrial society is different from that of a society in the midst of industrial development. The view that the classes of such a society would be so qualitatively different that they could not be reflected in a party system such as has existed in the past is less convincing. The coalitions of support for the parties might well be different, the differences between (or among) the parties might reflect cleavages of a different type, but parties could remain the mechanism through which these cleavages are represented in politics. As we have noted, there is no persuasive evidence showing that the parties have disappeared as objects of political significance to the voter at present, and there is no commanding evidence to demonstrate that societal change will necessarily render them irrelevant in the future.[19]

Loss of confidence and increasing cynicism are also seen as related to the decline of political parties. It is certainly well established that there is less trust and confidence in political parties, and since this development is presumably the public's reaction to the performance and behavior of political leaders, it is hardly surprising. By the same process, it can be imagined, sound and meaningful policy and the appearance of skilled leaders could restore confidence and reduce cynicism, although it may be easier to destroy than to create trust and confidence. Furthermore, this trend in attitudes is almost certainly not unique to the 1960s and 1970s, nor is it limited to parties or political leaders. It extends to all of government and most social institutions. Cynicism may remain high, but it is not in itself fatal to all the institutions it touches. Loss of confidence and trust in political and social institutions in the last decade should not be ignored and in fact suggest a contemporary crisis. It appears unwarranted, however, to conclude that existing levels of mistrust and cynicism will necessarily prevent the recovery of the party system.

A final argument upon which predictions of the demise of parties are sometimes based has to do with problems and difficulties confronting the United States. In this view, the problems confronting the nation are insoluble, at least through the instrumentalities of present political and governmental mechanisms, and increase in dissatisfaction produced by the failures of government will continue. From this perspective, declining support for political parties is only one of many symptoms of the collapse of the American governmental system. This is an alarming prospect, but it is not one that can be inferred in any straightforward way from historical political patterns or demonstrated with certainty on the basis of contemporary evidence. If it is an accurate prophecy, the least of our problems is declining partisan loyalties.

There is little disagreement that the data of the 1960s and 1970s provide evidence of the disaggregation of the old party alignment and of an increase in the pool of voters and potential voters detached from traditional party loyalties. It also appears that the political environment has become less congenial to political parties than in the past. On the other hand, there is little empirical support for the argument that the observed dealignment has progressed to a point from which the parties cannot recover and that many of their traditional functions will disappear, along with the party system as we know it. In the paragraphs above, we have attempted to show that it is plausible and in keeping with the evidence to believe that the parties reached an equally low state in the 1920s but still recovered. We see no evidence that some threshold has now been reached from which the parties cannot recover as organizers of political information for the public or as aggregators of issues and interests linking the public to the governing process. Clearly, the parties are less effective in performing these functions than in the past, but we see no evidence that the parties are somehow incapable of carrying out these functions.

Obviously, partisan realignment did not occur in the 1960s or 1970s. It is also the case that a longer time period has elapsed since the New Deal realignment than intervened between earlier realignments. But these facts in themselves do not demonstrate that partisan realignment of the historical form is no longer possible. There is no reason to believe, moreover, that partisan realignment and revitalization of political parties can only come, as in the past, with relative suddenness and in response to clear, short, and obvious crisis. It is also possible to imagine a more gradual process in which electoral support for the parties would develop over a prolonged period in response to party policies which appeared reasonably coherent and realistic and which could be taken as a meaningful response to national problems.

We have argued, however, that a vital element of historical realignments was action by government that could be seen as effective. Opportunities for realignment and revitalization of the parties have occurred in the 1960s and, it appears, again in the 1970s. The fact that these opportunities went unrealized was the consequence of failures of leadership and perhaps of the intervention of unforeseen and uncontrollable events rather than of any incapacity of voters to orient themselves toward and to support political parties. Thus, we can only conclude that the possibility of partisan realignment and revitalization of the parties in any form is critically dependent upon the behavior of the political leadership and the performance of government.

That the tasks of political leadership and of forming sound public policy have become more difficult seems undeniable. The problems confronting the nation are massive, diffuse, and probably insoluble without sacrifice. Certainly, they are insoluble without effective leadership. The current disjuncture between the presidency and Congress and the apparent propensity of political leaders to disassociate themselves from the parties pose a major uncertainty both for public policy and for the possibility of revitalization of the parties. The consequence of these tendencies is to fragment further an already fragmented political system. If these tendencies continue and become more pronounced, it would be unlikely that successful government by a majority party could occur and that credit for successful government could strengthen the party in power. Unless the electorate could make the connection between policy-making perceived as successful and candidates running for office under a party label, a supportive response to the parties would not occur. As we have argued, the widespread availability of mass media can be an asset, not a hindrance, in facilitating the transmission of information on these points. Whether policy-making is successful and whether successes are treated as party rather than personal efforts depends once again upon the behavior of party and governmental leadership.

Even considerable confidence in our descriptions of historical political patterns would not entail confidence in diagnoses of future development based upon those descriptions. We are less willing to argue the certain applicability to the future of the generalizations developed here than we are to urge the value and utility of a perspective on American politics that includes political leadership and governmental performance as well as the electorate. The perspective urged here corrects the tendency to view the electorate as the main or even the sole driving force in American politics.

The American electorate has been and remains, we have argued, a responsive and responsible electorate. Thus, alleged change in the electorate is not a crucial consideration. However, the role of the electorate is reactive; initiative for policy action and change lies with the political leadership. The leadership offers voters opportunities to "throw the rascals out" in response to inadequate performance, to respond to a newly established administration with enthusiasm, to align themselves with a successfully governing party, and to support effective policy action. The voters contribute a crucial element to these processes, but so indeed do the leaders. Both successes and failures in realigning the party coalitions depend heavily on the leaders, since they, in contrast to ordinary voters, appear historically to have been much more unevenly equipped for the challenges facing them.

The conditions confronting political parties in the 1960s and 1970s appear radically different from those of the latter nineteenth century, and the obstacles in the way of development and maintenance of strong political parties are considerably greater. We do not mean to argue that the health of the party system is good; we do argue, however, that the state of health is still better than it is sometimes made out to be, and that improvement is possible. Thus, we do not yet need to contemplate with certainty either a coming Caesarism as governmental power inevitably drifts to a presidency unrestrained by partisan ties, organization, or responsibility; unfettered domination over government by powerful and irresponsible interest groups; or a utopian age in which the more humane and rational values of postindustrial society dominate politics and government untrammeled by the venality and cynical compromise of political parties. The health of the parties may not be good, but predictions of their imminent demise are debatable.

The evidence summarized here does not lead us to conclude that political parties can no longer survive or marshall public support for complex governmental programs. We are prepared to believe that the challenge to political leaders in performing party functions successfully is indeed greater than in the past. The failures of the political system in the future, and they may be awesome, will be failures of leadership, and not in any significant degree the products of new characteristics of the electorate. The way in which American citizens respond to the successes and failures of political leaders is more properly viewed as relatively constant than as another erratic variable menacing the future.

NOTES

1. See, for example, Walter Dean Burnham, "The Changing Shape of the American Political Universe," *American Political Science Review* 59 (March 1965), pp. 7-28; Jerrold G. Rusk, "The Effect of the Australian Ballot Reform on Split Ticket Voting, 1876-1908," *American Political Science Review* 64 (December 1970), pp. 1220-1238; Philip E. Converse, "Change in the American Electorate," in Angus Campbell and Philip E. Converse (eds.), *The Human Meaning of Social Change* (New York: Russell Sage, 1972), pp. 263-337; and the exchange between Burnham, Converse, and Rusk in *American Political Science Review* 68 (September 1974), pp. 1002-1057.

2. The most significant statements are: Walter Dean Burnham, "American Politics in the 1970's: Beyond Party?" in William Nisbet Chambers and Walter Dean Burnham (eds.), *The American Party Systems* (New York: Oxford University Press, 1975), pp. 308-357; Walter Dean Burnham, *Critical Elections and the Mainsprings of American Politics* (New York: Norton, 1970); Everett Ladd with Charles Hadley, *Transformations of the American Party System* (New York: Norton, 1975); Norman Nie, Sidney Verba and John Petrocik, *The Changing American Voter* (Cambridge, MA: Harvard University Press, 1976).

3. William H. Flanigan and Nancy H. Zingale, *Political Behavior of the American Electorate* (Boston: Allyn and Bacon, 1979), pp. 14-20.

4. The most persuasive analysis we have found is Ray M. Shortridge, "Methodological Problems with Nineteenth Century Turnout Estimates," undated manuscript, University of Louisville.

5. See, for example, Lee Benson and Joel Silbey, "American Political Eras, 1788-1984: Toward a Normative, Substantive, and Conceptual Framework for the Historical Study of American Political Behavior," presented at the annual meeting of the Social Science History Association, 1978.

6. The social psychological theorizing about reference groups in the voting literature would appear to be directly applicable to the nineteenth-century social and political conditions, although analysts of the era have neglected this argument. See especially Angus Campbell, Philip E. Converse, Warren E. Miller, and Donald E. Stokes, *The American Voter* (New York: John Wiley, 1960), Ch. 12.

7. Robert H. Wiebe, *The Search for Order: 1877-1920* (New York: Hill and Wang, 1967).

8. Lee Benson, *The Concept of Jacksonian Democracy* (Princeton, NJ: Princeton University Press, 1961); Paul Kleppner, *The Cross of Culture* (New York: Macmillan, 1970); Samuel McSeveney, *The Politics of Depression* (New York: Oxford University Press, 1972); Richard Jensen, *The Winning of the Midwest* (Chicago: University of Chicago Press, 1971); Ronald Formisano, *The Birth of Mass Political Parties* (Princeton, NJ: Princeton University Press, 1971); Michael Holt, *Forging a Majority* (New Haven, CT: Yale University Press, 1969); Frederick Luebke, *Immigrants and Politics* (Lincoln: University of Nebraska Press, 1969).

9. James Wright, "The Ethnocultural Model of Voting: A Behavioral and Historical Critique," in Allan Bogue (ed.), *Emerging Theoretical Models in Social and Political History* (Beverly Hills, CA: Sage Publications, 1973); Richard McCormick, "Ethno-cultural Interpretations of Nineteenth-Century American Voting Behavior," *Political Science Quarterly* 89 (June 1974), pp. 351-377; Allan G. Bogue, Jerome M. Clubb, and William H. Flanigan, "The New Political History," *American Behavioral Scientist* 21 (November/December 1977), pp. 201-220.

10. Richard Jensen, "American Election Analysis," in S. M. Lipset (ed.), *Politics and the Social Sciences* (New York: Oxford University Press, 1969), especially pp. 228-230.

11. Rusk, "The Effect of the Australian Ballot Reform on Split-ticket Voting: 1876-1908."

12. Nelson W. Polsby, Miriam Gallaher, and Barry Spencer Rundquist, "The Growth of the Seniority System in the U.S. House of Representatives," *American Political Science Review* 63 (September 1969), pp. 787-807.

13. The best statement of the first view is in Burnham, "The Changing Shape of the American Political Universe." For the second view, see Jerrold Rusk, "Comment: The American Electoral Universe: Speculation and Evidence," *American Political Science Review* 68 (September 1974), pp. 1028-1049.

14. Converse, "Change in the American Electorate."

15. It may be that the progressive reformers' attack on political parties was carried to its greatest extreme in California, with the consequence of major reductions in political competition through institutional modifications that facilitated and encouraged cross-filing. In the congressional elections of 1926, in that state, for

example, cross-filed candidates ran unopposed as either "Republican-Democrat" or as "Democrat-Republican" in five of the eleven districts; in two districts, Republican candidates ran unopposed; and in two of the remaining four districts, there was opposition, involving in one case a Republican opposed by a "Prohibition-Democrat" and a Socialist candidate, and in the other a "Republican-Democrat-Prohibition" candidate opposed by a Socialist. In only two districts did a Republican candidate confront a Democratic candidate.

16. Philip E. Converse, "Public Opinion and Voting Behavior," in Fred Greenstein and Nelson Polsby (eds.), *Handbook of Political Science*, Vol. 4 (Reading, MA: Addison-Wesley, 1975), p. 144.

17. Burnham, "American Politics in the 1970's: Beyond Party?"; Ladd with Hadley, *Transformations of the American Party System*.

18. Thomas E. Patterson and Robert C. McClure, "Political Advertising: Voter Reaction to Televised Political Commercials," *Citizen Research Foundation Monograph* 23, 1973.

19. The best estimates of influences on vote choice continue to show party as a major factor. See Nie et al., *The Changing American Voter*, pp. 289-306.

APPENDIX

DATA SOURCES AND MANAGEMENT

Four data collections from among the rich holdings of the Inter-university Consortium for Political and Social Research constitute the primary empirical bases for this study. Our second, third, and fourth chapters draw on the collection of county and state level historical election returns maintained by the Consortium.[1] This collection was made possible by an initial award to the Consortium from the Social Science Research Council and by subsequent awards from the National Science Foundation. The data were collected from original sources by scholars throughout the nation and processed, maintained, and extended by the Consortium. Lee Benson, Warren E. Miller, Walter Dean Burnham, and Howard W. Allen, along with numerous other scholars, played primary roles in the creation of this massive collection of original research data.

Our fourth chapter also draws, often through the research of others, on the continuing series of National Election Studies conducted since 1952 by the Survey Research Center and the Center for Political Studies of the Institute for Social Research, University of Michigan. These studies were carried out under the direction of Warren E. Miller with support provided by diverse funding sources. Access to these data was also provided by the Consortium.

Our sixth and seventh chapters are largely based on two additional data collections. The first of these, bearing on the partisan composition of state legislatures and executive offices, was originally compiled by Walter Dean Burnham and subsequently continued and extended by the Consortium staff.[2] The historical core of the congressional voting records employed in our seventh chapter was originally organized under the auspices of the Works Progress Administration in the 1930s. An award to the Consortium from the Ford Foundation supported an extension of the collection and its conversion to computer-readable form. The collection has been subsequently maintained by the Consortium.[3]

Our treatment of the survey data, the data on partisan composition of state governments, and the congressional voting data was relatively straightforward and is described in notes and textual references where appropriate. The collection of historical election returns is intrinsically more complex, and its use required substantive judgments at a number of points.

As noted above, the core of the collection was originally compiled and transcribed from original sources, usually official state publications, which were identified by informed scholars. Extensive error checking procedures were carried out by the Consortium staff to assure the conformity of the computer-readable version of the data to the original sources and to assess in more limited ways the internal consistency of the original sources. To the degree possible, all errors so identified were corrected. Errors and anomalies discovered through further processing or research use of the data were also corrected by the Consortium staff. In some cases, superior or more complete sources were identified and substituted for those originally used.

Several potential sources of distortion characterize these data. The possible impact of corrupt practices, particularly during the latter nineteenth century, has received some discussion in the recent literature.[4] These discussions have concerned the possible inflation of voter participation rates through corrupt practices, although it appears equally possible that such practices could work artificially to deflate the number of votes recorded as cast. While these discussions have examined the impact of corruption on calculations of voter participation, it is obvious that this factor could also be a source of distortion of the recorded partisan distribution of the vote. There is some disagreement among scholars about the magnitude and significance of these distorting influences, and we know of no means by which their impact could be systematically assessed.

Analogous sources of distortion are difficulties in accurately determining the size of the eligible electorate, again particularly during the nineteenth century, due to lack of precise information about voting requirements and their enforcement and to the underenumeration that was very probably larger in the case of earlier national population censuses than recent censuses.[5] Such distortion would not influence our analyses of the partisan distribution of the popular vote, but it would affect turnout estimates.

Change in the boundaries of the geographical units for which the election data are recorded also constitute a source of distortion. This characteristic of the data is not a major difficulty where states are concerned, but it is substantially more troublesome in our county level analysis. For a variety of reasons, newer states do not enter our county level analysis until sometime after their establishment, when a measure of stability in county boundaries was attained. This reduces the amount of distortion produced by boundary changes. Even so, county boundary changes occurred in many states after the temporal points at which those states enter our analysis, and we did not undertake the large, and in many cases impossible, task of correcting for these changes. Such changes introduce a degree of spurious variation in the vote, which we believe to be small but which is unknown. This possible spurious variability is, of course, most marked for the western states during their earlier years.

Rapid population change similarly constitutes a source of what might be seen as spurious variability in the partisan distribution of the vote. That is, shifts in the partisan distribution of the vote in a state or county could be the product of immigration or emigration rather than of change in the partisan predilections of more permanent residents. To some degree, this influence is reduced by omitting the newer states from our analysis during their earlier years when the rate of population change was usually at its highest. But high population mobility has been a constant factor in American history and has been a characteristic of older and established states as well as newer ones. Thus the secular realignment of Massachusetts and Rhode Island in the twentieth century was probably a product of immigration from other states and from abroad rather than of change in the partisanship of long-term residents and their descendents. From our perspective, of course, partisan change produced by population mobility is not spurious, but it is one source of the derangement of partisan alignments and of the formation of new distributions of partisan strength.

The final and in some respects the most difficult problem to be touched on here has to do with party labels. In converting election returns to computer-readable form, the Consortium has followed the rule of recording, to the degree possible, the full detail characteristic of the original sources. Thus the basic collection records the vote for all known parties and candidates that contested elections, and all differences in party labels are preserved. As a consequence, the collection records the vote cast for candidates who ran under more than 1100 party labels, not to mention the vote for candidates who ran without party labels and "scattering" votes for unidentified candidates.[6] This approach preserves the analytical and substantive flexibility of the collection and leaves decisions concerning such matters as combination of parties and candidates to be made by the analyst in terms of specific research applications.

Our concern in examining mass voting behavior is with change and stability in popular support for the major parties and their candidates. Hence, as a general rule (but with some exceptions), we attempted to employ a "pure" major party vote for Democrats, Whigs, and Republicans. One consequence of this rule was that the vote for well over 90% of the third-party and unidentified candidates could be treated effectively as an "other" vote, as deviation from support of one or the other of the major parties, and as a source of instability in major party alignments. In the remaining cases, application of this rule involved judgments that might appear contestable.

A few categories and examples of such decisions will serve to illustrate the application of this approach and its implications. Cross-filed candidates (Democrat-Progressive-Socialist or Republican-Prohibition) were treated as third-party candidates, and their vote was not assigned to a major party when that vote was not differentiated by party in the original sources. When the vote for such candidates was recorded separately under each party label, the vote under the major party label was assigned to that party, and the vote recorded under other labels was treated as a minor party vote. The Roosevelt vote in New York in 1936 and 1940 is an example. In that election, Roosevelt appeared on the New York ballot as both a Democratic and an American Labor candidate, and his vote was recorded separately under the two party labels in the official returns. For the purposes of our analysis, only the vote he received under the Democratic label was treated as the Democratic vote. The vote for candidates who ran for office under a minor party label but who upon election served in Congress or other office as a major party member was treated as a minor party vote and not included in the major party vote. As a further illustration, the vote for candidates who ran in Minnesota under the Farmer-Labor Party label was not treated as part of the Democratic vote until the two parties effectively fused in 1944.

The presidential vote presented the most severe difficulties of classification, and in a few cases, our treatment of that vote involved deviation from our general rule. In the case of major party splits—the four-way race in 1860, the Bull Moose-Republican schism in 1912, or the Truman-Wallace-Thurmond-split in 1948—only the "loyal" party vote was treated as the major party vote. In some instances, and as indicated in notes, we also combined the loyalist and "bolting" components and report analytical results for both the loyalist vote taken separately and for the combined vote. The Union vote in 1864 was treated as the Republican vote; otherwise, no Republican vote would have been available. In some cases, the national nominees of major parties for president ran in most states under a major party label but under different labels in other states. Thus, Grover Cleveland, the Democratic nominee in 1884, ran under the Democratic label in most states but under different labels in two states. In this case, Cleveland's vote in all states was treated as the Democratic vote in order to avoid anomalous analytical results. The same practice was followed in other similar instances.

It is, of course, possible to contest our judgments in classifying and combining, or not combining, the vote cast under different party labels. We doubt, however, that different decisions would undermine our primary findings. In any event, the combined and collapsed files we created for the purposes of our analysis are available from the Consortium along with, of course, the basic files with complete detail.

NOTES

1. *Guide to Resources and Services 1979-1980* (Ann Arbor: Inter-university Consortium for Political and Social Research), pp. 263-264. This massive data file now has the following title: "United States Historical Election Returns, 1788-1978."

2. *Guide to Resources and Services 1979-1980,* p. 163. These data are titled "Partisan Division of American State Governments, 1834-1974. '

3. *Guide to Resources and Services 1979-1980,* pp. 214. This file is titled "United States Congressional Roll Call Voting Records, 1789-1979."

4. See, for example, Philip E. Converse, "Change in the American Electorate," in Angus Campbell and Philip E. Converse (eds.), *The Human Meaning of Social Change* (New York: Russell Sage, 1972), pp. 263-337; Walter Dean Burnham, "Theory and Voting Research: Some Reflections on Converse's 'Change in the American Electorate,'" *American Political Science Review* 58 (September 1974), pp. 1002-1007, and Howard W. Allen, "Vote Fraud and the Validity of Election Data," presented at the annual meeting of the Organization of American Historians, 1977. (mimeo, Southern Illinois University)

5. Ray M. Shortridge, "Methodological Problems with Nineteenth Century Turnout Estimates," 1979. (mimeo, University of Louisville)

6. For a partial indication of this diversity, see *Guide to U.S. Elections* (Washington, DC: Congressional Quarterly, 1975).

EPILOGUE

The election of George Bush marked the passage of more than fifty years without a partisan realignment of the form of the Civil War era, the 1890s, or the New Deal. The years since the late 1940s have eroded the alignment of political forces that grew out of the New Deal and the related events of the 1930s. In the terms introduced in the preceding chapters, the deterioration of the New Deal alignment can be seen as similar in many of its characteristics to the "decay phases" of political coalitions that followed earlier partisan realignments (see especially Chapters 1 and 4).

These decay phases were marked, as we have suggested, by progressive decline of the salience of issues and symbols that were associated with the preceding realignment. During these periods, new issues appeared that cut across realignment issues and could not be accommodated and reconciled by the symbols of the old realignment. With the passage of time following a realignment, the attachment of the electorate to the parties tended to weaken under the impact of new and discordant issues, with the waning salience of realignment symbols, and as new voters entering the electorate gradually replaced an older generation that had directly experienced the realignment crisis.

Through these processes, the constituency bases of the parties were progressively weakened and undermined. As a consequence, these periods were marked by more frequent deviating elections, an increased incidence of divided partisan control of government at both the state and national levels, a propensity toward policy deadlock, and a tendency to avoid rather than confront the major policy issues.

As we argued in Chapter 3, these decay periods were marked by both deviating and realigning change in voting behavior. In each period, the partisan attachments of particular voting groups underwent lasting change. These shifts in partisan attachments did not, however, give rise to a new or strengthened partisan alignment. Rather, they were a part of the partisan dealignment of these periods as the arrangement of political forces gradually lost its old structure.

These were not, of course, periods of unrelieved policy deadlock and inaction. Major governmental actions did take place during these periods, and policy action was not limited to periods of partisan realignment and their immediate aftermaths. We need only think of the reforms of the Progressive years or the enormous changes associated with the mobilization and demobilization at the beginning and end of World War II, all initiated in circumstances other than realignment.

It would be a mistake, therefore, to see these decay periods as significant only as preludes to the next partisan realignment. They were marked by electoral change—some of which was lasting—and by instances of major policy action. The propensity was, however, toward governmental deadlock and against innovative policy action.

Moreover, neither the realignment of particular groups nor policy action during these periods produced the narrowed issue consensus, the deepened and dedicated partisan attachments, or the configuration of widely shared symbols that appeared during the Civil War, the 1890s, and the 1930s. Rather, these decay periods involved weakening of partisan attachments and coalitions within the electorate. This weakening was a necessary step in making future realignment possible, although nothing in the process itself made that eventuality inevitable.

In our view, the Reagan years and the immediately preceding decades have been a continuation of the decay of the New Deal alignment. Some of the indicators of decay have evidenced further deterioration over the past decade, others have changed very little.

TABLE E.1   Unified and Divided Control of State Governments, 1976–1988

	Following the election of . . .						
	1976	1978	1980	1982	1984	1986	1988
Democratic Unified Control	26	20	17	23	16	12	15
Republican Unified Control	0	4	7	4	4	5	5
Divided Control	24	26	26	26	30	33	30

Source: *Statistical Abstract of the United States,* 1982–1983 (103rd edition), pp. 486–487, and 1988 (108th edition), pp. 245–246, U.S. Bureau of the Census, Washington, DC; *The World Almanac and Book of Facts 1989,* Pharos Books, New York, 1988, pp. 317–321.

Divided control of the national government has become the norm, with the Republicans having a string of successes in the White House, while the Democrats have maintained control of the House of Representatives. If we follow the perspective formulated in the preceding chapters, the absence of unified control of the national government during the Reagan years rules out the possibility that a partisan realignment has occurred.

The erosion of unified control of state governments has also characterized the 1980s, so the disarray in partisan voting patterns is not limited to elections for national office. Indeed, as Table E.1 reveals (when compared with Figure 6.2), the high levels of divided control since World War II have continued through 1988, and it might be noted in passing that Republicans have not strengthened their position in the states in recent years.

The evidence on electoral behavior reinforces the view that there is a high degree of volatility and independence in the American electorate. As can be seen in Table E.2, over a third of the electorate remained independent of the political parties through the 1980s. The recent increase in partisans enjoyed by the Republicans brings their strength back to the levels of the 1950s and early 1960s. Over the thirty years or so of dealignment, the significant change is the increased number of independents and the corresponding decline in Democratic identifiers.

TABLE E.2 Party Identification in the American Electorate, 1952–1988

	1952	1956	1960	1964	1968	1972	1976	1980	1984	1988
Strong Democrats	22%	21%	20%	27%	20%	15%	15%	18%	17%	17%
Weak Democrats	25	23	24	25	25	26	25	23	20	18
Independents	22	23	22	22	29	35	36	34	34	36
Weak Republicans	14	14	14	13	14	13	14	14	15	14
Strong Republicans	13	15	15	11	10	10	9	8	13	14
Apolitical, DK	4	4	5	2	2	2	2	2	2	2
Total	100%	100%	100%	100%	100%	100%	101%	99%	101%	101%
n =	1799	1762	1954	1571	1557	2705	2872	1614	1989	2040

Source: National Election Studies, Center for Political Studies.

TABLE E.3 Percentage of Party Identifiers[a] Defecting, 1952–1976

	Nation		Nonsouth		South	
	President	Congress	President	Congress	President	Congress
1952	15	13	15	14	29	6
1956	16	9	14	9	25	7
1960	14	11	9	7	24	9
1964	16	15	17	15	16	14
1968	23	18	19	18	34	18
1972	27	18	22	18	38	17
1976	17	21	17	21	17	22
1980	20	22	23	22	17	23
1984	14	22	13	21	18	23
1988	12	20	10	18	17	24

[a]Strong and weak partisans are included here. The findings would be changed little by adding leaners.
Source: Survey Research Center/Center for Political Studies election studies.

Another major contributor to electoral volatility is the low level of party-line voting during this period. Ticket splitting and defection from party continue to characterize American voting behavior; even though there has been some increase in strong partisans, there has been no corresponding increase in party-loyal behavior.[1] As can be seen in Table E.3, defections from party in voting for Congress remain at high levels through the 1980s, although defections from party in voting for President were at relatively low levels in 1984 and 1988. Data on ticket splitting for state and local offices are similar. Slightly over half of all voters reported splitting their tickets in 1984, in contrast to slightly over 60 percent a decade earlier.[2] These data suggest that party loyalty has not continued to deteriorate in the 1980s, although it has stayed at generally lower levels than the 1950s.

In his seminal works on electoral change, V. O. Key noted two kinds of electoral change: the sudden dramatic change that occurs in critical elections; and the slower, gradual change among subgroups of the population that he termed *secular realignment*.[3] Several discussions of the contemporary electorate suggest that secular realignment has occurred, particularly in the South and particularly in response to issues of race.[4]

This southern electoral realignment can be viewed as a shift
toward the Republican party or several more or less compensating
shifts involving Democratic blacks mobilizing and migrating, conservative whites becoming Republicans, and the in-migration of
several groups such as northern Republicans. Other accounts note
a movement toward the Republican party in the West, particularly
the mountain states and of the compensating pro-Democratic drift
of the Northeast.[5] Within the North, movement toward the Republicans by the white working class has been offset by pro-
Democratic moves within the white middle class.[6]

Several analysts use the term "realignment" to refer to this
shifting of voter attachments. A good example is the work of John
Petrocik, which refers to shifts in individual partisan loyalties as
"realignment" when these shifts alter the social bases of party
support.[7] Petrocik is explicit that this may not involve net gains
or losses for the political parties, but it is quite enough, he argues,
if changes occur in the composition of party coalitions. He offers
an interesting analysis of electoral alignments and, by implication,
the nature of representation they produce; it is not the same
meaning of "realignment" used here or in most of the literature,
however.

Although Edward G. Carmines and James A. Stimson are
reluctant to use the term "realignment," in their recent work *Issue
Evolution* they describe a similar reshuffling of voters as fundamentally transforming the partisan coalitions.[8] They persuasively
argue that racial policies and attitudes toward blacks have led,
since the early 1960s, to a new pattern of electoral alignments,
and that racial issues are the key to increased ideological constraint
during this period. Unlike most who examine public opinion, they
link the changes in mass behavior to the activities of party leaders
and activists. Carmines and Stimson contend that leadership on
racial policies was almost accidental, unlike the patterns of leadership that characterize partisan realignments. The public was
responding to themes and cues on which the leadership was not,
in fact, attempting to lead.

A number of points can be made about the apparent reshuffling
of voters between the parties. First, it has been in progress for

roughly twenty-five years; it is not a product of the Reagan years. Second, it has its clearest behavioral impact in presidential voting and is far less apparent in congressional voting or at lower levels. Third, changes in partisanship have tended to be movements toward political independence rather than adoptions of a new partisan affiliation. For example, in the South over the period from 1978 to 1988, Democratic identifiers among both southern whites and blacks declined, but Republican identifiers increased very little. Harold Stanley concludes that the South is undergoing both "realignment" and "dealignment" simultaneously; that is, voters are shifting around, and their attachments to their parties are weakening.[9]

Within the context of the realignment perspective presented here, Petrocik and Stanley, as well as Carmines and Stimson, document forms of individual change that we regard as the deterioration of electoral alignments. These are forms of often lasting change in the electorate that cut across previous electoral coalitions. (It is interesting and a bit ironic that these changes that undermined the composition of the New Deal coalition have contributed to a somewhat stronger division between Democrats and Republicans in the alignment of attitudes toward New Deal–like issues.[10]) Secular realignment, from our perspective, is another element in the deterioration of electoral coalitions and is the form of change frequently seen in the regional patterns presented in Chapter 3 (in particular, see Table 3.3). Secular realignment is purely an electoral phenomenon unless it is associated with shifts in the balance of power between the parties that lead to unified control of government.

Another indicator of electoral dealignment is the disjunction between the popular vote for President and the vote for Congress—which, of course, has led to divided control of government. Throughout the latter 1970s and the 1980s, the interelection correlations between the state-level vote for Congress in adjacent years remain at relatively high levels (see Table E.4). The same pattern appears in the case of the presidential vote in the elections of 1976 through 1988. In contrast, the correlations between the state-level vote for Congress and the presidential vote are signif-

TABLE E.4 Correlations of Democratic and Republican Voting for President
and Congress with States as Units, 1964–1988

	President-President	
	Democratic	Republican
1964–1968	.86	−.38
1968–1972	.86	−.24
1972–1976	.08	−.02
1976–1980	.88	.74
1980–1984	.71	.85
1984–1988	.86	.87

	President-Congress	
	Democratic	Republican
1964	−.24	−.29
1968	−.19	.81
1972	−.02	.02
1976	.63	.59
1980	.31	.23
1984	.45	.43

	Congress-Congress	
	Democratic	Republican
1966–1968	.90	.92
1968–1970	.89	.90
1970–1972	.78	.77
1972–1974	.61	.63
1974–1976	.80	.79
1976–1978	.67	.71
1978–1980	.85	.85
1980–1982	.82	.82
1982–1984	.89	.85
1984–1986	.82	.79

icantly lower, which reflects the ticket splitting throughout the
1980s that produced substantial victories for Republican presidential candidates while leaving the House firmly under Democratic
control.

Some analysts, such as John Chubb and Paul Peterson,[11] have
suggested that it is no longer necessary to control Congress in
order to effect the policy changes associated with partisan alignment. The presidency, the argument goes, has become so powerful,
so much the focus of important policy-making, that controlling
the White House is the crucial element in the control of govern-

ment. If this were the case, a new pattern of stable support for the presidential candidates of one party would be all that would be required of the electorate to create a partisan realignment, and the disjuncture in voting would not matter.

Certainly considerable evidence exists that such a new pattern of support for Republican presidential candidates has developed. As shown in Table E.4, inter-election correlations of the state vote for President show a sharp break in the 1960s and 1970s, which indicates a rearrangement of the party coalitions.[12] A lasting shift in favor of Republican presidential candidates can also be seen in 1972. In September 1988, the Gallup Poll showed the public viewing the Republican party as better able to manage prosperity *and* international relations—both, arguably, perceptions that shape presidential vote choices. One could make a case, then, that a change in the partisan balance has occurred in the only area that matters in policy-making; that this shift was in response to, and as a reward for, successful policy-making by the President, and that this shift will enable the presidental party to continue in office long enough, with enough resources, to consolidate its policy gains—in short, that in a president-centered system, a partisan realignment has occurred.

Despite the appeal of such an argument, we are inclined to see the disjunction between presidential and congressional voting as a symptom of continued dealignment rather than a new type of realignment. Although there are occasions when the President takes the initiative with little or no regard for congressional power, these are invariably brief episodes, usually in international matters. No policy initiatives of any consequence, especially domestic ones, are sustained without the involvement of Congress.

Our contention that the 1960s, 1970s, and 1980s reveal the deterioration of the earlier alignment ought not to be interpreted to mean that nothing of consequence has happened. There have been dramatic political events and major policy developments as well as significant changes in individual electoral behavior. It has never been contended that nothing important happens outside of a partisan realignment or that the realignment perspective explains all that is interesting in American politics.

Still, the decay of the New Deal alignment has extended longer than any previous such period, and it raises questions about the possibility of systemic changes that have lessened the capacity of the system to realign. One suggestion to explain the failure of the political system to realign offers the view that there has been no crisis serious enough to shake the system. Putting aside the tautological aspect of this argument (that is, there have been no realigning crises—otherwise there would have been a realignment), one could argue that a number of candidates for realigning crisis— Vietnam, Watergate—have arisen in the past thirty years that could have led to realignment had other conditions been present.[13] Another such candidate is race, which, as discussed above, may well have led to considerable rearrangement of partisan loyalties if not a shift in the partisan balance of power.

A variation on these themes suggests that the political system has developed the ability to manage small crises, particularly of an economic nature. The government's tools for economic management, internally and internationally, ward off politically damaging recessions and depressions. Although it is conceivable that political leaders have been handling crises and solving problems with greater and greater skill over recent years, this idea is hardly consistent with most commentary on American politics.

A more common contention, best articulated by David Brady,[14] focuses on the increased insulation of American political institutions from electoral forces—an insulation that makes the system less vulnerable to, and less responsive to, crises than in the past. In effect, it takes a much greater crisis in the twentieth century to provoke the same kind of response that would have resulted in a sweeping realignment in the nineteenth century. Focusing upon the role of the House of Representatives in realignments, Brady argues that a critical element is the amount of turnover in the House. With a sizable amount of turnover in membership in the House as a whole comes "sharp and inclusive" turnover on committees, including new committee leadership. Both leaders and followers on critical committees, not wedded to the normal patterns of decision-making, take their cues from party leaders, allowing for nonincremental policy changes that respond to national political forces. The turnover is crucial for the House of Representatives to overcome its normal tendencies toward localism and incrementalism. In the 1890s, as Brady shows, the large number of competitive seats allowed for a relatively minor shift in electoral sentiments to lead to a substantial amount of turnover in the House of Representatives, unified control of government, and non-incremental policy-making. In the less competitive 1930s, it required far more electoral change to create the same conditions for innovative policy change. Given the large number of safe seats in the House of Representatives today, quite massive electoral change would seem to be required.

Others have advanced similar arguments. John Chubb and Paul Peterson suggest that not only has Congress insulated itself from national electoral forces, but state governments have also done so by such tactics as scheduling gubernatorial and state legislative elections in nonpresidential years.[15] A pattern of low turnover similar to that found in the U.S. House of Representatives has been documented by Malcolm Jewell and David Breaux in state legislatures.[16] There is relatively low turnover in state legislatures, as in the U.S. House of Representatives, because so many incumbents run for reelection and almost all are successful. Such insulation decreases the likelihood of putting together the conditions for the sweeping policy changes associated with partisan realignment.

Although these developments normally would be seen as stabilizing the political system, from another perspective the system has lost its ability to respond to manageable problems with party-controlled policy-making. Although not always a prominent feature when the analysis focuses on electoral change, partisan realignments with their unified control of government offer an opportunity for political parties to rule with some cohesion and purpose for an extended period. Realignment eras have afforded rather rare occasions for widespread popular concern to be translated into a range of public policies.

If the system can suppress or ignore the minor political alarms that crises provide, we must be concerned that only a large, perhaps devastating, crisis will lead to substantial leadership changes. It is surely contrary to the interests of office-holders to keep the political system sensitive to minor crises, as they are the rascals who get thrown out, but from the point of view of system survival, correcting problems before they become unmanageable or insoluble is a valuable characteristic. It would be extremely difficult to demonstrate that the system has learned to avoid small crises or become insensitive to a given level of crisis, but it is not implausible on the face of it.[17]

We conclude, then, that a partisan realignment has not occurred since the 1930s. Although it is clear that there has been considerable shifting in individual partisan attachments, these changes have not produced clear dominance for either of the parties. On balance, the strength of partisan attachments in the electorate has not increased, divided control of government remains the rule rather than the exception, and a clear and sharply focused issue agenda has not emerged. Although lasting change in voting behavior and partisan attitudes has occurred at the individual level, those changes have not been accompanied by the other circumstances of realignment that characterized the Civil War years, the 1890s, and the New Deal.

This extended period without realignment, this prolonged "decay phase," has raised questions about the realignment perspective itself. These circumstances have led some observers to conclude with more than a hint of despair that a realignment is no longer possible. Others have drawn the more sweeping conclusion that the realignment perspective is without utility as a means to comprehend and interpret the political life and history of the nation.

In our view, such conclusions seem premature and may rest upon disagreement concerning elements of the realignment perspective. One source of these conclusions is the periodicity that has appeared to be a characteristic of historical realignment patterns. To state this argument in exaggerated form, partisan realignments have occurred on a seemingly regular basis about every thirty-six years. From this point of view, a realignment has been "due" for some years but none has occurred. Therefore, either realignment must no longer be possible or the concept itself must be defective. In fact, of course, little theoretical support for the view that realignments must occur on some periodic basis has been offered, and the empirical evidence is weak at best.[18]

This view is related to conceptions—misconceptions, to our minds—of the processes at work during interrealignment periods. The tendency in much of the earlier scholarship was to see these periods as little more than unproductive and uninteresting interludes leading to the next realignment. A further tendency has been to see the decline in the strength of partisan attachments and the dealignment of partisan coalitions that occurred following historical realignments as somehow leading necessarily to a new realignment. We remain convinced, however, that a somewhat different view better fits the facts. As we have noted in preceding chapters, the relaxation of partisan attachments and the shifts of partisan coalitions that occur during decay phases is a precondition of realignment. This process produces a sufficient pool of voters who are detached from or only weakly attached to the parties to provide the basis for a new partisan majority.

Although it is a necessary step in the realignment process, the development of a pool of unattached votes is not sufficient to produce a realignment. A triggering event in the form of a crisis and its successful handling by political leadership are also necessary for the consummation of a realignment. It may be, as we suggest above, that the propensity to governmental inaction and deadlock during these periods increases the likelihood of a precipitating crisis, but nothing about the characteristics of decay phases makes realignment inevitable.

A partisan realignment has not occurred in the contemporary period because a triggering event that is of a nature and magnitude sufficient to produce realignment has not taken place. We suspect that because of electoral and institutional change of the sort described by Brady, obstacles to realignment have increased, and under these circumstances a realignment has probably become less likely. However, realignment remains possible even under these circumstances if a crisis of sufficient magnitude occurs and if it is successfully handled by new political leadership. Nothing, moreover, makes the barriers to realignment unchangeable in the future.

The realignment perspective has not been presented, here or elsewhere, as a predictive theory; instead, it attempts to specify the conditions under which a realignment *could* happen and to explain a realignment after it has happened, but it makes no predictions about when political leadership will successfully turn an electoral advantage into a permanent shift in the partisan balance. Indeed, the notion of abortive realignments—realignments that might have been, had political leaders been successful in handling a crisis—attests to the lack of predictability in the phenomenon.[19]

We find ourselves ending this epilogue on much the same note of cautious optimism on which we concluded in 1980. We see nothing in the national situation, even in the absence of realignment, that precludes wise leadership. We find no reason to believe that the electorate is without capacity to recognize and reward sound policy action and to reject unwise actions. The responsiveness of institutions to small amounts of electoral change has doubtless been lessened, and this may eventually be seen as an enduring systemic change. Nonetheless, our view remains that a crisis of sufficient magnitude, coupled with innovative and successful policy-making by a unified governmental leadership, may still result in a lasting shift in the partisan balance in the United States—but it has not done so yet.

NOTES

1. Helmut Norpoth and Jerrold Rusk, "Partisan Dealignment in the American Electorate," *American Political Science Review* 76 (September 1982), pp. 522–537; Martin P. Wattenberg, *The Decline of American Political Parties, 1952–1980* (Cambridge, MA: Harvard University Press, 1984.

2. National Election Studies data.

3. V. O. Key, "A Theory of Critical Elections," *Journal of Politics* 17 (February 1955), pp. 3–18; and "Secular Realignment and the Party System," *Journal of Politics* 21 (May 1959), pp. 198–210.

4. John R. Petrocik, "Realignment: New Party Coalitions and the Nationalization of the South," *Journal of Politics* 49 (May 1987), pp. 347–375; Edward G.

Carmines and James A. Stimson, *Issue Evolution: Race and the Transformation of American Politics* (Princeton, NJ: Princeton University Press, 1989); Raymond Wolfinger and Michael Hagen, "Republican Prospects: Southern Comfort," *Public Opinion* vol. 8, no. 5; Earl Black and Merle Black, *Politics and Society in the South* (Cambridge, MA: Harvard University Press, 1987).

5. J. Clark Archer and Peter J. Taylor, *Section and Party* (New York: Wiley, 1981).

6. John R. Petrocik, *Party Coalitions: Realignments and the Decline of the New Deal Party System* (Chicago: University of Chicago Press, 1981).

7. Petrocik, *Party Coalitions.*

8. Carmines and Stimson, *Issue Evolution.*

9. Harold W. Stanley, "Southern Partisan Changes: Dealignment, Realignment or Both?" *Journal of Politics* 50 (February 1988), pp. 64–88.

10. Stuart Elaine Macdonald and George Rabinowitz, "The Dynamics of Structural Realignment," *American Political Science Review* 81 (September 1987), pp. 775–796. See also George Rabinowitz, Paul-Henri Gurian, and Stuart Elaine Macdonald, "The Structure of Presidental Elections and the Process of Realignment, 1944–1980," *American Journal of Political Science* 28 (November 1984), pp. 611–635.

11. John E. Chubb and Paul E. Peterson, eds., *The New Direction in American Politics* (Washington, DC: Brookings Institution, 1985).

12. Because of the influence of third party candidacies, the timing of the shift in presidential voting depends on whether one looks at the Democratic vote or the Republican vote.

13. Huntington, for example, designates the 1960s as an era of "creedal passion" that might have produced a realignment in the party system except that the parties and partisan loyalties had become too weak to matter. Samuel P. Huntington, *American Politics: The Promise of Disharmony* (Cambridge, MA: Harvard University Press, 1981).

14. David W. Brady, *Critical Elections and Congressional Policy Making* (Stanford, CA: Stanford University Press, 1988).

15. Chubb and Peterson, *The New Direction in American Politics.*

16. Malcolm E. Jewell and David Breaux, "The Effect of Incumbency in State Legislative Elections," *Legislative Studies Quarterly* 13, pp. 495–510.

17. So far as we are aware, no one has undertaken a systematic study of the nature of crisis in American political history. In the realignment perspective, crisis is treated primarily as an exogenous variable. Certainly a careful analysis of the magnitude and effects of various types of crises would be a useful addition to scholarship.

18. The best theoretical explanation for the observed regularity in realignment cycles is Paul A. Beck's article "A Socialization Theory of Partisan Realignment" (in Richard G. Niemi & Associates, *The Politics of Future Citizens* [San Francisco: Jossey-Bass, 1974]), although he does not argue that they must occur on schedule. The present authors used data from the Niemi political socialization study to test Beck's hypotheses for the New Deal generation and found little empirical support. Clubb, Flanigan, and Zingale, "Family Socialization by the New Deal Generation:

A Test of Beck's Thesis," presented at the annual meeting of the Midwest Political Science Association, 1984.

19. Lest the reader feel that the failure to predict is evidence of a lack of rigor, we would point to astronomers being able to explain but not predict the appearance of a nova, evolutionary biologists explaining but not predicting the appearance of new species, and to the lines of inquiry associated with chaos theory.

INDEX

ABOUT THE AUTHORS

JEROME M. CLUBB is Program Director of the Center for Political Studies of the Institute for Social Research, Executive Director of the Inter-university Consortium for Political and Social Research, and Professor of History at The University of Michigan. He received his Ph.D. in history from the University of Washington. He is an author or editor of various volumes and his publications are largely concerned with American legislative and electoral history.

WILLIAM H. FLANIGAN is Professor of Political Science at the University of Minnesota. He received his Ph.D. in political science from Yale University. His previous publications include (with Nancy H. Zingale) *Political Behavior of the American Electorate* and as editor (with Joel H. Silbey and Allan G. Bogue) *The History of American Electoral Behavior.*

NANCY H. ZINGALE is Professor of Political Science at the College of St. Thomas. She received her Ph.D. degree in political science from the University of Minnesota. She is coauthor (with William H. Flanigan) of *Political Behavior of the American Electorate* and author of "Third Party Alignments in a Two-Party System: The Case of Minnesota" in *The History of American Electoral Behavior.*